The Teaching Assistant Training Handbook

How to Prepare TAs for Their Responsibilities

edited by

Loreto R. Prieto, Ph.D.
Collaborative Program in Counseling Psychology
Department of Counseling and Special Education
University of Akron
Akron, OH 44325

Steven A. Meyers, Ph.D.
School of Psychology
Roosevelt University
430 S. Michigan Avenue
Chicago, IL 60605

NEW FORUMS PRESS INC.
Stillwater, Okla. U.S.A.

ISBN 10: 1-58107-031-4 / ISBN 13: 978-1-581070-31-6

This book is available at a special discount when ordered in bulk quantities. For more information, contact New Forums Press, Inc., P.O. Box 876, Stillwater, OK 74076 USA. Visit our web site at www.newforums.com.

Printed in the United States of America.

Contents

Acknowledgments

As a graduate student embarking on my own first appointment as a TA, I had no idea how lucky I was to have received some training and supervision of my teaching duties. It wasn't until much later, after talking with other TAs from across my college and university, that I realized just how many TAs literally had no preparation for their teaching duties or for the tasks and challenges they would face in the classroom. The questions and anxieties most TAs had were ones I had been fortunate enough to have answered and assuaged by my TA supervisor during my very first semester of graduate teaching. With my interest in teaching assistant issues sparked, I conducted my first empirical study as a graduate student - exploring the effects of training and supervision on the self-efficacy of teaching assistants. My interest in teaching assistant issues has continued unabated to this day.

Along the way, I have been fortunate enough to work with my co-editor, Dr. Steve Meyers, on several projects concerning TA training. My collaborations with Steve have not only broadened my own perspectives, knowledge and skill with respect to investigating the area of TA training, but I have also greatly appreciated being able to explore these issues of interest with such a competent and wonderful friend and colleague. I would also like to thank all of the contributors to this text, both for the privilege of working with them and for how much I learned in the process of editing this book. Being a part of this project has clearly shown me just how many people share a concern for the development of teaching assistants as effective classroom teachers and educators; it has been an honor to work on this text with such a distinguished set of scholars.

Finally, I would like to express my deepest gratitude to my wife and colleague, Dr. Karen R. Scheel, for her support, patience, wisdom, and encouragement of me and my efforts during the planning and completion of this book. I have learned much from her with regard to understanding what being a good teacher really means; she will always remain my chief source of inspiration both personally and professionally.

Loreto R. Prieto
November, 2000

Acknowledgments Continued

I am indebted to many people who have provided support in completing this project. First, I want to highlight the efforts of my co-editor, Dr. Loreto Prieto. His dedication as a colleague is only matched by his kindness as a friend. Second, I am grateful for the commitment and skill of the authors who contributed to this book. They not only have improved many TAs experiences at their home institutions, but they now extend their reach by adeptly sharing their wisdom to those who read and will benefit from this volume. Third, I am grateful for those faculty and administrators who had confidence in my teaching abilities during by graduate education. I acknowledge the kindness and consistent support of mu graduate mentor, Dr. Gary Stollak, who shares my commitment to teaching; I also express my gratitude to Dr. Gordon Wood, who as chairperson of the Department of Psychology at Michigan State University was exceptionally generous in providing me with teaching opportunities. Fourth, I thank Drs. Jonathan Smith and Edward Rossine for supporting and valuing my efforts toward improving the teaching skills of graduate students at Roosevelt University. Finally, I am most indebted to my family who provides me with the foundation for all that I do. I am thankful for the love and care of my mother, Marsha Meyers, who modeled skillful teaching throughout my life. I am also grateful for the love and support of my wife, Elaine Allensworth. She is a constant source of friendship, inspiration and joy.

Steven A. Meyers
November, 2000

Introduction

Loreto R. Prieto, Ph.D.
University of Akron

Steven A. Meyers, Ph.D.
Roosevelt University

Teaching assistants (TAs) play an indispensable role in higher education. Approximately 30 to 40% of the undergraduate courses at most major universities are taught by GTAs (Nyquist, Abbott, Wulff, & Sprague, 1991). Moreover, these teaching responsibilities are held by increasing numbers of graduate students, as most doctoral recipients report teaching during their graduate education (Henderson & Woods, 1998).

Despite their importance in college classrooms, many TAs are poorly prepared for their teaching responsibilities. Many TAs — even those who assume full responsibility for a course — receive only an initial orientation to teaching and occasionally meet with a faculty supervisor during the semester (Gray & Buerkel-Rothfuss, 1991; Prieto & Altmaier, 1994). Although model TA training programs do exist, research suggests that the training and supervision of TAs is highly inconsistent among departments and universities. Many faculty, staff, and administrators are committed to the growth and development of their TAs, but are uncertain about how to best proceed.

The Teaching Assistant Training Handbook: How to Prepare TAs for Their Responsibilities is designed for college faculty, staff, and administrators who train and supervise TAs in all disciplines. This edited book presents readers with a wealth of information that is essential for designing, implementing, or improving a TA training program in a department or university-wide office. The authors illustrate a wide range of strategies to prepare TAs for their teaching responsibilities, including orientation programs, workshops, courses, on-going supervision, and experiential activities. In addition, chapters address critical topics in college teaching, such as increasing TAs' awareness of ethical issues in the classroom or enhancing TAs' sensitivity to issues of gender and racial/ethnic issues when teaching.

In each chapter, authors present material in a way that can be easily used or adapted by faculty or staff who train TAs. For each training method (e.g., TA orientation programs or workshops), authors discuss the particular technique in detail, offer detailed and concrete examples that illustrate its implementation across disciplines, and provide helpful hand-outs, checklists, or forms. Moreover, authors summarize past research and writings for each training technique that is presented. Readers will not only learn from the authors' own experiences and expertise in preparing TAs, but will also learn about effective training techniques that have been documented in the literature.

In the first chapter, Meyers provides supervising faculty (i.e., university-level and department-level staff who train or supervise TAs) with both a conceptual framework to promote effective TA training as well as specific strategies to accomplish this goal. He first presents a process model of TA training that can guide the creation or expansion of development programs. More specifically, Meyers emphasizes that TAs' performance is ultimately shaped by graduate students' initial skills and level of motivation; the nature and number of teaching assignments that TAs receive; the rigor of training offered by the department and university; TAs' active engagement during training; and the broader departmental and institutional culture regarding teaching. Second, the author discusses five overarching principles that can galvanize such efforts. Finally, Meyers presents numerous active learning techniques that supervising faculty can use to increase graduate students' involvement and participation during TA training.

In Chapter 2, Goss Lucas offers a detailed template of a four-day long TA orientation program that can be used by readers to develop their own department-based TA orientations. She discusses the comparative benefits of offering TAs a departmental orientation program versus a university-wide orientation program, covers the "must have" components of an effective orientation, and provides examples of detailed handouts that can be used by readers in their own orientation programs. Highlights of important topics for TA orientation programs include presentations on teaching methods, campus guidelines and resources, testing and evaluation of students, classroom management, and many others.

Hainline, in Chapter 3, explains how to construct a seminar course and teaching practica to prepare TAs for the realities of university teaching. Completed as part of their own graduate training curriculum, TAs enroll in her seminar to learn valuable skills and information to help them succeed in their teaching role. Hainline presents possible course topics (e.g., exposure to various pedagogical approaches, the use of technology in the classroom, the psychology of human cognition and learning) and describes experiential aspects of the course that are intended to demystify teaching (e.g., consultations with experienced faculty, peer discussions of common insecurities and difficult experiences as a TA). In addition, the course enhances TAs' professional development by addressing academic career pathways as well as non-university career choices.

In Chapter 4, Maslach and her colleagues review microteaching, a powerful technique that allows TAs to refine their teaching behaviors. Microteaching is a structured, "hands-on" procedure in which TAs conduct a very brief lecture or discussion, receive feedback on their performance from peers and supervising faculty, and then re-teach the material. The authors review the process of microteaching, summarize empirical research about this technique, and explain how to incorporate microteaching into TA training programs. They also provide illustrations from their own TA training course, co-taught by a faculty member and a "veteran" TA, in which they use microteaching to help TAs master the myriad of tasks involved in their first teaching experiences. The chapter features step-by-step procedures, exercises, and forms for readers to use when employing microteaching with TAs.

In Chapter 5, Prentice-Dunn and Pitts provide a valuable and thorough discussion of how to supervise TAs, and offer detailed information on using videotaping as a tool for helping TAs develop their instructional skills. They explain their approach, refer to important empirical literature in the area, and offer readers concrete advice and methods so that they can effectively supervise TAs. Highlights of the chapter include an overview of a structured approach that uses both observation and videotape technology to help TAs evaluate their classroom performance; suggestions on how to prepare TAs to review their own videotapes in a way that will maximize skill development; identifying strategies to adopt (and pitfalls to avoid) when consulting with TAs to reinforce good teaching behaviors and use less productive teaching behaviors as a catalyst for change; providing checklists and other tools for use during supervision; and describing how observation and videotaping can be integrated into course work on teaching.

In Chapter 6, Prieto presents a theoretical model for conceptualizing the supervision of TAs from a developmental perspective, the Integrated Developmental Model for Graduate Teaching Assistants (IDM-GTA). Details of the model are outlined, explicating the anticipated developmental stages that GTAs will pass through as well as the teaching skills they will acquire in their development as classroom instructors. Faculty members who supervise GTAs are offered concrete tips regarding supervisory interventions and appropriate supervisory styles to employ with GTAs. In addition, the details of an empirical study offering preliminary validation of the IDM-GTA is provided in the chapter. Finally, a discussion of the group supervision of GTAs is offered, which outlines both conceptual as well as concrete information for GTA supervisors, and concludes with examples of how various teaching issues could be handled within a GTA supervision group. Throughout the chapter, relevant conceptual and empirical literature from the education and applied psychology literatures is cited and discussed.

In chapter 7, Keith-Spiegel and her associates outline critical issues regarding the ethics of teaching that TAs must be aware of in the course of their duties. Highlights of the chapter include a discussion of the "ambiguous" nature of the TA role (e.g., TAs are not experienced educators who hold formal faculty positions, but they still have high levels of responsibility in the classroom); typical ethical dilemmas that TAs encounter in their roles (e.g., dual role relationships, issues of confidentiality, misuses of power); ethical issues in the supervision and mentoring of TAs (e.g., evaluation concerns, inappropriate relationships with faculty); and helpful guidelines that TAs can use when making complicated ethical decisions. The authors supplement topics in this chapter with numerous case stories that clarify the main issues involved, connect ethical dilemmas to "real life," and illustrate possible solutions to ethically problematic teaching situations.

In Chapter, 8, Fencl addresses a frequently overlooked issue in TA training: How to ensure that TAs are sensitive to the role that gender plays in the college classroom. Fencl first provides readers with a definition of "gender conscious teaching" and thoughtfully explains how students' gender influences classroom dynamics. The majority of this chapter focuses on practical suggestions for gender conscious teaching, which include ways to create a "gender-friendly climate," encourage the participation of all students, and foster an inclusive environment in a variety of teaching settings. Fencl also provides examples of specific techniques for TAs to utilize, such as cooperative learning strategies and the gender equitable use of praise, questioning, discussion, and classroom exercises.

In chapter 9, Reid, Lewis, and Flores present important information about the need to foster an awareness of racial/ethnic issues in TA training programs. The authors address two main themes: (1) the need to increase the number of racially/ethnically diverse students who hold positions as TAs, and (2) the need for all TAs to possess a sound awareness of the racial/ethnic issues that impact both students and the material they teach. Reid and her colleagues discuss the benefits associated with extending teaching opportunities to graduate students of color, the need for academic departments and their TAs to address the changing demographics and educational needs of diverse students, and the barriers that prevent the retention of students of color who might later become valued faculty members. They also suggest ways to make courses more inclusive of the scholarly contributions of persons of color, explain how TAs can increase their awareness and responsiveness to the needs of the diverse students they teach, and describe how TAs can create and maintain classroom environments with positive racial climates that are conducive to the needs of all students.

In Chapter 10, Feldman and Coughlan offer a wealth of informational resources about college teaching that can be used in departmental TA training efforts. Divided into relevant major sections (e.g., course development, goals of education, classroom tools and strategies), this annotated bibliography and list of references covers many critical and useful topics such as understanding various styles of student learning, teaching students critical thinking skills, using Internet resources on teaching, and many others. This chapter can serve as a handy guide so that readers can immediately identify and incorporate important sources of information and knowledge into their TA training programs.

It is our hope that this text informs and inspires all those who are involved with teaching assistant training and serves to add to our ability to make the graduate teaching assistant experience a solid foundation for the future professional development of our students who serve in this important role.

References

Gray, P. L., & Buerkel-Rothfuss, N. L. (1991). Teaching assistant training: The view from the trenches. In J. D. Nyquist, R. D. Abbott, D. H. Wulff, & J. Sprague (Eds.), *Preparing the professoriate of tomorrow to teach* (pp. 40-54). Dubuque, IA: Kendall/Hunt.

Henderson, P. H., & Woods, C. (1998). *Summary report 1996: Doctorate recipients from United States universities.* Washington, DC: National Academy Press.

Nyquist, J. D., Abbott, R. D., Wulff, D. H., & Sprague, J. (Eds.). (1991). *Preparing the professoriate of tomorrow to teach.* Dubuque, IA: Kendall/Hunt.

Prieto, L. R., & Altmaier, E. M. (1994). The relationship of prior training and previous teaching experience to self-efficacy among graduate teaching assistants. *Research in Higher Education, 35,* 481-497.

SECTION I

THE TRAINING & PREPARATION OF GRADUATE TEACHING ASSISTANTS

The Teaching Assistant Training Handbook

Conceptualizing and Promoting Effective TA Training

Steven A. Meyers, Ph.D.
Roosevelt University

Many faculty and administrators are highly committed to the professional development of their teaching assistants (TAs), but are uncertain about how to proceed. In this chapter, I provide supervising faculty (i.e., university-level and department-level staff who train or supervise TAs) with both a conceptual framework to promote effective TA training as well as specific strategies to accomplish this goal. First, I present a process model of TA training that can guide the creation or expansion of development programs. Second, I discuss five overarching principles that can galvanize such efforts. Finally, I present numerous active learning techniques that supervising faculty can use to increase graduate students' involvement and participation during TA training.

Conceptualizing Effective TA Training

Figure 1 presents a conceptual model that summarizes the process of comprehensive TA training. First, supervising faculty must remember that graduate students approach their teaching responsibilities with different levels of pedagogical expertise and motivation. For example, students vary in terms of their initial ability to communicate in an organized and persuasive manner, their fear of public speaking, and their commitment to teaching. Thus, TA training must be mindful of and address individual differences in graduate students' initial proficiencies and dedication to refining their teaching skills. Assessing TAs' competence and confidence is a relative and idiosyncratic process in which progress is best judged by comparing TAs' initial and current classroom performance.

Second, supervising faculty must be sensitive to "who TAs become" as they advance through graduate school. Teaching assistants' abilities, attitudes towards teaching, and concerns evolve as they gain more experience in the classroom. This implies that graduate students need progressively more challenging teaching assignments in order to grow. Whereas TAs benefit from structured teaching apprenticeships in the first semesters of graduate school (i.e., primary responsibilities can include grading, delivering guest lectures, tutoring during office hours), TAs need to assume greater responsibilities in subsequent semesters to become independent and effective college teachers. Supervising faculty must tailor training and supervision experiences to TAs' stage of development rather than relying on a one-size-fits-all approach.

Third, supervising faculty and administrators must keep in mind that TA training is a essential and powerful tool that improves TAs' performance. Comprehensive preparation is facilitated by both department-based and university-based TA training. That is, services offered by campus-wide offices and individual departments are complementary rather than mutually exclusive. University-based training guarantees that all TAs have access to professional development services. Because TA training varies consid-

Figure 1. A process model of comprehensive TA training.

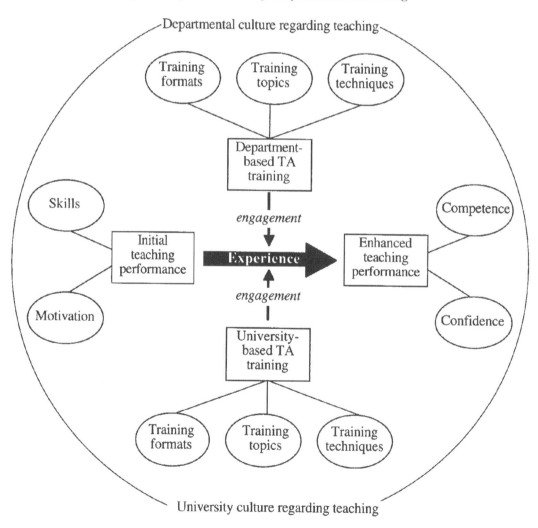

erably among departments, campus-wide preparation ensures that a minimum level of training can be established or required. University-wide offices also typically have greater resources than individual departments for training. The staff of centralized programs have cutting-edge knowledge about teaching and faculty development. Moreover, university-based programs often offer a greater range of services, such as an extensive resource library, expert presentations, and the administration of certificate/award programs (Mintz, 1998).

On the other hand, departmental preparation can be tailored to TAs' duties for particular disciplines. For example, the skills needed to effectively run a lab section of a physical science course are not the same as those required to adeptly lead a section of a course emphasizing foreign language conversational skills. Departmental TA training can focus more specifically on the academic content knowledge and the pedagogical content knowledge (i.e., ways to teach the specific content) of TAs' disciplines (Ronkowski, 1998). Finally, departmental training permits greater interaction between TAs and their immediate supervisors (Weimer, Svinicki, & Bauer, 1989). This facilitates mentoring and allows graduate students to observe faculty in their discipline valuing teaching.

Regardless of the location of training, TA development will be influenced by the extensiveness of such preparation. The rigor of TA training varies dramatically among departments and universities. In some cases, TAs receive hardly any preparation for their teaching responsibilities. For instance, Prieto and Altmaier (1994) found that 25% of TAs in their university-wide sample reported that they were teaching without any faculty supervision, whereas another quarter of those surveyed indicated that they met only monthly or by appointment with their supervisors. Similarly, Gray and Buerkel-Rothfuss (1991) reported that 88% of TAs in their national survey were prepared in less than one week for their teaching responsibilities. Most recently, Meyers and Prieto (2000) documented that psychology graduate students in their national sample reported an average of 22 hours of TA training. Thus, TAs' performance can flounder because of few opportunities for skill development; conversely, TAs' abilities can be bolstered by rigorous training that includes classes and workshops on college teaching, supervised teaching practica over the course of multiple semesters, or ongoing mentorship and peer support (e.g., Benassi & Fernald, 1993).

Although TA orientation programs, training workshops, and pedagogy classes are often necessary to enhance TAs' performance, the mere presentation of information is not sufficient to produce deep and enduring changes in their teaching. Rather, the effect of training on TAs' classroom behaviors is moderated by graduate students' level of active engagement during the training process. That is, how material is taught in TA training programs is as important as what material is taught. This assertion is buttressed by those researchers, theorists, and instructors who advocate the use of active learning methods in the college classroom (Johnson, Johnson, & Smith, 1991). Supervising faculty can maximize TAs' engagement during training by adopting a "microskills" approach. This basic training sequence involves supervising faculty presenting and modeling different teaching methods, TAs practicing these teaching skills, and TAs reflecting on and receiving feedback about their performance.

Finally, university and departmental cultures regarding teaching have significant effects on the development of graduate students' teaching skills. Graduate schools transmit values to graduate students in many ways; TAs internalize these views as they become socialized. First, TAs' financial compensation reinforces or undermines the belief that teaching is an important activity. Altbach (1970), for example, emphasized that graduate students are often exploited for the work that they perform. This assertion remains valid today in many institutions. Meyers and Prieto (2000) found that psychology TAs earned as little as $1.94 per hour (including both salary and tuition remission) as compensation for their teaching responsibilities; the lowest paid 10% of their national sample only earned about $1.50 more per hour than the national minimum wage for such highly specialized labor.

The norms and values of higher education that are reflected in the priorities used to assess faculty productivity also influence how graduate students are prepared to teach. Hutchings (1993) gleaned this sentiment from her survey of faculty and administrators who conduct department-based and university-wide TA training programs: "it's research that faculty and institutions really care about, research that brings money and reputation, research that's rewarded with promotion and tenure" (p. 127). When departments and institutions adopt broader definitions of scholarship (cf. Boyer, 1990), they are more likely to embrace rigorous pedagogical training for graduate students. This cultural shift challenges the supremacy of research training and helps graduate students learn about becoming an effective teacher, the norms of academia, and becoming a member of a college community (Schuster, 1993; Slevin, 1992).

In sum, the process model of TA training described in Figure 1 provides a conceptual framework to guide the development of comprehensive programs. Against this backdrop, I encourage supervising faculty to carefully consider the needs and resources of their graduate students, faculty, and university when preparing TAs for their responsibilities. Importantly, this process model emphasizes that TAs' performance is ultimately shaped by graduate students' initial skills and level of motivation; the nature and number of teaching assignments that TAs receive; the rigor of training offered by the department and university; TAs' active engagement during training; and the broader departmental and institutional culture regarding teaching. Based on the process model, I derive five general principles to help supervising faculty initiate or extend TA training efforts.

1. **Keep in mind that preparing TAs for their teaching responsibilities is important and worthwhile.** In addition to gaining competence in their specialized area of expertise, graduate students need to develop college-level teaching skills for several

reasons. First, preparing doctoral students to teach is important because the majority hold teaching assistantships during their graduate school education (Henderson & Woods, 1997). Many of these TAs play a major role in higher education; approximately 30 to 40% of undergraduate courses at research universities are taught by TAs (Nyquist, Abbott, Wulff, & Sprague, 1991). Moreover, formal training enhances TAs' performance. Teaching assistants who have preparation receive course evaluation ratings comparable to those of experienced faculty members (Benassi & Fernald, 1993; Rickard, Prentice-Dunn, Rogers, Scogin, & Lyman, 1991), and possess a greater sense of self-efficacy toward their teaching duties compared to those who do not receive training (Prieto & Meyers, 1999). Second, teaching preparation is essential because many future doctorates will be employed in college and university settings. Fifty-five percent of all doctorate recipients in 1996 with employment plans sought or obtained a position at an educational institution and identified teaching as their primary or secondary job activity (Henderson & Woods, 1997). This percentage is even higher among those graduate students who hold a teaching assistantship during graduate school (Diamond & Gray, 1987). Third, the development of teaching skills is related to graduate students' later success as faculty members. The extent to which new faculty are prepared to teach has been related to their job acclimation and stress level (Boice, 1992; Sorcinelli & Austin, 1992). This finding makes intuitive sense as several studies have reported that the majority of faculty work time is devoted to teaching and preparing for teaching (e.g., Astin, Korn, & Day, 1991).

2. **Provide more TA training rather than less**. The amount of preparation that graduate students receive for teaching is very low in comparison to other areas of their professional training. For example, doctoral students in the social sciences generally complete a multiple-course sequence in statistics and research design; they also conduct at least one independent research project under the supervision of a faculty member. The actual quantity of teaching-related training that supervising faculty offer graduate students is extremely modest in comparison to these standards (Gray & Buerkel-Rothfuss, 1991; Prieto & Altmaier, 1994). If faculty and administrators are truly committed to the development of competent scholar-educators, then graduate training must reflect this balance.

Rigorous training must broach topics that are central to TAs' day-to-day classroom responsibilities. Table 1 lists subjects that are important to address during training; these include course preparation, dissemination techniques, evaluation techniques, interacting with students, and institutional issues. The salience of different topics may be influenced by when training is provided. For example, TAs may want to learn how to select a textbook or develop a syllabus before they teach. On the other hand, TAs may find a discussion of ways to handle conflicts with students more meaningful if this topic is broached while they teach.

Training must not only prepare TAs for their current duties, but it must also provide the foundation for them to assume full course responsibility. Even if graduate students are not expected to design syllabi or select a textbook as part of their assistantships, it is nevertheless important for them to know how. Moreover, training cannot be limited to the mechanics of teaching. For example, TAs must understand how issues of cultural diversity can be infused into curricula and ways that students' racial and ethnic backgrounds affect classroom dynamics and the learning process (see Reid, Lewis, & Flores, this volume). Graduate students must learn how to create a gender-friendly climate in their classes and appreciate how certain teaching strategies differentially affect men's and women's learning (see Fencl, this volume). Similarly, supervising faculty must not only model ethical behavior, but encourage TAs to grapple with ethical dilemmas frequently encountered by college teachers (see Keith-Spiegel, Perkins, Whitely, Balogh, & Wittig, this volume).

Table 1
Topics Frequently Addressed During TA Training

Course preparation
    Developing a teaching philosophy
    Developing course policies and procedures
    Writing course objectives
    Writing a syllabus
    Selecting a textbook
    Developing lesson plans
    Preparing for the first day of class
    Integrating technology into courses
Dissemination techniques
    Lecturing
    Leading discussions
    Using active learning
    Using visual aids
    Running a lab section
    Developing critical thinking and writing skills
Evaluation techniques
    Developing assignments
    Writing objective tests
    Writing essay exams
    Grading course assignments
    Evaluating instructor effectiveness

Table 1 (Continued)

Interacting with students
    Building classroom climate and rapport
    Promoting student involvement and motivating students
    Managing classroom and student-teacher conflict
    Providing constructive criticism
    Understanding different student learning styles
    Understanding ethical issues in teaching
    Understanding the effects of race, ethnicity, and gender
    Interacting with disabled students
    Teaching international students
Institutional issues
    Understanding the TA role
    Understanding department and university policies
    Understanding institutional resources and supports

From: Bort & Buerkel-Rothfuss, 1991; Gray & Buerkel-Rothfuss, 1991; Lowman & Mathie, 1993; and Marincovich, 1998.

To accomplish these ends, supervising faculty must train TAs using multiple formats. The most frequently used approaches include:

a. **Readings and resource materials on teaching.** One of the easiest ways to provide information to graduate students about teaching is through reference materials. Many well-written texts address teaching at the college level. Authors of exemplary books include McKeachie (1999), Davis (1993), Lowman (1995), and Eble (1988). Helpful complementary texts are available that focus on specific pedagogical topics, such as grading (e.g., Ory & Ryan, 1993) and active learning (e.g., Meyers & Jones, 1993). In addition to books on teaching, TA manuals are at the core of many training programs. They often include important references and include institution-specific policies, procedures, and resources (Lowman & Mathie, 1993). Professional organizations are another source of resource materials that provide information for both TAs and faculty through their newsletters, journals, conferences, and web pages. Finally, Feldman and Coughlan (this volume) present a wealth of informational resources about college teaching that can be used in TA training efforts.

b. **Teaching orientation programs and workshops.** Orientation programs and workshops, which range in duration from less than one day to several days, typically concentrate on the immediate needs of TAs and have a circumscribed focus. Brief orientation programs generally aim to transmit information to graduate students. They allow supervising faculty to effectively familiarize TAs with their duties, campus policies, resources, and guidelines for interacting with students (Stout, 1998). Goss Lucas (this volume) provides detailed recommendations for developing TA orientations and encourages supervising faculty to focus sessions on teaching survival skills. Longer workshops, however, can address additional pedagogical topics and allow participants to practice teaching skills (Eison & Hill, 1990). They can also be targeted to the unique needs that are identified by faculty and graduate students.

c. **Courses on college teaching.** A semester- or year-long course on college teaching allows greater depth and breadth of coverage in comparison to orientations and workshops. Coursework provides graduate students the opportunity to complete and discuss relevant readings, refine important pedagogical skills, and participate in many structured learning experiences (e.g., microteaching sessions and role-plays). Courses in college teaching frequently have objectives beyond refining basic instructional skills and often include goals such as developing a philosophy of teaching, becoming a reflective practitioner, and understanding professional issues in higher education. Moreover, coursework on pedagogy can be integrated with TAs' teaching responsibilities so that topics are presented at opportune times. Hainline (this volume) provides detailed information regarding the content and structure of courses on college teaching.

Importantly, the distribution of reference materials, orientation programs, workshops, and courses on college teaching are not mutually exclusive. Rather, departments and universities must integrate these approaches to provide graduate students with a comprehensive preparatory experience for academic careers. For example, TA certificate programs typically offer rigorous training opportunities. Certification requires supervised teaching experience, completing university-wide and discipline-specific courses on college teaching, participating in teaching workshops, constructing a teaching portfolio, and eventually mentoring junior TAs in their department (Tice, Featherstone, & Johnson, 1998).

3. **Be sensitive to TAs' needs and abilities and encourage others to do so as well**. One important determinant of TAs' performance and satisfaction is the manner in which faculty relate to them. In a cross-disciplinary survey, Meyers (1996) reported that TAs associated their most positive teaching experiences with "authoritative instructors" who frequently encouraged verbal give-and-take, discussed their expectations with TAs, provided clear but flexible standards for TA behavior, offered direction for TAs' activities, and appreciated differences in opinions. Moreover, perceptions of instructor authoritativeness predicted TAs' self-rated job satisfaction and effectiveness. In contrast, the "authoritarian" (or overly demanding and strict) authority style was negatively associated with TAs' job satisfaction and competence. Authoritarian instructors typically did not permit TAs to question their decisions, required immediate TA compliance to their requests, became upset when TAs disagreed with their decisions, and expected that TAs conform to their expectations out of respect for their authority.

Supervising faculty must educate their colleagues about ways to establish productive relations with TAs. Meyers (1995) listed five suggestions for instructors who supervise and regularly work with TAs. These included: (a) treat TAs with respect (i.e., be open to TAs' input and participation, view TAs like colleagues and collaborators); (b) provide structure for the TA experience (i.e., provide TAs with clear guidelines, share advice and support); (c) display interpersonal sensitivity in interactions with TAs (i.e., be kind and approachable, express interest); (d) assign appropriate responsibilities and grant TAs sufficient autonomy (i.e., trust TAs' capabilities, be sensitive to TAs' developmental level); and (e) model enthusiasm for teaching and concern for undergraduate students (i.e., emphasize and demonstrate the importance of teaching).

As graduate students gain additional teaching experience, supervising faculty must attend to TAs' changing abilities and needs. Sprague and Nyquist (1989) presented a 3 stage model of TA development and stated that graduate students progress from senior learners to colleagues-in-training to junior colleagues. These developmental phases differ in terms of TAs' concerns, discourse level, approach to authority, and relationships with students (Nyquist & Sprague, 1998). Prieto's (1995) Integrated Developmental Model for Teaching Assistants (IDM-TA) shares this developmental framework and directs attention to TAs' changing levels of self-versus-other awareness, motivation, and autonomy across a range of important teaching domains (e.g., presentation skills, organizational skills, ethics).

Both of these conceptualizations emphasize that TA training and supervision must be tailored to TAs' developmental phase to have the greatest impact on their performance. As TAs acquire more experience, supervising faculty should delegate greater course responsibilities to them; grant more autonomy; provide reflective, rather than directive, feedback; and develop increasingly collegial relationships with TAs (Sprague & Nyquist, 1989). In addition, supervising faculty should focus on TAs' developmental levels within different teaching domains (Prieto, 1995). That is, TAs may require less directive supervision for certain teaching tasks (e.g., lecturing skills), but may still need more concrete training and feedback for other teaching domains (e.g., understanding the role of culture and ethnicity in the classroom) at the same point in time. Prieto (this volume) offers more detailed and helpful recommendations in this regard.

4. **Establish departmental and institutional cultures that value teaching and nurture professional development.** Incrementally changing departments' and universities' overarching views regarding teaching is a formidable task, but is needed to improve how graduate students are prepared for their teaching responsibilities (Hutchings, 1993). Despite the difficulties involved in questioning institutional norms, many faculty have a great deal of personal investment in their teaching and would support efforts to challenge its undervaluation in their departments and universities (Olson & Sorcinelli, 1992).

Some strategies to establish a culture that values teaching require a broad commitment and consensus among graduate students, faculty, and administrators. For instance, creating a centralized TA training/faculty development center or ensuring that the university appropriately compensates TAs for their labor need considerable political and financial support within the institution. However, such measures are likely to genuinely enhance TAs' perceptions of the importance of teaching and increase their skill development in this area.

Other ways to change attitudes towards teaching are local in nature and involve the creation of "caring communities" within departments and universities that focus on improving college teaching. Caring communities require meaningful relationships between faculty and graduate students. For instance, the professional development of graduate students can be furthered by structured mentorship experiences. In addition to meeting with TAs on a regular and frequent basis, mentors provide graduate students with advice, listen to their ideas, demonstrate and explain how to approach the process of teaching, and offer constructive feedback (Boice, 1992; Nyquist & Wulff, 1996). Moreover, supervising faculty can actively encourage peer mentoring. Not only will experienced student instructors gain from discussing pedagogy, but they also feel a sense of accomplishment when sharing their classroom successes (Meyers, Reid, & Quina, 1998).

Caring communities are not restricted to one-on-one relationships. Rather, groups of faculty and TAs can regularly meet to increase members' instructional expertise. For instance, teaching circles and collegial support groups (e.g., Johnson, Johnson, & Smith, 1991) provide members with support, guidance, observation, and respectful feedback. Group meetings allow members to discuss resources (e.g., readings on pedagogy, teaching-related web sites), share information, and may even inspire department-wide colloquia that promote TA and faculty development.

Caring communities are not bounded by disciplinary or institutional borders. For instance, mentoring relationships are effective even when the mentor and protégé are from different disciplines (Boice, 1992). Similarly, teaching circles can include TAs and faculty members from departments across the university. Caring communities can also extend beyond the home university. Professional organizations within disciplines can facilitate mentoring by matching senior faculty with less experienced instructors from different institutions. Ambitious demonstration projects that bring together graduate students, faculty from research institutions, and faculty from liberal arts colleges have also been shown to widen TAs' views of teaching and academic life. Slevin (1992) described a project in which graduate students received intensive mentoring experiences from faculty at neighboring liberal arts colleges and participated in seminars focusing on higher education to expose them to a broad array of institutional cultures.

5. **Ensure that teaching assistants are active learners during training**. Regardless of the training format and location, TAs are more likely to gain increased com-

petence and confidence if they are actively involved during training. Although the overall effectiveness of active learning techniques has been well-documented in research studies (cf. Johnson, Johnson, & Smith, 1991), relatively few publications have described how these strategies can be used to enhance graduate students' teaching skills. As such, the remainder of this chapter focuses on three sets of active learning strategies for use in TA training programs: in-class activities, written assignments, and modeling/ performance feedback.

Active Learning Strategies for TA Training

Promoting Effective TA Training Through In-Class Activities

In-class activities are exercises that encourage TAs to analyze their teaching or are strategies that allow TAs to practice a specific skill. Activities that promote reflection are especially useful in the beginning of TA training programs. One effective way for TAs to examine their training needs and teaching goals is to provide an opportunity for them to complete questionnaires. For example, the Self Efficacy Towards Teaching Inventory-Adapted (SETI-A; Prieto & Altmaier, 1994) assesses TAs' confidence in their ability to perform 32 teaching behaviors (e.g., plan lectures, write a course syllabus, draw students into discussions). Supervising faculty can examine TAs' responses to ensure that training meets TAs' needs. In addition, faculty can administer the SETI-A at the conclusion of training to measure changes in TAs' confidence levels.

Teaching assistants reflect on the goals that guide their teaching by completing the Teaching Goals Inventory (Angelo & Cross, 1993). This questionnaire provides TAs with feedback on the extent to which they choose to foster undergraduates': higher-order thinking skills, basic academic success skills, discipline-specific knowledge, liberal arts and academic values, work and career preparation, and personal development. After completing and scoring these measures, TAs contrast their responses with those of their peers for further consideration.

Supervising faculty also encourage reflection when they allocate time for TAs to share their teaching successes and difficulties with each other. Teaching assistants meet in small groups during these "check-in periods" so that each can speak for several minutes. These opportunities provide TAs with peer support, promote cohesion, provide new ideas, and normalize many of the frustrations that they experience.

In-class activities can also involve analyzing and discussing challenging situations that TAs encounter. These exercises often adhere to a general framework. The supervising faculty member first presents TAs with a teaching dilemma (e.g., "Two students who are sitting at the back of your lab section are talking to each other. This continues for five minutes and it begins to distract your lecture"). Supervising faculty can elicit TAs' actual experiences for these activities or can develop scenarios beforehand. Fictitious teaching dilemmas can be presented briefly, but detailed case studies (Tillson, 1997) or videotaped vignettes (Bach, 1992) are likely to be more productive.

After presenting the stimulus for the exercise, TAs engage with the material and relate it to their own teaching. Supervising faculty encourage analysis by stimulating discussion. For example, Tillson (1997) recommended posing the following questions to TAs: (a) Who are the main characters?; (b) What problems are evident?; (c) What solutions can be identified?; (d) What is the best solution?; (e) Why?; and (f) How do pedagogical concepts apply to this case? During discussion, supervising faculty encourage the participation of all TAs, periodically summarize discussion content, connect and reconcile differing points of view, and explicitly connect the discussion to concepts reviewed during training.

In addition to presenting and discussing teaching dilemmas, supervising faculty can provide participants with sample syllabi, tests, and project assignments to review as in-class activities. Sample syllabi, exam questions, or project assignments can be obtained from TAs themselves, departmental faculty, or ancillary materials developed for textbooks. Teaching assistants then critique these materials using a set of guidelines that are provided by supervising faculty.

For example, TAs can analyze syllabi for several courses and note whether the following information is present in each: (a) course number and name; (b) current year and semester; (c) instructor's name; (d) instructor's office hours and office location; (e) instructor's telephone number, e-mail address, or voice mail; (f) required texts and readings; (g) course prerequisites; (h) course overview, objectives, and goals; (i) description of the content of tests, quizzes, essays, and projects; (j) relative weight of tests, quizzes, essays, and projects in grade computation; (k) dates that tests, quizzes, essays, and projects are due; (l) description of policies about attendance, late work, and make-up work; (m) list of topics for each class session; and (n) list of readings expected for each class session.

Similarly, TAs can examine multiple choice questions from a test bank or those that they have developed and answer the following questions: (a) Are students instructed to select the best answer, not the correct answer?; (b) Is the stem clear and concise?; (c) Is the stem stated in positive form?; (d) Is the full problem and all relevant material presented in the stem?; (d) Is the intended answer is clearly the best?; (e) Do the alternatives avoid the choices "all of the above" or "none of the above?"; (f) Are alternatives equal in terms of length, complexity, plausibility, and grammatical consistency?; and (g) Do the alternatives avoid words such as always, never, all, none, sometimes, may, and usually?

Finally, in-class activities help TAs plan and practice teaching skills. These exercises allow TAs to gain firsthand experience designing lectures, discussions, or active learning activities during training. After providing a topic with which the TAs are familiar, representative assignments include: (a) make this lecture relevant or interesting;

(b) design a discussion around the content of this topic; or (c) develop an active learning strategy that involves a small group activity for this topic.

Moreover, supervising faculty can use microteaching to allow TAs to practice these techniques in a supportive environment. Microteaching is a training activity in which instructors teach a brief lesson, analyze their performance, and reteach the same material (Allen & Ryan, 1969). It typically isolates a single teaching skill or task, such as posing stimulating questions, exemplifying a concept, or reviewing a syllabus on the first day of class. Teaching assistants prepare and present a 5 to 10 minute lesson to peers or to a small number of undergraduates recruited for this exercise. After the initial presentation, supervising faculty solicit written or oral feedback from the mock class. Because many TAs feel anxious during this exercise, supervisors attend to positive aspects of these presentations and ensure that peer comments are constructive. In addition, TAs are involved in their own critiquing process. As such, microteaching lessons are videotaped to promote TAs' awareness of their teaching style, and are played back to illustrate relevant points during the feedback phase (Wulff, 1992). In the final phase of microteaching, TAs incorporate these suggestions, reteach the same material, and receive additional feedback. During reteaching the mock class can be composed of the same audience members or a different group of students. Because microteaching focuses on the accomplishment of specific teaching tasks, these exercises can be used throughout TA training programs so that participants rehearse a wide range of skills. Finally, supervising faculty can modify or abbreviate the microteaching process to meet programmatic needs, but still generally follow the teach, analyze, and reteach sequence. Maslach, Silver, Pole, and Ozer (this volume) provide more detailed instructions about ways to incorporate microteaching into TA training programs.

Promoting Effective TA Training Through Written Assignments

Written assignments foster an ongoing dialogue between supervising faculty and TAs who participate in training programs. Regularly collected journals provide TAs with a forum to record problems and successes from class, document strategies for improvement, and note reminders for subsequent semesters (Vanderford, Eison, & Olive, 1996). Journal writing also allows TAs to reflect on their teaching as well as integrate readings and topics addressed during training with their own classroom experiences.

Journals can be used in different ways. Some supervising faculty adopt an unstructured approach and encourage TAs to maintain a teaching diary in which they record their thoughts about and reactions to teaching. A somewhat more structured approach is to provide TAs with a general framework for journal entries. For instance, supervising faculty can provide the following instructions to guide journal writing:

Briefly summarize one or two significant events that occurred in your class during the past week. Focus on a teaching-related issue that you struggled with, found intriguing or confusing, or about which you would like feedback. Try to relate your experiences to the seminar material and readings if possible. Bach (1992) provided another general framework for TAs' classroom communications and behaviors. Teaching assistants profile a teaching success and failure by: (a) describing their behavior, (b) describing the students' reaction, (c) analyzing why the behavior was successful or failed, and (d) developing possible solutions for the problematic situation.

Alternatively, supervising faculty can tailor the focus of TAs' journals to a specific topic that is addressed in a seminar or workshop meeting. Sample assignments for structured journal entries include:

1. Think back upon all the college instructors that you have had. Select the person who you believed was the most effective. Describe that instructor's teaching behaviors. Why was this person an effective instructor? What do you think the goals for this class were, and why was the class successful in meeting these goals?

2. Describe an incident in which you had a conflict with one of the students enrolled in your class. Describe how you handled the situation and ways that you wished you had dealt with the situation. How could the conflict have been prevented?

3. List several goals that guide or permeate your course. After each, explain how you assess whether students have accomplished this objective. For instance, one course goal can be: "students will be able to apply theories presented in this course to real-world problems." In addition to stating this goal, please describe how you assess whether students can actually do this (e.g., "Exam 2 presents students with the following problem. They are asked to use two theories to explain the origins of this problem.).

Hainline (this volume) provides additional suggestions and topics for journal assignments for use in TA development seminars.

The teaching portfolio is a written assignment that documents TAs' growth as an instructor. Graduate students often view the construction of teaching portfolios as an opportunity to examine their professional development and consider them a useful way to document teaching expertise for later academic job searches. Teaching assistants' portfolios include: (a) a statement of teaching experience that lists the scope of their responsibilities and profiles the courses that they have taught; (b) a statement of teaching philosophy; (c) sample syllabi, if they have developed any; (d) sample lecture outlines and handouts; (e) representative class assignments, including tests, papers, and projects; (f) sample student work, such as graded essay assignments or term papers; and (g) teaching evaluations and observational feedback (Freeman & Schmidt, 1997; Vanderford et al., 1996).

Constructing a teaching portfolio is a demanding task and some TAs need assistance beyond these instructions. One helpful strategy is to encourage TAs to carefully examine several model teaching portfolios that have been assembled by faculty and senior TAs. Another way to facilitate TAs' portfolio development is to require several smaller assignments (i.e., journal entries and in-class exercises) throughout the training program that allow them to compile and write parts of the portfolio over a greater period of time.

Promoting Effective TA Training Through Modeling and Performance Feedback

Finally, modeling, observation, and feedback are three powerful techniques that help TAs develop teaching abilities. In modeling, TAs acquire skills by watching and imitating experts; observation and feedback involve other individuals examining or critiquing TAs' performance while teaching.

Modeling activities can be used with TAs regardless of their level of experience or the nature of their job responsibilities. However, the success of a modeling activity is increased if supervising faculty carefully plan the assignment and provide TAs with detailed instructions beforehand. First, supervising faculty determine the specific teaching skills that they want TAs to develop as a result of the modeling activity. For example, TAs can examine how a model stimulates discussion, summarizes points during a lecture, uses visual aids, or redirects classroom conflicts. The choice of target teaching tasks should be related to the topics that are addressed during training so that TAs have the opportunity to discuss and learn about the skill in greater detail.

Second, supervising faculty select one or more models for TAs to observe. Possible teaching models include faculty members, senior TAs, and videotaped experts. Modeling will likely be enhanced when: (a) the model is highly adept at performing the teaching task, (b) the model demonstrates a teaching task that seems relevant to the TA, (c) the model presents the teaching task several times in a clear fashion, (d) the model appears friendly and pleasant, and (e) TAs have the opportunity to view different models perform the teaching task (cf. McGinnis & Goldstein, 1997). Regardless of the model's identity, TAs will benefit from conversations with him or her after the observation period.

The most common model for TAs to observe is a faculty member in TAs' own department. These observations can occur in the context of a one-on-one mentoring relationship (Beaudoin & Felder, 1997) or TAs can ask faculty members for permission to observe their teaching. Alternatively, supervising faculty can direct TAs to observe advanced graduate students who display teaching excellence. One variation of this idea is to use a demonstration class in which all new TAs observe the same model, who has been selected on the basis of his or her teaching skill and willingness to be scrutinized throughout the semester (Strozer, 1993). Participating TAs and supervising faculty consequently have a shared understanding when they refer to the demonstration class. Finally, TAs benefit from analyzing videotaped model teachers. These films are available commercially (see Bach, 1992 for a brief description and ordering information for several videotapes) or can be created by supervising faculty who videotape skilled colleagues.

Teaching assistants may gain further insights through guided discussions about the teaching behaviors that they observed. For example, supervising faculty can ask TAs to explain why and when the observed teaching task is appropriate, to describe the behaviors of the instructor and students during the teaching task, and to relate the teaching task to seminar readings and past discussions (Sherer, 1991).

Unlike modeling, observation entails TAs performing rather than watching teaching behaviors. The setting for observations depends on the TA's job responsibilities. Observations can easily be scheduled for those TAs who have full course responsibility or who lead discussion or laboratory sections. However, supervising faculty have to arrange for TAs to guest lecture for those who have few classroom duties. Several people can observe TAs and provide them with feedback. Most frequently, supervising faculty visit during a class or review a videotape of the session. Faculty observations of TAs are important for ensuring the quality of undergraduate education, determining future assistantship assignments, and collecting observations for writing letters of recommendation for graduate students. Moreover, faculty are uniquely qualified to assess certain aspects of TAs' performance that others (e.g., students, peers) cannot. These areas include accuracy of information, consistency of lectures with course goals, and skill using discipline-specific pedagogy (Wulff, 1992).

Other writers have underscored that non-faculty observers also make important contributions. Jones and Makinen (1991) emphasized that undergraduate students have the most valid judgments with regard to TAs' level of presentation and the effectiveness of TAs' presentation techniques; they also provide useful suggestions for improvement. Similarly, Allen (1991) suggested that participants in TA training programs observe each other. This approach may be less intimidating than observations by faculty and may decrease TAs' performance anxiety. Finally, TAs can observe and critique their own videotaped performance. Self-review increases TAs' awareness of their communication idiosyncrasies (i.e., distracting behavioral mannerisms and speech patterns) and highlights areas in need of improvement in a minimally threatening environment. Importantly, these techniques are not mutually exclusive; TAs benefit from multiple observers.

Observation must be coupled with constructive feedback so that TAs appreciate their strengths and weaknesses as well as identify strategies to improve their performance. Prentice-Dunn and Pitts (this volume) provide supervising faculty with detailed instructions on ways to prepare TAs for feedback as well as how to conduct a consultation session. Although faculty and peers can spontaneously organize and discuss their classroom observations with TAs, the use of checklists helps observers offer more thorough and constructive feedback. Helling (1988) provided an extensive checklist that is tailored to the format of the observed session (i.e., teaching through presentation, teaching through involvement, teaching through questioning). Raters indicate whether concrete teaching behaviors are present during their observation. Moreover, all teaching behaviors are positively worded so that TAs receive specific and constructive recommendations for improving their performance. Briefer checklists are also available. For instance, the Center for Teaching and Learning at University of North Carolina, Chapel Hill (1992) developed a 20-item inventory that is scored on a 3-point scale. Observers rate TAs' organization (e.g., "presented an overview of the lesson"), presentation (e.g., "explained things with clarity"), interaction (e.g., "actively encouraged student questions"), and content knowledge (e.g., "demonstrated command of the subject matter"). Observers also indicate TAs' strengths and suggest ways to improve their teaching.

Teaching assistants can also critique their own performance. The Center for Teaching and Learning, University of North Carolina at Chapel Hill (1992) developed several self-evaluation forms for TAs to use when analyzing their own videotaped teaching. Fourteen questions direct TAs' attention to selected aspects of their presentation (e.g., "What do you do with your hands?;" "When do you speak faster/slower?;" "How do you emphasize main points?"). A more detailed 46-item checklist encourages TAs to rate their clarity of presentation, class structure, excitement of student interest, questioning technique, and communication style on a 3-point scale.

Finally, TAs can anonymously collect student feedback during the semester to enhance their teaching skills. Although student evaluation is often conducted at the end of the course, evaluation before the middle of the semester suggests areas to be improved while the course is in progress (Duba-Biedermann, 1991). If TAs want informal feedback, they can ask undergraduates to write three aspects of the course that they enjoy and to indicate three ways that the course could be improved. Alternatively, TAs can distribute course evaluations that their universities traditionally use at the end of the semester. If such evaluation forms are not readily available or appear inadequate, supervising faculty can provide TAs with Marsh's (1982) SEEQ instrument that assesses instructors' ability to stimulate learning, convey enthusiasm, organize material effectively, promote student participation, establish rapport, present a breadth of information, develop fair examinations, design valuable assignments, as well as their overall teaching ability.

Conclusions

Supervising faculty have a wide range of training options to choose from when creating or expanding TA training programs. The ultimate determination of the "who-what-when-where-and-how" of TA training must be tailored to the needs of each department and university. Just as there many ways to be an effective instructor, there are also many ways to help instructors become more effective. This statement, however, is not intended to lessen the responsibility of departments and universities to prepare their doctoral students for teaching. As Slevin (1992) argued, faculty development must begin in graduate school.

References

Allen, D., & Ryan, K. (1969). *Microteaching.* Reading, MA: Addison-Wesley.

Allen, R. R. (1991). Encouraging reflection in teaching assistants. In J. D. Nyquist, R. D. Abbott, D. H. Wulff, & J. Sprague (Eds.), *Preparing the professoriate of tomorrow to teach* (pp. 313-317). Dubuque, IA: Kendall/Hunt.

Altbach, P. G. (1970). Commitment and powerlessness on the American campus: The case of the graduate student. *Liberal Education, 56,* 562-582.

Angelo, T. A., & Cross, K. P. (1993). *Classroom assessment techniques: A handbook for college teachers* (2nd ed.). San Francisco: Jossey-Bass.

Astin, A., Korn, W. S., & Day, E. L. (1991). *The American college teacher: National norms for the 1989-1990 HERI faculty survey.* Los Angeles: Higher Education Research Institute, Graduate School of Education, UCLA.

Bach, B. W. (1992). A professional course on college teaching. In J. D. Nyquist & D. H. Wulff (Eds.), *Preparing teaching assistants for instructional roles: Supervising TAs in communication* (pp. 214-222). Annandale, VA: Speech Communication Association.

Beaudoin, S. P., & Felder, R. M. (1997). Preparing for the professoriate: A study in mentorship. *Journal of Graduate Teaching Assistant Development, 4,* 87-91.

Benassi, V. A., & Fernald, P. S. (1993). Preparing tomorrow's psychologists for careers in academe. *Teaching of Psychology, 20,* 149-155.

Boice, R. (1992). Lessons learned about mentoring. In M. D. Sorcinelli & A. E. Austin (Eds.), *Developing new and junior faculty* (pp. 51-61). San Francisco: Jossey-Bass.

Bort, M., & Buerkel-Rothfuss, N. L. (1991). A content analysis of TA training materials. In J. D. Nyquist, R. D. Abbott, D. H. Wulff, & J. Sprague (Eds.), *Preparing the professoriate of tomorrow to teach* (pp. 243-251). Dubuque, IA: Kendall/Hunt.

Boyer, E. L. (1990). *Scholarship reconsidered: Priorities of the professoriate.* Princeton, NJ: Carnegie Foundation for the Advancement of Teaching.

Center for Teaching and Learning, University of North Carolina at Chapel Hill. (1992). *TAs and professors as a teaching team: A faculty guide to TA training and supervision.* Chapel Hill, NC: Author.

Davis, B. G. (1993). *Tools for teaching.* San Francisco: Jossey-Bass.

Diamond, R. M., & Gray, P. (1987). *National study of teaching assistants.* Syracuse, NY: Syracuse University Center for Instructional Development.

Duba-Biedermann, L. (1991). Changes in teaching behavior reported by teaching assistants after a midterm analysis of teaching. In J. D. Nyquist, R. D. Abbott, D. H. Wulff, & J. Sprague (Eds.), *Preparing the professoriate of tomorrow to teach* (pp. 289-292). Dubuque, IA: Kendall/Hunt.

Eble, K. E. (1988). *The craft of teaching: A guide to mastering the professor's art* (2nd ed.). San Francisco: Jossey-Bass.

Eison, J., & Hill, H. H. (1990). Creating workshops for new faculty. *Journal of Staff, Program, and Organization Development, 8*, 223-234.

Freeman, P. R., & Schmidt, J. Z. (1997). An interdisciplinary teaching assistant training program at an M.A. institution. *Journal of Graduate Teaching Assistant Development, 4*, 93-99.

Gray, P. L., & Buerkel-Rothfuss, N. L. (1991). Teaching assistant training: The view from the trenches. In J. D. Nyquist, R. D. Abbott, D. H. Wulff, & J. Sprague (Eds.), *Preparing the professoriate of tomorrow to teach* (pp. 40-51). Dubuque, IA: Kendall/Hunt.

Helling, B. B. (1988). Looking for good teaching: A guide to peer observation. *Journal of Staff, Program, and Organization Development, 6*, 147-158.

Henderson, P. H., & Woods, C. (1997). *Summary report 1996: Doctorate recipients from United States universities.* Washington, DC: National Academy Press.

Hutchings, P. (1993). Preparing the professoriate: Next steps and what we need to do to take them. In L. M. Lambert & S. L. Tice (Eds.), *Preparing graduate students to teach: A guide to programs that improve undergraduate education and develop tomorrow's faculty.* Washington, DC: American Association for Higher Education.

Johnson, D. W., Johnson, R. T., & Smith, C. A. (1991). *Active learning: Cooperation in the college classroom.* Edina, MN: Interaction Book Company.

Jones, R. W., & Makinen, A. L. (1991). Instructional preparation program for TAs in Michigan Tech's General Chemistry program. In J. D. Nyquist, R. D. Abbott, D. H. Wulff, & J. Sprague (Eds.), *Preparing the professoriate of tomorrow to teach* (pp. 210-214). Dubuque, IA: Kendall/Hunt.

Lowman, J. (1995). *Mastering the techniques of teaching* (2nd ed.). San Francisco: Jossey-Bass.

Lowman, J., & Mathie, V. A. (1993). What should graduate teaching assistants know about teaching? *Teaching of Psychology, 20*, 84-88.

Marincovich, M. (1998). Teaching teaching: The importance of courses on teaching in TA training programs. In M. Marincovich, J. Prostko, & F. Stout (Eds.), *The professional development of graduate teaching assistants* (pp. 145-162). Bolton, MA: Anker.

Marsh, H. W. (1982). SEEQ: A reliable, valid, and useful instrument for collecting students' evaluations of university teaching. *British Journal of Educational Psychology, 52*, 77-95.

McGinnis, E., & Goldstein, A. P. (1997). *Skillstreaming the elementary school child* (Revised ed.). Champaign, IL: Research Press.

McKeachie, W. J. (Ed.). (1999). *Teaching tips: Strategies, research, and theory for college and university teachers* (10th ed.). Boston: Houghton-Mifflin.

Meyers, C., & Jones, T. B. (1993). *Promoting active learning: Strategies for the college classroom.* San Francisco: Jossey-Bass.

Meyers, S. A. (1995). Enhancing relationships between instructors and teaching assistants. *Journal of Graduate Teaching Assistant Development, 2,* 107-112.

Meyers, S. A. (1996). Consequences of interpersonal relationships between teaching assistants and supervising faculty. *Psychological Reports, 78,* 755-762.

Meyers, S. A., & Prieto, L. R. (in press). Training in the teaching of psychology: What is done and examining the differences. *Teaching of Psychology.*

Meyers, S. A., Reid, P. T., & Quina, K. (1998). Ready or not, here we come: Preparing psychology graduate students for academic careers. *Teaching of Psychology, 25,* 124-126.

Mintz, J. A. (1998). The role of centralized programs in preparing graduate students to teach. In M. Marincovich, J. Prostko, & F. Stout (Eds.), *The professional development of graduate teaching assistants* (pp. 19-40). Bolton, MA: Anker.

Nyquist, J. D., Abbott, R. D., Wulff, D. H., & Sprague, J. (Eds.). (1991). *Preparing the professoriate of tomorrow to teach.* Dubuque, IA: Kendall/Hunt.

Nyquist, J. D., & Sprague, J. (1998). Thinking developmentally about TAs. In M. Marincovich, J. Prostko, & F. Stout (Eds.), *The professional development of graduate teaching assistants* (pp. 61-88). Bolton, MA: Anker.

Nyquist, J. D., & Wulff, D. H. (1996). *Working effectively with graduate assistants.* Thousand Oaks, CA: Sage.

Olson, D., & Sorcinelli, M. D. (1992). The pretenure years: A longitudinal perspective. In M. D. Sorcinelli & A. E. Austin (Eds.), *Developing new and junior faculty* (pp. 15-25). San Francisco: Jossey-Bass.

Ory, J. C., & Ryan, K. E. (1993). *Tips for improving grading and testing.* Newbury Park, CA: Sage.

Prieto, L. R. (1995). Supervising graduate teaching assistants: An adaptation of the Integrated Developmental Model. *Journal of Graduate Teaching Assistant Development, 2,* 93-105.

Prieto, L. R., & Altmaier, E. M. (1994). The relationship of prior training and previous teaching experience to self-efficacy among graduate teaching assistants. *Research in Higher Education, 35,* 481-497.

Prieto, L. R., & Meyers, S. A. (1999). The effects of training and supervision on the self-efficacy of psychology graduate teaching assistants. *Teaching of Psychology, 26,* 264-266.

Rickard, H. C., Prentice-Dunn, S., Rogers, R. W., Scogin, F. R., & Lyman, R. D. (1991). Teaching of psychology: A required course for all doctoral students. *Teaching of Psychology, 18,* 235-237.

Ronkowski, S. A. (1998). The disciplinary/departmental context of TA training. In M. Marincovich, J. Prostko, & F. Stout (Eds.), *The professional development of graduate teaching assistants* (pp. 41-60). Bolton, MA: Anker.

Schuster, J. H. (1993). Preparing the next generation of faculty: The graduate school's opportunity. In L. Richlin (Ed.), *Preparing faculty for new conceptions of scholarship* (pp. 27-38). San Francisco: Jossey-Bass.

Sherer, P. D. (1991). A framework for TA training: Methods, behaviors, skills, and student involvement. In J. D. Nyquist, R. D. Abbott, D. H. Wulff, & J. Sprague (Eds.), *Preparing the professoriate of tomorrow to teach* (pp. 257-262). Dubuque, IA: Kendall/Hunt.

Slevin, J. F. (1992). *The next generation: Preparing graduate students for the professional responsibilities of college teachers.* Washington, DC: Association of American Colleges.

Sorcinelli, M. D., & Austin, A. E. (Eds.). (1992). *Developing new and junior faculty.* San Francisco: Jossey-Bass.

Sprague, J., & Nyquist, J. D. (1989). TA supervision. In J. D. Nyquist, R. D. Abbott, & D. H. Wulff (Eds.), *Teaching assistant training in the 1990s* (pp. 37-53). San Francisco: Jossey-Bass.

Stout, F. (1998). Getting started with TA training on your campus. In M. Marincovich, J. Prostko, & F. Stout (Eds.), *The professional development of graduate teaching assistants* (pp. 121-144). Bolton, MA: Anker.

Strozer, J. R. (1993). Using modeling to develop teaching effectiveness and "classroom sense" in graduate teaching assistants. In K. G. Lewis (Ed.), *The TA experience: Preparing for multiple roles* (pp. 167-173). Stillwater, OK: New Forums Press.

Tice, S. L., Featherstone, P. H., & Johnson, H. C. (1998). TA certificate programs. In M. Marincovich, J. Prostko, & F. Stout (Eds.), *The professional development of graduate teaching assistants* (pp. 263-274). Bolton, MA: Anker.

Tillson, L. D. (1997). Preparing tomorrow's professoriate: GTA development and the case method. *Journal of Graduate Teaching Assistant Development, 5,* 31-42.

Vanderford, M. L., Eison, J., & Olive, T. (1996). Challenges and strategies for helping GTAs develop teaching portfolios. *Journal of Graduate Teaching Assistant Development, 3,* 61-68.

Weimer, M., Svinicki, M. D., & Bauer, G. (1989). In J. D. Nyquist, R. D. Abbott, & D. H. Wulff (Eds.), *Teaching assistant training in the 1990s* (pp. 57-70). San Francisco: Jossey-Bass.

Wulff, D. H. (1992). Essential elements of TA training. In J. D. Nyquist & D. H. Wulff (Eds.), *Preparing teaching assistants for instructional roles: Supervising TAs in communication* (pp. 114-127). Annandale, VA: Speech Communication Association.

Departmental Teaching Assistants' Orientation

Sandra Goss Lucas, Ph.D.
University of Illinois

Note: This departmental orientation was jointly developed and would not have been possible without Douglas A. Bernstein, Professor Emeritus at the University of Illinois. Special thanks to John Ory, Marne Helgesen, and Nancy Diamond from the University of Illinois Office of Instructional Resources, and John Fiore from the University of Illinois Department of Psychology for all of their help in developing this orientation. Thanks, also, to the University of Illinois Department of Psychology for its continued support of this orientation.

Overview

This chapter will focus on practical information that departments can use in the development of their own Teaching Assistants' Orientation. It contains an outline of a two day departmental orientation (plus microteaching and feedback on microteaching) with enough detail that it could serve as a guideline for the development of any departmental orientation. Included are numerous handouts that could be duplicated, or adapted to meet the specific needs of the department.

The focus will be on two important questions:

1. Why a departmental TA Orientation instead of an All-Campus Orientation?
2. What are the basic "MUST include" topics for a TA Orientation?

Departmental vs. All-Campus TA Orientation

Our campus has an outstanding Office of Instructional Resources that presents a TA Orientation every semester for first-time TAs across the campus. When we began our program, we had our TAs attend this All-Campus Orientation, while attending small group activities that were led by people from our department. This model worked well the first couple of years because it allowed us to focus on small group activities while our TAs received good information on general issues such as lecturing, grading, etc. It also allowed us to focus our resources, given a limited budget.

However, as we received feedback from our TAs, we found that they were dissatisfied with this model for two important reasons. First, they received little information that was specific to the department. TAs told us that they needed answers to some very basic departmental questions, such as how to get a desk copy of the textbook, where to check out audio-visual equipment, who would type and reproduce tests, how class rosters would be distributed, what their specific duties were, where to go if they had a "problem" student, who to talk to if classroom management problems emerged, etc. These issues could not be dealt with in an All-Campus Orientation.

In addition, TAs reported some of the concepts presented at the All-Campus TA Orientation, for example learning styles, were new ideas to many TAs from other departments, but "old hat" to our TAs. They were "turned off" by their perception of a very simplistic presentation.

Because of the feedback that we received from our TAs we decided to develop a departmentally focused TA Orientation. We have never regretted that decision. We also were very careful that we continued to make use of the excellent resources from our campus Office of Instructional Resources. We were able to continue the microteaching component of the experience and have a presentation by an expert in test development, thanks to this office.

The format of the orientation team has varied, but it is very important that "senior" graduate students, with considerable teaching experience, be part of the team. Our orientation team has evolved into one faculty member (due to the retirement of the other co-developer) and two graduate students. It is difficult for one person to "be on" for two solid days, and having three people involved allows for other important activities to take place simultaneously (such as choosing sample exam questions and xeroxing). It is also excellent experience for the graduate students to be involved in planning and implementing such a program.

We have now presented five departmental TA Orientations and are working on the next one. While much of the "core" of the Orientation remains the same, there are other topics and issues that have evolved as we integrate the feedback from our past participants. The basic tenet that has evolved from our departmental orientations is that the focus of the orientation must be on the essentials of teaching. Most of the participants in our orientation will be TAs in one week and most have no previous experience. Their feedback to us continues to be that we need to give them the teaching skills now and focus on philosophical issues of teaching later, when they are in a position to appreciate and understand the bigger picture. While many teacher training experts will disagree with this perspective, our program has evolved into a very practical orientation with major emphasis on teaching "survival skills" and available resources. Philosophical discussions are reserved for a future "Teaching Psychology at the College Level" course.

Basic "Must Include" Topics

This leads to the second question, what are the basic concepts/skills that need to be included in an orientation, whether departmental or all-campus?

I believe it is essential to address the teaching concerns of the participants. Their concerns about teaching are of overwhelming importance to them. We have learned to address these concerns at the very beginning of the program. Otherwise, some participants experience such anxiety that they aren't able to concentrate on other important issues.

After introductions, participants are given a blank 3 x 5 card. They are instructed to not put their names on the cards but write their major concern(s) about teaching on one side and why they are excited/looking forward to being a TA on the other. The cards are collected, shuffled, and randomly handed back. Participants then share a concern listed on the card they were given, not their own. If the concern is a simple one, we provide an answer. For example, if the question is, "Where do I get a copy of the textbook?," we provide the information. If the issue is more complicated, we point out when we will present information on that issue. We promise to address all concerns before the orientation ends. I take the cards home that evening and read them. If there are questions/concerns that have not been addressed and were not on the outline to be addressed, then I incorporate them into the next day's presentations. (Often that issue will get added to the next year's outline.) This lowers the anxiety and stress level of the entire room, and leads to a better focus on other issues.

Another basic is some "hands on" experience writing exam questions. The first day of orientation includes a presentation by the head of our Office of Instructional Resources who is renowned for his expertise on developing exam questions. Following this presentation, we distribute a copy of a section from an introductory textbook and ask the participants to return the next day with exam questions covering that material. We ask them to write definitional and application multiple choice questions, as well as an essay question with a scoring grid. Each question is submitted on a separate piece of paper in as large a font as possible with no names on them. The next morning, the graduate student presenters look through the questions and pick examples of common problems and examples of very good questions. The questions are duplicated onto transparencies and we discuss the them, applying the concepts presented by our "expert".

Some type of microteaching or practice teaching experience is an essential component of a TA Orientation. Following our two day orientation, participants present an 8-minute "mini-lesson" on a topic of their choice. We encourage them to choose a topic that they are likely to teach. Groups of ten participants present their "mini-lessons" to their peers and receive immediate feedback (via evaluation sheets) from them. All of the "mini-lessons" are videotaped and viewed later with one of the orientation presenters. This component, the most dreaded as participants come into the program, has consistently been evaluated as the most important and useful part of the entire orientation. Nothing is more powerful than actually seeing yourself in a teaching role.

Finally, every orientation must contain a good evaluative component so participants can note what they found most useful, what they felt was missing, what information they didn't need, etc. We ask for evaluations of the orientation at two different points in time. The first evaluation is completed at the end of the two day orientation, before the microteaching component. The second evaluation is distributed at mid-semester, to see if other issues have emerged from their TA experience. These evaluations have been very useful in adapting the orientation to meet TA needs.

Outline and Handouts developed for
University of Illinois Psychology Department's
Teaching Assistants' Orientation
Overview

Orientation Topics	Handouts	Chapter Appendix
DAY ONE		
Welcoming remarks		
Introductions		
Teaching methods		
TA concerns/hopes	3 x 5 blank index cards	
Tips on lecturing		
Leading discussions		
Asking questions		
Active learning strategies	Active learning handout	
Evaluation		
Grading		
Writing test items	Jacobs & Chase excerpt	
Textbook excerpt		
Evaluating students		
Teacher evaluation		
Effectively using informal early semester feedback		
Written and verbal methods for early semester feedback		
Analyzing student evaluations		A
Posting grades		
Campus guidelines/resources		
Departmental resources	"Numbers that might come in handy"	

Orientation Topics	Handouts	Chapter Appendix
Add/drop & credit/ no credit	General policies	
	Student information card	
Make-up policies	Conflict exam request form	B
Rehab policies/procedures	Teaching students with disabilities	
	Guide to disability resources and services	
Handicapping language		
Counseling Center	Self-help pamphlets	
Identifying and referring troubled students		
Helping students' get a first time appointment at the counseling center		
Instructor responsibilities	Job description	C
DAY TWO		
Student-faculty relations	Faculty-student relationships in class	
Power and dating		
Problems related to minority status		
Sexual harassment	U of I sexual harassment policy	
	Warming the Chilly Classroom Climate	
	The student in the back row	
Discrimination based on sexual orientation	Preventing discrimination based on sexual orientation	
Who are your students?	Who are your students?	
Classroom management techniques		
Survival skills		
Importance of rules		
Consistency		
Academic integrity		
Capricious grading		
Academic dishonesty	Sample letters	
Practical approaches to dealing with cheating on exams		
Returning quizzes and exams	Request to review an exam item	D
Sample item analysis		
Preparing for the first day	Preparing for the first day	E
Syllabus construction	as an instructor	
Wrap-up	Orientation evaluation form	
DAY THREE		
Microteaching		
Feedback on microteaching (Faculty guidelines)		

Day One

Welcoming Remarks by the Department Head

It is essential that the Department TA Orientation be sanctioned by the department hierarchy. This provides credibility to the entire experience. We ask our department head to make welcoming remarks and to emphasis the importance that the department places on quality teaching.

Introductions of Facilitators, Presenters, and Participants

It is much more comfortable to talk with a group of people you know than with a group of strangers. Therefore, we spend time introducing ourselves and having the participants introduce themselves. Name tags would be an additional way to get to know the people in the group.

The first handout is an outline of the entire program and a listing of all of the handouts they will receive. At our first departmental orientation, several presenters talked about the importance of outlining each day's class for our students. But a participant pointed out that we had not provided them with an outline of the orientation. Feedback is essential! This outline helps TAs understand the scope of the orientation and often guides them in writing their concerns.

Teaching Methods

As discussed previously, after introductions we distribute 3 x 5 cards and ask for participant concerns regarding their upcoming teaching. Then we discuss some of the concerns and collect the rest to read later so they can be incorporated into the orientation.

Most participants are very worried about their microteaching. In their notification letter they were told to bring their microteaching outline with them. So, at this point we tell them that past participants have consistently identified microteaching as the most important component of the entire orientation. We also reassure them that there will be an opportunity to consult with a presenter and fellow participants to review their outlines and that microteaching isn't meant to be evaluative.

Lecturing, Using Small Groups, Leading Discussions, and Asking Questions

Most college instructors use a combination of teaching strategies in their classroom. Rather than just discussing these strategies, we show videotape of TAs using many of them. For example, we have three short videotape clips of three different TAs lecturing, using very different styles. All three are excellent teachers, they just have different personalities and different size classes. This leads to a discussion of being yourself in front of the class (instead of trying to be a clone of your favorite instructor), the impact of class size on teaching style, etc. It is important that TAs realize very early that there is no one model of good teaching and that everyone, if motivated, can become a good teacher. (Note: We put together our own videotape of former TAs who had been videotaped in their classrooms and who gave us permission to use the video. These were edited so that each segment is only a few minutes in length.)

Active Learning Strategies

Recent research on teaching has found that active learning techniques are superior to standard lecture formats. To demonstrate this principle, the two graduate student presenters cover the same material, one in a lecture format and one in a more active format. The first presenter discusses the concept in a short, well-done lecture. The second presenter covers exactly the same material, but does so through a classroom demonstration that actively involves the participants. This demonstration shows participants that "lecture material" can be covered in a more interactive way.

Our active learning handout lists teaching techniques, ranging from low risk activities to high risk ones. This handout is adapted from material from his book Bonwell and Eison, 1991.

Evaluation

Evaluating Students

Evaluating students through the use of quizzes, exams, papers, and projects is the next topic. We have a guest speaker from the campus Office of Instructional Resources discuss writing good multiple choice items (since many courses in our department use multiple choice items exclusively or in combination with other types of test questions). In addition to providing information and handouts on developing exam questions, our speaker also discusses different types of grading schemes that can be used.

We then hand out copies of the chapter from a current introductory textbook and ask participants to write exam questions covering that material. We also cite information from the excellent book by Lucy Cheser Jacobs and Clinton Chase, *Developing and using tests effectively: A guide for faculty.*

Teacher Evaluation

Student evaluation of teaching is another issue. We emphasize the formative (or feedback) value of student evaluations rather than the summative (or evaluative). Therefore, we encourage all TAs to collect feedback about their teaching in the 3rd or 4th week of class. Several handouts are provided, including different methods of obtaining early feedback, how to use informal early feedback, and analyzing student evaluations (Appendix A). TAs are often very hard on themselves and focus on negative comments. Thus, it is important that they have some guidelines (and resource people) to help them interpret their student evaluations.

Campus Guidelines/Resources

Our department requested that a media specialist present information concerning the use of the department's A-V equipment, primarily the overheads and VCR set-ups. The specialist provides a handout with a list of do's and don'ts, but most importantly does a hands-on demonstration of such common procedures as changing the bulb. Because of this 20 minute segment, there have been many fewer problems with the departmental A-V equipment and TAs have felt more competent using the equipment.

Most importantly, we compile a list of people in the department who would be resource persons for particular TA needs and include their office and phone numbers. The list includes the people to contact when faced with such issues as ordering textbooks; computer questions/problems; reserving A-V equipment; where to obtain films/ videotapes; the office that grades objective exams; where to get office supplies as well as test forms; rehabilitation center contacts for students with special needs; university proctor service; room reservations; concerns about undergraduate students including registration, class enrollments, rosters, advising, etc.; subject pool; teaching concerns; and duplicating procedures.

Campus Information/General University Rules

We distribute the Campus Handbook which contains the campus "code" or general university rules. One issue that we discuss from this handbook involves the rules for posting students' grades. This is a major issue on many campuses. We encourage TAs (and professors) to get students' written permission to post their grades by the last 5 digits of their Social Security number. This is achieved through the use of the Student Information Card. The student information card is a printed version of the blank 3 x 5 cards that many professors use. It asks students to identify their major, to provide contact information (e-mail address, phone number) and it asks them what they are looking for from the course. Many TAs will compile this information and present it back to the class, letting them know about the composition of the class and the topics of interest. However, it also contains the statement, "I give my permission for my grade to be posted by the last five digits of my Social Security Number", and then has a line for the student signature.

Another handout provides campus information about adding and dropping a class, the rules for section changes, proficiency exam rules, an explanation of our campus' satisfactory/unsatisfactory and credit/no credit grading options, and a list of courses available in our department—including prerequisites. Students will inevitably ask TAs about these basic deadlines and procedures, so it is important that the TA have the information. We also let TAs know about our Psychology Student Information Center (PSI Center) which is staffed by undergraduate honors students who provide free tutoring.

Make-up Policies (Including Religious Holidays)

This is a difficult issue for any teacher, beginning or experienced. Many campuses, including ours, provide guidelines for offering students make-up exams. This is an issue that is very important for TAs, or their course supervisor, to think through. We encourage the TAs to specifically state their make-up policies in their syllabus. In general, our advice has been to always schedule more graded exercises/quizzes than will count. Then students who must miss class will not be penalized and the TA will not have to provide make-ups. We also distribute a list of major religious holidays so that TAs and instructors can avoid scheduling quizzes or exams on those days. However, midterm and final exams present special problems.

It is often difficult to decide who should be allowed to take a conflict exam; who has legitimate reasons. For our introductory psychology course, we developed a conflict exam request form that outlines the university rules for conflict exams. Use of this form has reduced the number of conflict exams given in our introductory course from 200 to 45. The key is to require documentation of all excuses (Appendix B).

Rehabilitation Center Policies and Procedures: Dealing with Students with Special Needs

Our campus has a world-wide reputation for excellence in dealing with students with special needs. Until recently, the majority of these students have been students with sensory or motor deficits. That has changed dramatically over the last several years and now students with cognitive learning disabilities are the group making the most use of our Rehabilitation Center. This has major repercussions for TAs and instructors, as we are asked to make more accommodations in our classrooms. We distribute three handouts to the TAs which are published by the Division of Rehabilitation Education Services at the University of Illinois (although they make use of material from other sources). These handouts detail specific information about services provided, suggestions for working with students with special needs, and a guide to preferred language when discussing student disabilities. (See University of Illinois: Division of Rehabilitation Education in references.)

Counseling Center

In general, undergraduate students feel more comfortable talking with a TA about personal problems than the professor. Therefore, it is important that TAs are familiar with the counseling resources on campus.

One resource, developed by our Counseling Center, is a series of self-help pamphlets that students can pick up from a display in the main library. The pamphlet topics range from eating disorders to test anxiety to stress management.

Another campus resource is a handbook, "Identifying and referring troubled students: A handbook for campus professionals". The idea behind the handbook is that the classroom instructor has more contact with students than do the professionals at the Counseling Center. Therefore guidelines are provided for the lay person to help deal with troubled students.

A one page handout describing the exact procedures for helping students obtain a first-time appointment at the counseling center has proved an invaluable resource, as has a list of mental health resources with phone numbers, including our local crisis line. We strongly encourage TAs to refer students with problems to the appropriate campus resource and caution them NOT to become a student's pseudo-therapist. (See University of Illinois: Counseling Center in references.)

E-mail, Web, Campus Resource Groups

E-mail groups that deal specifically with teaching issues are quickly emerging. We provide information on how to access some of these groups. We also set up our own departmental e-mail group, so that those of us involved in the orientation can continue to discuss teaching issues as they arise throughout the school year. This also allows us to make TAs aware of campus workshops or seminars on teaching.

Instructor Responsibilities

The entire TA orientation focuses on information about the generic duties of being a TA, including keeping grades, having office hours, and interacting with students.

But, because specific TA appointments also vary within our department, not all TAs will be doing the same job. Some will be grading only, some will be holding office hours and attending faculty taught lectures, and others will be engaging in "real teaching". Unfortunately, TAs are often unsure of their exact responsibilities. So, we developed a form titled "Information for New TAs" (Appendix C). We first asked the faculty supervisor of each course to fill out the form. But later, we found that the supervisor's perception of the job did not always match the TA's experience. Now we have the TA who held the job previously, complete the form. We then distribute them at this point in the orientation to relieve anxiety and to allow participants to ask questions. This also gives the new TA a resource person who has actually been in the position before.

Day Two

Problems, Issues and Policies

Student-faculty relations. TAs are often perceived as bridging the gap between being a student and being an instructor. They are often unsure as to how they should interact with their students. This creates some unique problems. After supervising many beginning TAs, we find "figuring out" that relationship is often the most difficult aspect of their job. Some TAs want to be students' friend and thus have a difficult time fulfilling their responsibilities in grading and providing critical feedback. On the other hand, some TAs are so intimidated by their students that they revert to an extreme authoritarian position, thus alienating their students. We try to help TAs think about how they want to present themselves and to avoid potential "pitfalls" by discussing the student-instructor relationship.

The issues we discuss include sexual harassment and discrimination. A faculty member, whose research involves sexual harassment, makes a presentation about the definition of sexual harassment and students' perceptions of its occurrence on our campus. We also discuss our campus policies on these issues. (See the University of Illinois: Office of Affirmative Action in references.)

We also use an outstanding videotape produced by Myra and David Sadker titled *Breaking the silence: Equity and effectiveness in college teaching*. This video demonstrates the very subtle ways that women are "ignored" in classrooms. The format begins with a short clip of a staged class period. On the surface, it appears to be a routine class. However, upon analysis it becomes apparent that the men are encouraged to talk while the women are ignored. The best part of this video is that the "incidents" are very subtle and plausible. Most TAs know how to avoid being blatantly sexist or racist. It is the subtle discrimination that is more difficult to deal with.

We provide some very practical guidelines: DO leave your office door open when talking with students; DON'T date your students; DON'T make one person from a minority group the spokesperson for the entire group.

There are three excellent references that deal with gender inequity (which can be generalized to deal with any minority group's inequitable treatment in the classroom). These include *Teaching faculty members to be better teachers* (Sandler & Hoffman 1992); "The Student in the Back Row" from Michele Paludi and Richard Barickman's book *Sexual harassment on campus: A resource manual*; and *Creating gender equity in your teaching* from the College of Engineering at the University of California, Davis. In addition, the University of Illinois' Office of Minority Student Affairs has produced a handout of suggestions for faculty-student relations in class (based on materials from Ohio State University's Center for Teaching Excellence). This office has also developed excellent guidelines for tutoring. (See The University of Illinois: Office of Minority Student Affairs in references.)

It is important that teachers understand who their students are. At the University of Illinois we have a diverse student population, we also have a very "top-notch" student body. Our students score high on the ACT and SAT and are at the top of their high school classes. So, I compile information about the "average" first year student at the University of Illinois as well as some general information about first year students obtained from the American Freshman study (Astin, Parrott, Korn, & Sax, 1997; Dey, Astin, & Korn, 1991; Sax, Astin, Korn, & Mahoney 1998).

Classroom Management Techniques

For those TAs who will be facing a class for the first time, basic classroom survival skills are essential. We emphasize the basics, especially the importance of rules and thinking through the consequences of rules, being consistent, and the importance of learning your students' names. At this point we often address concerns that TAs expressed at the beginning of the orientation on their 3 x 5 cards.

Academic Integrity: Departmental and Campus Procedures and Policies

Our Associate Department Head for Undergraduate Affairs makes a presentation on capricious grading. He provides the university's definition of capricious grading and the procedural steps outlined when a student accuses an instructor of capricious grading. His emphasis is on setting up the classroom so that there can be no issue of capricious grading. He also discusses student academic dishonesty and the procedural steps outlined by our university to deal with such issues. Again, his emphasis is on prevention. Discussion centers on limiting cheating by exam procedures (random seating, multiple forms, etc.).

He provides sample letters to send to students who are suspected of academic dishonesty which follow Campus Code guidelines and outline the student's options and procedures.

At this point we also use another resource published by the Office of Instructional Resources at the University of Illinois, "Practical Approaches to dealing with cheating on exams." This is an excellent publication, full of practical advice. (See the University of Illinois: Office of Instructional Resources in the references.)

Evaluating Quiz and Exam Items

Returning quizzes and exams. When experienced TAs are polled about good and bad class days, they overwhelming say that the days they hand back quizzes or exams are among the worst of the semester. They report that their students complain about items, beg for points, and that they are pressured to make decisions in front of the class.

Some TAs (and professors) dread this so much that they just hand back the exams without going over the most missed items or providing students with feedback.

We provide some basic principles for handing back exams that take the confrontational aspect out of the experience. First, we tell our TAs to have a form ready for students to contest items. Then, when students begin to complain about an item, the TA tells them to pick up a Request to Review An Exam (or Quiz) Item form, fill it out, and return it (Appendix D). This eliminates the "frivolous" complaints because the form requests an argument as to why another answer should be considered correct, as well as requesting supporting evidence from the textbook. This also takes the pressure off the TA who no longer has to make such decisions in front of the class, but can evaluate the completed form in less stressful circumstances with advice from other TAs and faculty.

When dealing with essay exams or papers, we encourage the TAs to provide a scoring grid, or an outline of the number of points to be provided for each aspect of the writing, with the assignment. We also encourage TAs to grade written assignments without knowing the identity of the author (anonymously) and we provide procedures to streamline this. Then, when grading, the TA completes a grid for each paper. When handing back the graded written assignment, the TA states that s/he will reread any paper the student returns, but not during that class period. The student must take the paper home, read the TA's comments, respond to the comments, or mark on the paper where they believe the TA missed the points they made. Only then will the TA take the paper/exam back to reread.

These procedures work well because it communicates to students that the TA is willing to take student comments into account, but only if they are substantiated and well-thought out. It also gives all test constructors/paper graders a double check because there are times that we may write a bad item or "mis-read" a paper.

TAs are initially anxious about using these procedures because they believe that they will be overwhelmed with complaints. But experience shows that only the serious complaint is pursued, and it makes the day(s) of handing back an exam or paper much less confrontational and more of a learning experience.

At this time we go over the quiz items that the participants have written and the graduate student presenters chose earlier. There are no names on the items and as each item is put on the overhead we discuss what problems the item might have and how it might be better written. We are very careful not to criticize the item writer or make fun of an item. We try to demonstrate how difficult it is to write a good exam item and how this takes time and effort. Hopefully this experience will help TAs become better exam writers and teach them not to put off the chore of writing an exam until the day before it is to be given.

Preparing for the First Day

The TA who is going to be facing students as the instructor of a course for the first time is very interested in how to prepare for the first day of class. Incorporating information from my own experience, as well as obtaining information from two very experienced TAs, I wrote a checklist handout outlining preparation for that first day of class. Some of this information is adapted from Bette Erickson and Diane Strommer's excellent book, *Teaching college freshmen*. The handout discusses issues from checking out the classroom before the first day of class, to providing guidelines for constructing a syllabus.

Syllabus construction is a crucial issue given recent court decisions defining a course syllabus as a legally binding document. We try to give TAs an outline of what should be contained in the syllabus and some potential pitfalls to avoid on the first day of class (Appendix E).

Wrap-Up

Time for questions, evaluation of the orientation and help with microteaching outlines. We end the orientation with questions and discussion. We double check with participants that we have addressed all of the original questions that we received via the 3 x 5 cards at the beginning of the orientation. We ask the participants one last time for questions or concerns.

We also ask that all participants fill out the formal evaluation form for the orientation. We stress that the evaluations always have an impact on the next year's orientation. Finally, for those TAs who are anxious about their microteaching experience, we have small groups (each with a faculty or graduate student facilitator) that discuss the TA's outline and ideas for microteaching, while providing tips or suggestions for the presentation.

Day Three/Four

Microteaching

Microteaching involves a two hour block of time. It takes place in a normal classroom setting where both a chalkboard and overhead projector are available. In the classroom are approximately ten TAs, the graduate student or faculty moderator, and the video camera operator. Each TA presents an 8 minute lesson, while the other TAs act as the students. Each presentation is videotaped. After each presentation, the TAs acting as students and the moderator provide anonymous written feedback on the presentation.

The moderator keeps time, distributes blank feedback forms, then collects the completed forms and distributes them to the appropriate TA.

Feedback on Microteaching

In addition to the feedback from their peers, each TA signs up for a 20 minute consultation with a faculty or graduate student presenter who watches the videotape of the TA's "lesson" with the TA. The TA discusses their perception of their teaching and also brings the written feedback forms s/he received from the other microteaching participants. This is the time TAs can discuss personal reservations or fears about teaching.

Summary

A departmental TA Orientation is an excellent model of TA training for a variety of reasons. One of the most important outcomes of a departmental TA Orientation is the development of a relationship between the faculty presenters and the new TAs. TAs will now have resource people to approach for information or feedback or moral support during their teaching experience. This relationship did not arise in the All-Campus Orientation, primarily because the All-Campus Orientation involved over 800 participants and presenters from all across the campus, while our departmental orientation involves between 25 and 40 participants and the majority of presenters from within our department.

Another advantage is that the departmental orientation can address issues that are departmentally specific. In addition, the departmental orientation can introduce key resource people within the department.

Finally, departmental orientations demonstrate that the department itself, not just the campus in general, values quality teaching.

I would like to close with a caution to those of you planning a departmental orientation. Don't feel that you must "re-invent the wheel". There is enough to do without duplicating often excellent work done by others. Make use of the existing resources within your department, on your campus, and outside your campus.

Our departmental orientation is constantly changing on the basis of participant input and our discovery of additional resources. I would love to hear about your ideas for your departmental orientation and I would be happy to answer any questions you have about our departmental orientation.

References

Astin, A., Parrott, S., Korn, W., & Sax, L. (1997). *The American freshmen: Thirty year trends, 1966-1996.* Los Angeles: Higher Education Research Institute, Graduate School of Education, University of California.

Bonwell, C., & Eison, J. (1991). *Active learning: Creating excitement in the classroom* (ASHE-ERIC Higher Education Report No. 1, 1991). Washington, DC: The George Washington University.

Davis, B. (1993). *Tools for teaching.* San Francisco: Jossey Bass.

Dey, E., Astin, A., & Korn, W. (1991). *The American freshmen: Twenty-five year trends, 1966-1990.* Los Angeles: Higher Education Research Institute, Graduate School of Education, University of California.

Erickson, B., & Strommer, D. (1991). *Teaching college freshmen.* San Francisco: Jossey-Bass.

Goss, S. (1990). *Analyzing student evaluations.* Unpublished paper. See Appendix A.

Jacobs, L., & Chase, C. (1992). *Developing and using tests effectively: A guide for faculty.* San Francisco: Jossey-Bass.

McKeachie, W. (1986). *Teaching tips: A guidebook for the beginning college teacher* (8th edition). Lexington, MA: D.C. Heath and Company.

McKeachie, W. (1999). *Teaching tips: Strategies, research and theory for college and university teachers* (10th edition). Boston: Houghton Mifflin.

Ory, J., & Ryan, K. (1993). *Tips for improving testing and grading.* Newbury Park, CA: Sage Publications.

Paludi, M., & Barickman, R. (1991). The student in the back row. In M. Paludi and R. Barickman (Eds.), *Sexual harassment on campus: A resource manual.* Albany, NY: SUNY Press.

Sadker, M., & Sadker, D. (Producers). (1989). *Breaking the silence: Equity and effectiveness in college teaching.* (Videocassette) (Made possible by a grant to the Association of American College's Commission on the Status and Education of Women/administered by Bernice Sandler. Available from N.A.K. Production Associates: Silver Springs, Maryland)

Sandler, B., & Hoffman, E. (1992). Part Two: Warming the chilly classroom climate. In *Teaching faculty members to be better teachers: A guide to equitable and effective classroom techniques.* Washington DC: Association of American Colleges.

Sax, L., Astin, A., Korn, W., & Mahoney, K. (1998). *The American freshman: National norms for Fall 1996.* Los Angeles: Higher Education Research Institute, UCLA.

University of Illinois; Counseling Center. *Series of self-help pamphlets.* (Web Address: http://www.odos.uiuc.edu/Counseling_Center)

University of Illinois; Division of Rehabilitation-Education Services. *Information for instructors.* (Web Address: http://rehab.uiuc.edu)

University of Illinois; Office of Affirmative Action. (1990). *Preventing discrimination based on sexual orientation.* (Web address: http://www.oc.uiuc.edu/oaa/oaa.html)

University of Illinois; Office of Affirmative Action. (1998). *Sexual Harassment*. (Web address: http://www.oc.uiuc.edu/oaa/oaa.html)

University of Illinois; Office of Instructional Resources. (1987). *Instructor series #5: Effectively using informal early semester feedback*. (Web Address: http://www.oir.uiuc.edu/did)

University of Illinois; Office of Instructional Resources. (1987). *Instructor series #4: Practical approaches to dealing with cheating on exams*. (Web Address: http://www.oir. uiuc.edu/did)

University of Illinois; Office of Instructional Resources. (1987). *Instructor series #4: Written and verbal methods for early semester feedback*. (Web Address: http://www.oir. uiuc.edu/did)

University of Illinois; Office of Minority Student Affairs: *Faculty-student relationships in class/Tutor handbook*. (Web Address: http://www.omsa.uiuc.edu).

APPENDIX A

ANALYZING STUDENT EVALUATIONS

Typically, when we look at our student evaluations the negative comment(s) seem to leap off the page at us. But focusing only on the negative comments will ignore most of the valuable information that our students have given us.

The first decision is what evaluation instrument will provide the most information. Open-ended and free response questions provide the richest data, especially if you are gathering "early feedback" data rather than end-of-the semester data. Some sample evaluation questions are given at the end of this handout.

The second decision concerns when to administer the evaluation. The third or fourth week of class is often considered ideal — far enough into the semester that students have a sense of how the course is taught, but early enough in the semester that appropriate changes can be implemented. It is also a good idea to leave the classroom while students fill out the form and, of course, to make them anonymous. If you provide ten minutes at the end of a class period, you can wait outside until all forms have been completed and pick them up after class.

Once you have collected the student evaluations, you need an analytical way of evaluating them — a summary grid will help you categorize and find any recurring themes. We have developed a simple basic grid divided into four areas: Positive comments, Negative comments, Factors Outside of My Control, and Suggestions for Improvement. However, any type of summary sheet that is helpful to you will be fine.

As you read each evaluation jot down the most significant statements in the appropriate grid of the summary sheet. For example a student statement, "The quizzes were hard and confusing" would be entered under negative comments. Note that this statement makes 2 distinct comments, i.e., the quizzes were difficult and the quizzes were confusing. As you read through student comments also keep a rough tally of the number of students making each comment. Once you have categorized the student comments onto a summary grid, your job of analyzing the results really begins.

Factors which are outside of instructor control often surface in student evaluations. This involves such comments as "I hate having to get up for this class at 8 in the morning" or "The classroom is too far away from my previous class". Although these factors cannot be changed by you, they should be included in the summary sheet and addressed when you talk to the class about the results. By addressing such issues you allow students to understand that you cannot change such factors but that you are sympathetic to such problems. A statement such as "A lot of you dislike the fact that this class meets at 8 am. I understand that because I too have a difficult time getting up for class. But since none of us can change the time the class meets let's try to make the best of it. Does anyone have any ideas how we can "perk" things up?" However, it is important not to concentrate on issues that you cannot change. Summarize these statements, share the consensus with the class, and move onto issues that you can influence.

Analyzing positive and negative comments is similar. At this point the tally of the number of students making each statement is important. For example if you received 50 student evaluations and 40 of them mentioned difficult quizzes but only one mentioned confusing quizzes this provides different information than if 40 of them mentioned difficult and confusing quizzes. The tally is important to give you a sense of how prevalent that student attitude actually is. It is very difficult to overlook negative comments such as, "This instructor is the worst one I have ever had", however, such statements should be addressed only if the statement is consistently made on the evaluations. One comment like this would be more indicative of a problem with the student than with the instructor. The same holds true of positive comments. Look for the trends, consistencies, and patterns. Don't concentrate on the "stray comment".

The comments in the positive quadrant and the negative quadrant should be instructor controllable factors consistently mentioned in the student evaluations. Items on which there is a high consensus should be examined carefully. If most students say that your quizzes are too difficult that is an issue that you need to reexamine. Maybe it is your intention to have difficult quizzes because you think they better prepare students for exams. If this is the case then you need to tell the students that you are aware that they think the quizzes are very difficult but that they are devised to be preparatory to taking the examinations. On the other hand, you might not have realized just how difficult the quizzes were. In that case you might thank the class for pointing out how difficult the quizzes actually were and promise to try to devise clearer and more equitable quizzes for the remainder of the class. (An advantage of giving the evaluations early in the semester is the ability to make appropriate changes as the class progresses). The point is that comments are judged as negative or positive by you (e.g. it is good that the quizzes are difficult or it is bad that the quizzes are difficult). However, such high consensus comments need to be addressed when you talk with the class.

The tricky part of the evaluations comes when almost half of the class believes one thing and the other half believes the opposite. For example, when half tell you that the class is boring because it moves too slowly and half tell you that the class is difficult because you move through the material too quickly. In a situation like this you must remember that the class is not really a unit but a group of individual students with different backgrounds and skills. You can address such an issue in at least two ways. One is to try to help both sets of students, for example by providing study aides and handouts to help students finding the pace too fast, while providing extra types of papers, etc. for the students who find the pace too slow. Another way of addressing the problem is to admit to students that it is a problem and since there is not a consensus on class pace you will try to maintain a moderate pace but are open for people to ask questions, see you in your office, do individual projects in areas of interest, etc. The most important thing that you have done is to let your students know that you are aware of their individual differences and will do the best that you can.

The last section to look at is the suggestions for improvement. These suggestions can oftentimes be further categorized into three subcategories; suggestions that might work, suggestions that cannot be implemented, and "funnies". An example of a suggestion that might work is, "Give the quiz at the beginning of class time instead of the end so that I can concentrate on what you are saying instead of worrying about the quiz." An example of a suggestion which could not be implemented might be, "Change classrooms." And whenever you provide a space on student evaluations labeled "suggestions for improvement", you will get crazy statements such as, "Your clothes never match."

When you discuss these suggestions with the class, concentrate on the ones that you can implement and which seem to be a good idea. You also need to mention the ones that were a good idea but could not be implemented. We always mention the "funnies" casually and in a humorous context such as, "One person said that my clothes didn't match. I'm really sorry if you have such poor fashion sense."

At this point you have administered instructor evaluations, summarized the results onto a summary sheet, concentrated on the prevalent issues, and made decisions about changing (or not changing) some of your instructional practices. Now it is important to share the results with your students. It has been our experience that students are very surprised when the instructor discusses the results of the evaluation in class. Most students believe that the instructor will never look at such statements, let alone acknowledge them to the entire class. We feel that such a discussion is essential for good instructor-student rapport and we have tried to provide you with some examples of how to discuss each section with the class.

The last step is to implement the changes (if any) that you have decided to make. You can monitor such changes with the help of your class. They will be glad to tell you if the quiz was confusing, you are still talking too fast, or the pace of the class is better. We believe that student evaluations of teaching are absolutely vital for teacher growth and we encourage you to use them.

SAMPLE TYPES OF MIDTERM EVALUATIONS

I am very interested in your evaluation of this course. Please complete the following sentences. I take all of your comments seriously and will use them in planning this course.

1. The instructor
2. The textbook
3. The lectures
4. The quizzes
5. The paper

I am very interested in getting your impressions of the course and suggestions for improvement in the class format. Please respond to the following items and add any ideas you wish to offer. Thank you!

- The reason(s) I took this course
- The reason(s) other people take this course
- The people who are doing well in this course
- The people who are not doing well in this course
- Changes that would make this course better for me
- Other comments, complaints, or ideas

Please complete the following questions. Thank you!

- Three things that I like *best* about this course are
- Three things that I like *least* about this course are
- If I could change anything I would

I am extremely interested in providing this course as a valuable experience. I will appreciate and consider seriously your comments and suggestions to help improve this course. Please complete the sentences below.

- If only there would be
- The textbook
- The instructor should
- One thing I like about the instructor is
- The worst part of the course is
- Concerning my being prepared to take the midterm exam, I felt
- I'd like to see more

Please add any additional comments, complaints, compliments, etc.

Given the chance to start the semester over again, would you choose to take this course?

What suggestions do you have for improving the first half of the course? (Use the other side if you need more room.)

APPENDIX B

Application for Conflict Examination

Directions to the Student:

After completing the information requested below and obtaining the necessary signature(s), <u>please return this form to your instructor</u>. Once we have verified the accuracy of the information you have provided, you will be admitted to the conflict examination. The date, time, and place of that examination will be given to you when this form is returned.

Your Name _____

SS# _____

Section _____

e-mail address _____

Instructor _____

Today's date: _____

Your phone no. _____

I, _____, certify that I am unable to take the examination scheduled for _____ for the following reason (check one <u>and obtain confirming signature</u>):

( ) 1) Another examination or a regularly scheduled class at the same time as this examination.

The other examination or class session is for _____ and will take place on

(course)

_____ at _____ a.m./p.m.

(date)   (time)

Instructor's name _____

Instructor's signature _____

Office phone _____

( ) 2) A regularly scheduled performance or rehearsal (Describe):

_____

Supervisor's name _____

Supervisor's signature _____

Office Phone _____

( ) 3) Other extenuating circumstances (describe)

_____

_____

APPENDIX C

INFORMATION FOR NEW TAs

COURSE:
FACULTY SUPERVISOR _____

Description of TA's responsibilities (grading, leading discussions, lecturing, lab demonstrations, writing quizzes and/or exams, attending lectures, taking notes, meeting with students, etc.):

List all required and recommended material or equipment the TAs will need (e.g. books, lab supplies):

Other information that you think is important for new TAs to have:

TA supervisor if other than Faculty Supervisor:
SUPERVISOR'S NAME _____
OFFICE ADDRESS _____

If regular supervisory meetings are held throughout the semester when and where do such meetings generally take place?

Would you be willing to serve as a resource person for a new TA in this course?
_____ Yes _____ No

Other courses you would also be willing to be a resource person for:

PLEASE ATTACH A COPY OF THE LATEST SYLLABUS FOR THE COURSE.

APPENDIX D

REQUEST TO REVIEW AN EXAM ITEM

DATE _____
NAME _____
SECTION INSTRUCTOR'S NAME _____
EXAM FORM _____
QUESTION #_____
I believe that answer _____ should also be considered correct because
I found supporting evidence on page(s) _____ in the textbook.

APPENDIX E

PREPARING FOR THE FIRST DAY AS AN INSTRUCTOR OR TA

Before the first class meeting:

1. Know what textbook and ancillary materials are required. Become familiar with them so that you can answer questions about them.

2. Go to the classroom and "figure out" the physical set-up. Is the room kept locked and if so how do you get a key? Where are the light switches? Is there a desk, a podium, and an overhead in the room? If you are going to use an overhead, is there a place to plug it in? Is there chalk available at the chalkboard or do you need to bring your own? If you are going to show videos, are there shades at the windows or a way of darkening the room? Is any of the equipment locked in cabinets or closets for which you will need keys or combinations? How many student desks are in the room? Is there any missing or broken equipment?

3. Be sure that there is a syllabus for the course. You may even write a shorter syllabus covering aspects of the course you are responsible for. A good syllabus provides structure and direction for students (and the instructor) and helps to relieve anxiety (Erickson & Strommer, 1991). A syllabus is also a contract between you and your students, specifying the responsibilities and terms of conduct for both you and the students. Be aware that courts have interpreted a syllabus as a legally binding document. Your syllabus should include:

a. The course number and title.

b. When and where the course meets.

c. Your name, your office number, your office phone number and your office hours. (Whether or not to provide your home phone number is a personal decision. If you do so, provide parameters for its use, e.g. "Please do not call me after 10 pm unless it is an emergency.")

d. The required textbook and ancillaries.

e. A description of the evaluation procedures. This should include how the final grade is computed and an explanation of every graded component.

f. A course outline. The outline should include:

(1) Lecture/discussion topics and reading assignments.

(2) Quizzes, tests, and paper due dates.

(3) Your make-up policy concerning exams/quizzes and how late papers will be dealt with.

g. Optional but nice: A statement of course goals, a description of the course/subject matter (Erickson & Strommer, 1991).

4. When developing course presentations you should over prepare. Prepare enough material for two class periods and then you will not "run short." Prepare specific, concrete examples, handouts, class activities, etc.

a. Think about who your audience is. For the most part your audience is NOT faculty or graduate students (Gleitman, 1984). The level of presentation and the assumption of background knowledge must be based on who is taking the course. Teaching an undergraduate course is NOT like presenting a seminar to fellow graduate students. If you are teaching an undergraduate survey course your primary audience is students who will not take more courses in your discipline.

THE FIRST DAY OF CLASS DOs

1. Arrive early with all of the materials that you will need. Write the course name and number and your name on the overhead or blackboard.

2. Converse with students as they enter the classroom before class starts. Treat your students with respect.

3. Introduce yourself. Tell your students what your background is—your interests, etc. Tell them what you want them to call you; first name, Mr./Ms., etc.

4. Distribute your syllabus and cover the important points. Encourage students to come to your office hours. Once you have covered the course basics, be sure to ask for questions. Have specific questions ready in case students don't have any right away. For example, "You are sick next week when your first reaction paper is due. What do you do?" OR "Whom should you contact if you have to miss a lab, class, experiment, assignment due date, etc.?"

5. Stop periodically to ask for questions. When you do so, look at the students— scan the classroom. Be sure that you exhibit adequate wait time.

6. Provide an activity/demonstration/short writing assignment—something that demands that the students be active rather than passive.

EXAMPLE: Divide the class into small groups of 5 or 6 and give each group one blank 3x5 card. Give them 5 minutes to agree on one question that they would like the instructor to answer and have them write that question on the card. The instructor then reads the question and answers it (Erickson & Strommer, 1991). You might feel more comfortable phrasing the assignment so that they are to ask a question about the course content.

EXAMPLE: Provide a problem for students to analyze. Present a case study and ask students to discuss (Erickson & Strommer, 1991).

EXAMPLE: Ask students what problems/issues they want to discuss in the course. List all suggestions on the board. Discuss what course content areas relate to each issue (McKeachie, 1986).

EXAMPLE: Ask your students to write a paragraph about their expectations of the class.

EXAMPLE: At the end of class ask students to take 2 minutes to write down their reactions to the first day. This indicates that you are interested in learning from your students and it also provides you with feedback (McKeachie, 1986).

7. Try to make the activities, overheads, or demonstrations engaging and interesting (even fun) so that students leave the class with a good first impression.

8. Encourage student interaction. This might include breaking into small groups, setting up study groups, asking for general information that encourages students to talk (Who is from the Chicago area? What courses in this discipline have you taken before? Did you have a class in this area in high school? etc.)

THE FIRST DAY OF CLASS DON'Ts.

1. Arrive late.
2. Ignore students.
3. Distribute the syllabus and dismiss class. (What does this say about the importance of class time??)
4. Lecture the entire period.

Thanks to Amanda Allman and Joel Shenker for their contributions to this handout.

Teaching in the University Setting: A Course for Teaching Assistants

Louise Hainline, Ph.D.
Brooklyn College of CUNY

Note: Thanks are due to the many graduate students whose input and participation over the years have shaped the seminar described here. I especially acknowledge Jeanette Gong, who as a graduate student composed a memo to the faculty that was the original instigation to offer the teaching seminar, and Neil Macmillan who helped plan the course the first time it was given.

Redefining the Professorial Role

One of the most glaring paradoxes in graduate education is that although a large proportion of the PhDs in the US eventually take jobs teaching in colleges and universities, historically, the focus of doctoral education has been on research. Little effort has been expended on training students in effective teaching (Slevin, 1992). Most established faculty, if asked under the right circumstances, will share their war stories about their first, frightening weeks and months in front of the classroom. Most of us survived, but surprisingly have not been highly motivated to talk about it. A decade or so ago, my colleagues and I decided that we wanted something better, or at least different, for our students. Our choice has been to offer a regular semester-long seminar on various issues relating to college teaching. Thus, about every other year for the last 10 years, I have taught a seminar and practicum on undergraduate teaching for the students in our Experimental Psychology doctoral program. Although our program concentrates, for obvious reasons, on the teaching of various areas of psychology, many of the topics and themes that the course includes are general. To be sure, a course concentrating, for example, on the teaching of freshman English would naturally emphasize different things (such as teaching composition) that we cover only very briefly in our course, despite these considerations, there are many aspects of our course which have general application.

The course is designed to prepare our students for the university of the 21st century. As a university teacher with several decades of experience and the opportunity to think about university teaching biennially in this seminar, I am cognizant of how our profession is changing. When people in my cohort became teachers, we certainly worked at bettering our teaching, but the accepted model of what university teaching was about was not openly examined. Most of us received the implicit if not explicit message that research should have a higher priority than teaching as a professional activity. Currently, many of the old assumptions of how university teaching is done are being questioned (Gardiner, 1994). Even research-oriented universities are devoting resources and attention to the quality of their undergraduate teaching, although whether this will actually change the formulae for awarding tenure and promotion remains to be seen (Diamond & Adams, 1997).

The advent of technology has started to change many aspects of instruction at a pace that, one fears, is leaving many faculty members behind (Dolence & Norris, 1995; Oblinger & Rush, 1997). The traditional notion that students should sit passively and listen while instructors lecture is being seriously questioned; faculty with decades of experience are being asked to rethink their approach to students and their field's content (Bonwell & Eison, 1991; Bruffee, 1999; Meyers & Jones, 1993). The growing need to show accountability for the results of our education, both for universities themselves and for the politicians who fund much of our efforts, has focused our attention on the issue of outcomes assessment as never before (Angelo & Cross, 1993; Banta, 1996). Increasing diversity of ethnicity, age, and health status in many student bodies requires giving serious thought to how to present material that does not needlessly exclude significant portions of our audience (Asante, 1996; Smith, 1997). A growing tendency for litigation on everything from serious ethical issues such as sexual harassment to nuisance suits stemming from students' being dissatisfied with their grades requires more careful and measured consideration about the relationships we develop with our students (Fisch, 1996). It's an exciting and interesting time to take up the profession of college teaching, but it is also one in which the old practitioners aren't always the most reliable guides. Part of the plan of our course is intended to equip our graduate students to deal with our changing profession.

Major funding is also now being devoted to TA preparation. For example, a group of universities are participating in a collaborative Preparing Future Faculty project supported by the Pew Charitable Trust, the Council of Graduate Schools, the Association of American Colleges and Universities, and the Bush Foundation. The project is intended to develop a national model for the training of graduate students who select teaching careers; information on this program can be found on the Internet at *www.preparing-faculty.org*. The Preparing Future Faculty project has begun to circulate a directory of job candidates for consideration by colleges and universities seeking entry-level faculty, in order to market the graduate students who have completed their program. While not yet an accepted certification of teaching expertise in higher education, such efforts indicate that courses on preparing graduate students to teach may be an emerging model of a credentialing process for faculty positions in the future (Tice, Gaff, & Pruitt-Logan, 1998).

Higher-Order Course Goals

Our seminar has several goals, some general and some specific to the teaching that our students are engaged in. A major objective of the course is to encourage students to think about the goals of teaching and how different methods can achieve those goals. Typically, the first teaching experience is a study in survival – especially at the beginning of the semester, the new TA is often struggling to make it through each class intellectually and emotionally intact. Thoughts about higher-order goals seem irrelevant in the face of more immediate concerns. However, within a few class sessions, the new instructor typically begins to relax and to become acquainted with the class so that the students in the class are no longer critical strangers but individuals. Getting to know his/her students frees up enough mental energy to allow the TA to move beyond the act of teaching to reflect on the process of teaching, what we might call "meta-teaching." At this stage, it becomes possible to see the separate activities of the semester (examinations, lectures, discussions, collaborative exercises, demonstrations, laboratories, etc.) as part of a comprehensive 15-week plan for a particular class, rather than a series of ad hoc decisions of the moment.

I don't really expect that teaching assistants will "get" this higher order view of teaching immediately; the first few times they teach, they lack the perspective that comes from experience as teachers. They do, however, have a lot of experience at being students. Because they have spent much more time being students observing their professors than being teachers themselves, I start by asking them to introspect about their own experiences with successful and not-so-successful professors. The objective is to acquaint them with the habit of thinking about teaching goals and how the various activities of the semester are structured in support of those goals as soon as possible. So, while the course deals with matters of technique, I am constantly trying to point out how decisions about technique cannot be made independently of the goals for a particular class.

Another major objective is to help these new instructors to find a style of teaching that fits them (Parini, 1997). Faculty are invited to visit the seminar and speak about their development as teachers. By exposing the TAs to more and less experienced professors (some of whom they have had themselves as teachers) and even advanced graduate students who have taught for several years, the class is intended to help each person come to terms with what works for him/herself, for a particular subject matter and class size. These discussions are also designed to help our graduate students realize that even experienced teachers continue to have doubts about themselves as teachers and to fiddle with new ways of doing things.

We would like teaching to become an informed career choice for our students, not just a default activity that accompanies the awarding of a PhD. The general public and even our students don't understand very well what university professors actually do (AAUP Committee C on College and University Teaching, Research and Publications, 1994; Meiland & Rosenthal, 1994); the teaching component is public and visible, but the profession has many facets invisible to a casual observer. The academic world is a subculture of its own, and there is a lot of information that doctoral students and new PhDs are never told about what a career as a university professor entails (DeNeef, 1996). Those of us who survive in the university eventually learn these things on our own, but often at some cost to our career progress.

Also, with college and university jobs continuing to be scarce and highly competitive, fewer of our students will end up taking jobs as professors. Because of the scarcity of academic jobs, many of our students will probably not spend much if any time in academic positions, so I have begun to add readings and discussion about alternative, non-university careers for PhDs in our area of science (National Research Council Committee on Science, Engineering, and Public Policy, 1995; Robbins-Roth, 1998). Our students have requested more coverage of this topic, and I sense that they are relieved to have a professor admit in public that there are worthwhile careers other than our own. A final goal of the course is to let the students know that they have career options, at the same time that I try to make college teaching an attractive and compelling choice.

The Structure of the Course

The course has evolved substantially since it was first offered, with modifications based on written student evaluations done at the end of each semester. The course has been popular with students, being taken by almost all of them early in their graduate careers. Years afterwards, students who went on to teaching careers have told me that they still find the course notes and readings useful as they strive to improve as teachers. Most of our graduate students begin by acting as teaching assistants for laboratory sections. Because the model at our college de-emphasizes large lecture classes, there are not many opportunities for them to do recitation or discussion sections. Within a couple of semesters, those who have are ready are asked to teach full undergraduate courses independently, usually in an area of psychology related to their field of study. The teaching seminar is taken before they are given responsibility for a full class.

In its first incarnation, the course was offered on a non-credit basis as an informal seminar every other week. It became obvious over time that the material and assignments had increased to the level that the course merited being changed to a regular 3-credit, semester-long course with weekly meetings. When the course began to be graded, feeling a bit uncomfortable about being perceived to be grading the students in their roles as new teachers, I assigned pass/fail grades. I was surprised when the graduate students themselves requested that they be given regular letter grade in recognition of the effort that the course required. I have assigned regular grades since then.

One issue to consider is when graduate students should begin such training. We originally planned our course to have graduate students take the class *before* they enter the classroom; it seemed logical that students should cover some of this ground prior to beginning to teach. In retrospect, however, the seminar was least successful when we required students to take it before they had actual classroom experience. Discussions were too hypothetical and a bit flat. We now encourage students to defer the class until they are scheduled to teach for the first time. In fact, because we offer the course only in alternate years, students sometimes have one or two semesters of teaching under their belts by the time they take the class. In such cases, they have usually been laboratory teaching assistants working under a faculty member's supervision. Being in the throes of teaching as a novice serves as a very strong motivating force to consider seriously some of the basic issues involved in pedagogy. The questions that the class deals with are merely theoretical until a teaching assistant steps in front of a class, when they become more real and urgent. The discussions are thus enlivened by the many specific episodes that students bring from their classroom experiences. We have found that our graduate students learn best about teaching by teaching, with an opportunity for targeted readings and much group discussion of the process as a support.

Course Content

The course as it is structured now deals with most of the expected topics related to the logistics of teaching: how to design a syllabus, run the first day of class, design and grade exams, choose a textbook, cope with cheating, etc. Besides the question of how to plan and deliver effective lectures and lead successful discussions, as new forms of pedagogy have emerged in higher education, students read about and try methods such as collaborative learning, activity-based laboratories, and the use of technology such as computers and the resources of the World Wide Web in undergraduate education. Space does not allow inclusion of the full reading list or syllabus, but Table 1 contains abbreviated examples of some of the written assignments that have been developed for the course, to give flavor of the coverage and the kind of written work the graduate students are asked to do.

Table 1
Examples of Written Assignments for Teaching Seminar

Topic	Assignment
Goals of teaching	"You have now been on both sides of the desk with respect to college teaching. Discuss what you've learned about effective and ineffective teaching from being a student. Describe the teaching of someone who was, in your experience, a particularly effective teacher, and analyze why this person succeeded as a teacher. What were his/her goals? What are your goals for the course you are currently teaching?"
Self-evaluation of teaching components	"In Weimer (1993), there is a "bubble" diagram of what she believes are five basic components that comprise her teaching: enthusiasm, preparation and organization, ability to stimulate student thought and interest, clarity, and knowledge and love of content. Draw a Weimer diagram of your current teaching style, and explain what factors lead to this diagram. As part of your personal goals for this class, how would you like the bubbles to be rearranged." [Note: the "bubble" assignment is given twice – once early in the semester and once near the end, so students can see how their self assessment of their teaching styles has changed].
The first class	"Using material from the readings, discuss your higher and lower level goals for the course you are teaching, how you would go about preparing for the first day of class, and what you would do on the first day. Prepare a sample syllabus, which should reflect your own ideas about the course organization. Also, be prepared to "microteach" a 5-minute sample of the first day of your course."
Class materials, alternatives lecturing	"Either critique the text book for the class you are teaching, including any supplemental materials the book may have, or to surf the Web for materials that can be used to supplement your course . Explore relevant sites and pick two or three ideas for class materials to summarize for class, including an explanation of how you would use the materials in class. The goals is to go beyond simply lecturing about the material to alternative exercises that are both academically sound and involve students. Explain why you think that theoretically and practically these exercises will have the desired effect, state your goals in

	using them, and describe how you would evaluate whether they actually work."
Test construction	"Critique a multiple choice test from a class of your choice, from the perspectives described by Ory and Ryan (1993). Also do a more global critique about the teaching goals the test meets and fails to meet. Articulate your philosophy about student assessment in various levels of courses that under graduates take. In creating your own philosophy of teaching, what kind of examinations do you think make the most sense, and how frequently should exams be given?"
Grading, grade inflation, cheating	"Using information in the readings and your own experience, discuss the problems that the necessity of grading students creates. What is the purpose of student evaluation? Do you think that grade inflation is a problem, or just an indication that students are getting better? Faculty have been increasingly concerned about cheating, not necessarily because it is increasing, but because they feel that it is getting harder to detect. Discuss why students cheat (and what you've heard via the grapevine about novel methods for cheating) and what you feel faculty should do about it. If we didn't grade at all, cheating would probably disappear, but would that be a change for the better?"
Human cognition and college teaching	"Teaching and learning should, in principle, be related to each other. Based on your readings and your own studies discuss how one could apply sound psychological principles (and which ones?) to improve teaching. What factors of the teacher and the student are relevant to whether learning "of the right kind" takes place? What do we know about human motivation that contributes to learning? What is your opinion about whether research on cognitive or learning styles has any relevance to teaching at the college level?
Student issues	"*Either*: Analyze the current University and College policies on sexual harassment and discuss the adjustments in teaching and conduct that an instructor might make to avoid running afoul of such issues. *Or:* Using the College's *Manual for Students with Disabilities*, design an accommodation in an introductory course for a student who has a serious visual impairment, including consideration of the steps you would take to make sure that you comply with college regulations."
Evaluation of teaching	"There is some controversy about whether formal teaching evaluation actually improves teaching, but it is probably here to

stay, given the requirements of colleges and universities for faculty review. There is less controversy about the value of getting formal and informal feedback from your students while a class is underway. How else are we supposed to become better teachers? The class will divide into three teams, with each being asked to work on one aspect of evaluation. The goal of the assignment is for you to create evaluations that *you* think would be useful to you as you advance as teachers from your first semester onwards. One group will work on formal summative evaluation – that is, written evaluation from students at the end of the class on a formal instrument that might be used for hiring decisions, in a teaching portfolio, etc.; examples of two different CUNY summative evaluations are attached for your information, and there are others in your readings. The second group will work on formal (i.e., faculty) formative evaluation, based on some kind of teaching evaluation done by a faculty member that is intended to give you information about how you are doing and what you might do differently; attached is the form currently used in this department. The last group will work on informal methods, both formative and summative, to allow students to provide you, the instructor, with feedback about a course. The groups will resent to the class, and provide a rationale for the evaluation, a protocol for administration, a method of analysis, and a discussion of the strengths and limitations of the instrument."

Observing
professors

"To teach effectively, it helps to observe how different people do it. Do a systematic observation of two faculty members in the department. Explain to the professor that you are doing an assignment in this class and that you are interested in observing different faculty teach to improve your own classroom presentation. Before or after the class, speak with the instructor to get an explanation of his/her goals for that session and the course as a whole. For each observation, write a short summary of the method of delivery, mode of presentation, demeanor of the instructor to the class, and other reflections on the observation that flow from your readings and our discussions this semester. Don't be afraid to be critical, if this is appropriate. I will take the observations in confidence, and you can mask the identity of the instructor if you like. On your second observation, contrast the two performances. If you do a little research ahead of time, you can probably find two instructors with diverse styles, to make the contrast have a little more zip."

Videotaping

"Robert Burns ("To a Louse", 1786) prayed for the gift "to see ourselves as others see us". Today, the gift is the camcorder, which allows us without too much fuss to videotape our teaching so that we can observe ourselves. At least once, and preferably twice this semester, videotape yourself teaching. I suggest you team up, so that one person can work the camera while another teaches, and then switch roles. You can sign out a camcorder and tripod in my office. After the taping, go through the tape in private, using the guide provided by Davis (1993). Write an observation for yourself, akin to the ones you are doing for other faculty members. As intimidating as this exercise is at first blush, people generally find it is quite useful, after the initial shock wears off. I will not require it, but if there are portions of your taping that you think illustrate what you're doing well and not so well, I would appreciate it if you would be willing to show short segments to the class for discussion, but because this assignment always makes people nervous, I won't require this."

Careers

"You have chosen to enter a Ph.D. program which is the traditional training for a college or university faculty position. Tell me why you decided to pursue a Ph.D., and what type of job you imagine yourself in 7-10 years from now. If you're uncertain, try to imagine a best case/worse case scenario. If you were to pursue an academic career, what kinds of skills, strategies, planning. could you do now to prepare yourself for a career in the professoriate? Try to be more specific than "study hard and do good research". Where do you see the satisfactions of such a career, and where do you see problems that you might encounter?"

The course also includes discussion of the diversity of the student population at our urban public institution and how that diversity can be addressed in the content and style of presentation in teaching. Besides covering some of the general regulations of the College, we read descriptions of the national, ethnic, and socioeconomic demographics of our undergraduate student population, and the issues and opportunities that this glorious heterogeneity presents to the teacher. We cover the general professional problem of the ethics of teaching (e.g., Audi, 1994; Tabachnick, Keith-Speigel, & Pope, 1991). Some of the legalities of teaching in the 21st century are also presented, particularly in the context of our college's policies on sexual harassment and teaching students with disabilities. These documents are discussed, along with specific instances that the teaching assistants may have encountered in their classes. The class is also assigned to read the College's guidelines and procedures concerning academic honesty, plagiarism, and cheating and we talk about these matters in the context of a general discussion of testing and grading. The TAs are provided with information about the services that our college offers for dealing with problem students, including the availability of counseling services. Most importantly, I endeavor to make them realize the limitations of their expertise in such instances and encourage them to get help with problems they are not trained or hired to solve.

Non-classroom activities connected with teaching, including academic advising of students, writing letters of reference, and supervising independent study are also covered, if only briefly. As a faculty member myself, I am still struggling with how to deal with improving students' writing; I do not feel competent to be an English composition instructor, but as I assign a lot of written assignments, it seems logical that I should deal with the form as well as the content of what students submit as written work. In connection with this, the class discusses various perspectives on the role that individual faculty in the disciplines should play in developing students' skills in general areas such as writing, quantitative reasoning, and critical thinking. I don't pretend to have any answers here, but appreciate the opportunity to have a discussion on matters that concern me currently as an educator. Such discussions also communicate to the graduate students that their jobs as instructors ideally should involve more than just communicating information about their discipline.

Some of the topics covered are not in traditional books about teaching. For example, it often takes graduate students some time to develop the confidence to critique published works. In their research training, one of our teaching tasks is to help them develop the skills and confidence for the critical reading of research articles. Textbooks, which are delivered with lots of hype and frills, are a different kind of written medium. We discuss the politics and economics of college text books and how to deal intelligently with publisher's representatives and conference book exhibits. I explain how to get examination copies and evaluate and select text books by more than the supplemental materials offered by the publisher.

In the unit on university careers, we discuss what I wish I'd been told about the academic job search and how to turn their teaching experiences into a professional asset. Students are encouraged to develop a statement of their teaching goals and philosophy and begin assembling a teaching portfolio (Seldin, 1991). As the class usually consists of students in their first or second year of study, this at first seems a trifle premature to them, but their graduate careers progress quickly. In most cases, during their time as graduate students, they are not asked anything more about their teaching than "what courses have you taught," but increasingly, departments are requiring a statement on teaching philosophy as part of the application process. Smart applicants include one even if it isn't requested. A statement that has been developed over several years is usually more seasoned and thus more effective than one that is prepared at the last minute. I also encourage the graduate students to pay attention to the use of technology in teaching, and if possible to develop expertise in some aspect of this form of pedagogy in parallel to their research training. As older faculty retire and new faculty positions open up, a mastery of teaching technology is a strong advantage in the search for a faculty position.

Regardless of the academic area being taught, it is also important to present novice teachers with the best research we currently have on how people learn in college classes. To that end, I include readings from research on human cognition, higher order learning, and motivation. At this point, much of the literature on the direct educational applications of research on human learning and cognition has concerned K-12 education, but there are now attempts to feed this knowledge back into higher education to improve how we teach. This meager but promising literature is used to encourage students to bridge the gap between theoretical or purely laboratory knowledge and the application of such research in higher education practice. Wilbert McKeachie's classic book on teaching for years included a chapter or two on this topic, although to my regret, it has been dropped in the latest edition (McKeachie, 1999), perhaps to make the book have a more general appeal. As part of their efforts to improve teaching at all levels including college, the National Research Council has recently sponsored the publication of an excellent summary of human cognition and learning as it relates to education, which is a useful general source for material on this subject (Bransford, Brown, & Cocking, 1999).

A particular component of pedagogy that has been much discussed in the higher education literature is the evaluation of teaching and what has come to be called "outcomes assessment". An increasing number of books about teaching evaluation and outcomes assessment are addressing institutions' need to develop objective performance indicators for outcomes assessment in teaching (e.g., Banta, 1996; Nichols, 1995). McKeachie (1999) also has a good chapter on this topic that is not highly technical and is appropriate for a general audience. The course works through with students the differences between formative and summative evaluation and considerations for doing a good job on both types. We go over the form our college has been using for student evaluation of professors, a form which we agreed was not particularly well-done. In a recent semester, I had groups of students work on a new faculty evaluation form, input that I shared with a committee that has been redesigning the form currently in use. Some aspects of the new form were stimulated by the instrument devised by the graduate students.

While such formal assessment instruments are important concomitants of outcomes assessment, they are probably not as effective in improving what actually happens in a classroom as evaluation designed by the instructor for his or her own feedback during the semester. Thus, we also discuss how an instructor can get feedback about the impact of the course both during and at the end of the semester. A current favorite is the "one minute paper" idea described by Richard Light of the Harvard Assessment Seminar (Light, 1990) in which students are asked in a sentence each to state after each class what was the most important thing that they learned in that class and the biggest unanswered question remaining at the end. Many other ideas on classroom-based assessment can be found in Angelo and Cross (1993). One of the class exercises encourages students to develop and use specific formative and summative evaluations for their own use in particular courses.

Readings and Other Course Material

When I began teaching the course a decade ago, there were only a few books discussing pedagogy in higher education. In 1988, McKeachie's venerable book was already on its 8th edition. Now in its 10th edition, McKeachie's book is a virtual bible which continues to be valuable today. At the beginning, I also found useful chapters in the book edited by Guillemette (1982), *The Art and Craft of Teaching*, published for the Harvard-Danforth Center for Teaching and Learning. (The immediate predecessor of the Harvard-Danforth Center was where I received my first TA training in the early 1970's; the Center has been a pioneer in such efforts.) Early on, I also used material from another classic in the field, Eble's *The Art of Teaching* (Eble, 1976; 1988). I continue to assign selected chapters from each book today. Since our course began, the gates have been opened, and there is a veritable flood of new books on teaching in higher education. A particularly rich selection is published by Jossey-Bass, Sage, and Anker, but the American Association of Higher Education (AAHE) and other professional organizations also have relevant publications. My current reading list draws from these sources and also from widely distributed journal articles on higher education in general and in our own discipline.

Professional societies have also become interested in supporting better teaching. National professional organizations have begun to sponsor activities related to improving higher education in their fields at their conferences and in their house periodicals many now include articles on teaching undergraduates and on preparing graduate students to teach. One of our professional organizations (the American Psychological Society) has recently published a book with many helpful short articles that had appeared in their house journal (Perlman, McCann, & McFadden, 1999). Although the title implies that the work deals mainly with the teaching of psychology, actually the majority of the topics are general and quite well presented. Another excellent new work dealing with teaching in the sciences was recently published by the National Research Council's Committee on Undergraduate Science Education (Committee on Undergraduate Science Education, National Research Council, 1997, also available on-line at *www.nap.edu*). I also encourage my students to join the major professional organizations in our field (student membership is quite inexpensive) and to pay attention to teaching-related articles as their teaching and graduate careers progress.

Anyone preparing a course on teaching for teaching assistants will find useful some of the publications on preparing graduate students to teach, of which there were few when our course began. For example, a useful survey of what other institutions are doing to equip their graduate students for teaching careers can be found in Lambert and Tice's 1993 book *Preparing Graduate Students to Teach,* the results of a project by the American Association for Higher Education Teaching Initiative. The book is from a comprehensive national survey of teaching assistant programs and practices, across a wide variety of disciplines. It presents thumbnail descriptions of the varieties of teaching programs in the sciences, social sciences, and humanities that can be found at institutions across the country. The project was funded by the Council of Graduate Schools, TIAA-CREF, and the Pew Charitable Trusts. Other recent books are *Working with Graduate Assistants* (Nyquist & Wulff, 1996) and *The TA Experience: Preparing for Multiple Roles* (Lewis, 1993). The present book is another example of this genre. Articles on preparing teaching assistants also regularly appear in the *Journal of Graduate Teaching Assistant Development, Change, The Journal of Higher Education, Studies in Higher Education, The Teaching Professor, Improving College and University Teaching, Journal on Excellence in College Teaching,* and *Higher Education,* as well as many other general and discipline-specific materials on college teaching that are available in print and on the Internet.

Increasingly, the Internet is a rich source of material that can be used to improve higher education teaching. I routinely send my students to the Internet to look for materials for class demonstrations, suggestions for presentation of materials, ideas for laboratory and class exercises, etc. Professional organizations are increasingly including information and help on college-level teaching on their web sites. In my field, Psychology, the two major professional organizations have Web sites with information useful for teaching psychology and teaching in general (*www.apa.org* as well as *www.psychologicalscience.org*). In preparing for this chapter, I surfed at random for a short time and found useful information on college-level instruction in Sociology (*www.lemoyne.edu/ts*), History (*www.theaha.org*), Humanities and Social Sciences (*h-net2.msu.edu*), Chemistry (www.acs.org/education), Physics (*www.aps.org*), Classics (*www.scholar.ee.emory.edu/scripts/apa*)**,** Economics (*www.unc.edu/~saleni/AEA_CEE*), Anthropology (*www.ameranthassn.org*), Mathematics (*www.maa.org*), and Modern Languages (*www.smpcollege.com/modlang*). No doubt this is only the tip of the iceberg. Faculty in other areas will now find such web-based information in virtually all of their disciplines. What is available on-line is constantly undergoing revision and one would be advised to revisit the Web from time to time to see what new material on college teaching and the preparation of graduate teaching assistants has been posted.

My most recent surfing has found a new class of materials specifically oriented toward teaching methods. A useful site at *www.lemoyne.edu/-hevern/psychref2.html/* contains an extensive list of links to web-based materials on teaching Psychology, including information on conferences on teaching, but it has lists of links that are useful for TA training in any discipline; for example, it lists a number of links to on-line resources that individual colleges have developed for their teaching assistants, graduate students and new faculty. Some examples: The University of Massachusetts at Amherst posts their handbook for teaching assistants on line (*www.umass.edu/cft/tahtoc.html*). The University of Minnesota also has their handbook for teaching assistants on-line at *www1.umn.edu/ohr/ftae/ handbook.html.* In addition to names, contacts, and policies specific to U. Minn, the manual includes a list of printed materials on college teaching and some well-written material on teaching prepared for teaching assistants. One that is particularly interesting was compiled from a questionnaire given to graduate students who had survived their initiation into teaching, entitled "What I wish they'd told me." The TAs often poignantly described mistakes they made in their first teaching experiences. A list that reflects similar hints from a more experienced professor has been compiled by Lee Seidel, the Director of the Teaching Excellence Program at the University of New Hampshire (*www.unh.edu.teaching*). *Speaking of Teaching,* a newsletter on Teaching that often includes material on preparing teaching assistants and published quarterly by Stamford's Center for Teaching and Learning, is available on-line at the Center's site *www-ctl.stamford.edu*. This site also contains a list of links to the growing number of college and university Centers for Teaching, many of which also deal with suggestions for people who are beginning instructors. Dalhousie's handbook can be found at *www.da.ca/~oidt/taguide* and The Rutgers University TA Handbook is on-line at tapproject.rutgers.edu/pubs. The handbook for Queens University, posted at *www.queensu.ca/ idc/trainers* includes some useful case studies that can be used to stimulate class discussion in a TA course. The Instruction Innovation Network at *www.eminfo.maricopa.edu/innivation* deals with methodology across all disciplines. The on-line version of ERIC can also point one to resources in all academic fields (*www.accesseric.org*). It is very likely that this is only the beginning of web-based materials for higher education. These materials are useful both for those who are preparing teaching assistants and for the TAs themselves who should be encouraged to become familiar with this medium of information. Most of these sites contain the same kind of good advice that one can find in the many books being published on college teaching, but they have the advantage of being more readily accessible and more up-to-date. I plan to use them extensively in the next version of our seminar, because the content is good and because I want the graduate students to learn effective web-searching in support of their development as teachers.

Experiential Aspects

Most of the students in the teaching seminar have already stepped in front of classrooms or are doing so for the first time when they take the course. They need not only information on how to teach, but help in dealing with the issue of assuming the role of a teacher. Another very important function of the course is to serve as a kind of support group to help the graduate students through what for many is a difficult transition from one side of the desk to the other. As Mary Ellen Weimer pointed out in her very effective book for introductory teachers (Weimer, 1993, always a favorite with my students), there is a pervasive myth in our culture that teaching is a special gift that one either has (the master teacher) or does not have (the hack). Students frequently become very discouraged when they begin teaching to discover how hard it is to do well. They need assurance that like playing the guitar or programming a computer, people can learn to be effective teachers by practice and effort, as long as they are willing to work to improve.

In addition to problems of public presentation in a new role they feel somewhat fraudulent in assuming, students experience many role conflicts as they come to terms with being an authority figure for students who often are older than they are. The transition from seeing yourself as a student (which of course these individuals still are) to a teacher is difficult for many of them. A good part of class time each session is devoted to "war stories" and particular problems, sometimes technical but usually psychological, that students are having with their classes. Students have problems with the age differential between themselves and adult students. Dealing with flirtatious members of either sex is problematic, for personal and legal reasons. One of the students in a recent seminar was himself disabled, and the disability posed issues in dealing with both non-disabled and disabled students. Undergraduate students are quick to pick up on the new teachers' uncertainties and we discuss an amazing range of flimflam that they can throw at the nervous new instructor. A very common pattern is for the new teaching assistants initially to be extremely lenient with students (the "marshmallow" role). Fairly quickly, in most cases, the TA realizes the liabilities of this role, as the demands of continually preparing make-up examinations or serving as a tutor for individual students consume significant quantities of time. We discuss the importance of having high expectations for students, and setting and maintaining high standards to be really effective as a teacher. It doesn't take too long for them to learn the essentials of their new role, for self-preservation if nothing else.

I continuously emphasize how each of the TAs needs to find his/her own style or persona as a teacher; what works well for one person can fail miserably for another. A particularly effective device to bring this home to them has been the sessions in which we invite experienced and less-experienced faculty to reminisce about their development as teachers. In choosing faculty for these sessions, I deliberately choose faculty whose styles vary widely on any number of dimensions (looseness, sense of humor, organization, philosophy, etc.). The students have themselves had many of these professors in class and generally regard them as good teachers. The visits demonstrate that effective teachers continue to struggle with becoming better teachers, and that good teaching comes from some pretty divergent types of people. In a few cases, experienced faculty members are so insecure about their teaching ability that they have declined the invitation to visit the class. Despite the fact that they are known to be conscientious and effective teachers by the graduate students themselves, these professors are unable to acknowledge that they have anything of value to share. For the less secure students, it seems to help to know that some of your professors still have crises of confidence and get nervous and even ill before the first day of a new semester. More commonly, the faculty share that they continue to have a normal range of doubts about their teaching performances, but that they try new things both to keep themselves fresh and to keep up with new trends in pedagogy. This aspect of the course is uniformly rated by the students as their favorite part. For some reason, our tendency is to regard the act of teaching as private or secret – like other forms of private human activity, it does tend to take place behind closed doors, and it is not normally discussed openly in polite society.

One of the background activities we do is a search for what works for each person in the class. In what some of them regard as a rather cruel exercise but which students always agree is very helpful after the initial shock wears off, I have students videotape themselves teaching during the semester to give them some sense of how they appear and sound to their own students. They are encouraged to do two tapings, once early the semester and once later to see how they are developing as instructors. Davis (1993, ch. 42) provides a useful set of guidelines to point out things that students should look for in these videotapes. My next goal for myself is to develop more facility in helping the graduate students use these tapes for maximum gain. The chapter in this volume by Prentice-Dunn and Pitts is quite instructive on this topic.

Other Benefits of the Course

Because of the scarcity of graduate student support at the City University of New York, our students teach a lot for their support during graduate school. Traditionally, teaching during preparation for the Ph.D. has been regarded by many professors as an unfortunate interference with a student's "real" education in research and scholarship. Our students have been quite successful in securing teaching jobs, if they desire such positions. This is undoubtedly in part because of their natural abilities and the extensive teaching experience that they have during their graduate training. However, it is likely that some of their success comes from having the chance to think about teaching as part of our teaching seminar. The faculty believe that the course is a success, and this is corroborated by student ratings of the course. What I continue to be surprised at is how much I as a professor get out of the opportunity to consider teaching explicitly for an entire semester every two years. The course has become a stimulus to rethink my own teaching goals, an opportunity to be reminded of various practical matters involved in teaching, and a chance to catch up on latest articles on teaching methods and technology. It offers a forum for thinking about this important aspect of our profession that is found too rarely in our institutions of higher learning. While the ostensible goal is to prepare future faculty, in this one case, at least one experienced faculty member benefits mightily as well.

References

AAUP Committee C on College and University Teaching, Research and Publication. (1994). Report: The work of faculty: Expectations, priorities and rewards. *Academe, 80*(1), 35-48.

Angelo, T., & Cross, P. (1993). *Classroom assessment techniques: A handbook for college teachers.* San Francisco: Jossey Bass.

Asante, M. K. (1996). Multiculturalism and the academy. *Academe, 82*(3), 20-23.

Audi, R. (1994). On the ethics of teaching and the ideals of learning. *Academe, 80*(9), 27-36.

Banta, T. (1996). *Assessment in practice: Putting principles to work on college campuses.* San Francisco: Jossey Bass.

Bonwell, C. C., & Eison, J. A. (1991). *Active learning: Creating excitement in the classroom.* Washington, DC: ASHE-ERIC.

Bransford, J. B., Brown, A. L., & Cocking, R. R. (Eds.). (1999). *How people learn: Brain, mind, experience, and school.* Washington, DC: National Academy Press.

Bruffee, K. A. (1999). *Collaborative learning: Higher education, interdependence and the authority of knowledge* (2nd ed.). Baltimore, MD: Johns Hopkins Press.

Davis, B. G. (1993). *Tools for teaching.* San Francisco: Jossey Bass.

DeNeef, A. L. (1996). *The lessons of PFF concerning the job market.* An occasional paper from the Preparing Future Faculty Program. Washington, DC: American Association of Colleges and Universities.

Diamond, R. M., & Adam, B. E. (1997, November). *Changing priorities at research universities: 1991-1996.* Syracuse, NY: Center for Instructional Development, Syracuse University.

Dolence, M. G., & Norris, D. M. (1995). *Transforming higher education: A vision for learning in the 21st century.* Ann Arbor, MI: Society for College and University Planning.

Eble, K. E. (1976). *The craft of teaching: A guide to mastering the professor's art.* San Francisco: Jossey Bass.

Eble, K. E. (1988). *The craft of teaching: A guide to mastering the professor's art* (2nd ed.). San Francisco: Jossey Bass.

Fisch, L. (Ed.). (1996). *Ethical dimensions of college and university teaching: Understanding and honoring the special relationship between teachers and students.* San Francisco: Jossey-Bass.

Gardiner, L. F. (1994). *Redesigning higher education: Producing dramatic gains in student learning.* Washington, DC: ASHE-ERIC.

Guillemette, M. M. (Ed.). (1982). *The art and craft of teaching.* Cambridge, MA: Harvard University Press.

Lambert, L. M., & Tice, S. L. (1993). *Preparing graduate students to teach.* Washington, DC: American Association for Higher Education.

Lewis, K. G. (Ed.). (1993). *The TA experience: Preparing for multiple roles: Selected readings from the 3rd National Conference on the Training and Employment of Graduate Teaching Assistants.* Stillwater, OK: New Forums Press.

Light, R. M. (1990). *The Harvard Assessment Seminars: Explorations with students and faculty about teaching, learning, and student life: First report.* Cambridge, MA: Harvard University Press.

McKeachie, W. J. (1986). *Teaching tips: A guidebook for the beginning college teacher* (8th ed.). Lexington, MA: D.C. Heath.

McKeachie, W. J. (1999). *Teaching tips: Strategies, research, and theory for college and university teachers* (10th ed.). Boston: Houghton-Mifflin.

Meiland, J., & Rosenthal, J. T. (1994). Two faculty members' careers. *Academe, 80*(1), 28-32.

Meyers, C., & Jones, T. B. (1993). *Promoting active learning: Strategies for the college classroom.* San Francisco: Jossey Bass.

National Research Council's Committee on Science, Engineering, and Public Policy. (1995). *Reshaping the graduate education of scientists and engineers.* Washington, DC: National Academy Press.

National Research Council's Committee on Undergraduate Science Education. (1997). *Science teaching reconsidered: A handbook.* Washington, DC: National Academy Press.

Nichols, J. O. (1995). *The department guide and record book for student outcomes: assessment and institutional effectiveness.* New York: Agathon Press.

Nyquist, J. D., & Wulff, D. H. (1996). *Working with graduate assistants.* Newbury Park, CA: Sage Publications.

Oblinger, D. G., & Rush, S. C. (Eds.). (1997). *The teaching revolution: The challenge of information technologies in the academy.* Jaffrey, NH: Anker Publishing.

Ory, J. C., & Ryan, K. E. (1993). *Tips for improving testing and grading.* Newbury Park, CA: Sage Publications.

Parini, J. (1997). Cultivating a teaching persona. *Chronicle of higher education, 44(5)*, A92.

Perlman, B., McCann, L. I., & McFadden, S. H. (1999). *Lessons learned: Practical advice for the teaching of psychology.* Washington, DC: American Psychological Society.

Robbins-Roth, C. (Ed.). (1998). *Alternative careers in science: Leaving the ivory tower.* San Diego, CA: Academic Press.

Seldin, P. (1991). *The teaching portfolio: A practical guide to improved performance and promotion/ tenure decisions.* Jaffrey, NH: Anker Publishing.

Slevin, J. (1992). *The next generation: Preparing graduate students for the professional responsibilities of college teaching.* Washington, DC: American Association of Colleges and Universities.

Smith, D. G. (Ed.). (1997). *Diversity works: The emerging picture of how students benefit.* Washington, DC: American Association of Colleges and Universities.

Tabachnick, B. G., Keith-Spiegel, P., & Pope, K. S. (1991) Ethics of teaching: Beliefs and behaviors of psychologists as educators. *American Psychologist, 46,* 506-515.

Tice, S. L., Gaff, J. G., & Pruitt-Logan, A. S. (1998). Preparing Future Faculty programs: Beyond TA development. In M. Marincovich, J. Prostco, & F. Stout (Eds.). *The professional development of graduate teaching assistants: The practitioner's handbook.* Jaffrey, NH: Anker Publishing.

Weimer, M. (1990). *Improving college teaching: Strategies for developing instructional effectiveness.* San Francisco: Jossey Bass.

Weimer, M. (1993). *Improving your classroom teaching.* Newbury Park, CA: Sage.

Making the First Time a Good Time: Microteaching for New Teaching Assistants

Christina Maslach, Ph.D.
University of California at Berkeley

Lauren Silver, Ph.D.
Stanford University

Nnamdi Pole, Ph.D.
University of Michigan

Emily Ozer, M.A.
University of California at San Francisco

Overview

Teaching is an ongoing learning process, in which there is a continuing acquisition of both knowledge and skills. In that sense, the journey to good teaching does not have a specific endpoint. But it does have a clear beginning, when novice teachers have their first classroom experience. And if that first time is a good time, then subsequent steps on the teaching pathway are likely to be successful.

At Berkeley, our teacher training practicum course is specifically designed with that first time in mind. It is a one-semester course that prepares graduate students to master the myriad of tasks involved in their first teaching experience. The student trainees participate in a number of activities designed to increase their skill and effectiveness as teachers and to foster their confidence in their own capabilities. A particularly important facet of this "first-time" practicum is that the trainees "micro-teach" in front of their peers, and it is this aspect of the training that will be the focus of this chapter.

Before discussing the microteaching process in depth, we want to provide some of the context in which that occurs, and thus will say a bit more about the teaching training practicum. On the theory that two heads are better than one, the teacher training course is co-taught by a faculty member and a senior graduate student TA. Both have been selected for the role on the basis of their excellent teaching track record. Typically, both have regularly received exemplary teaching ratings from their students and have received teaching awards from the department and/or campus. Though both instructors provide feedback and advice, the graduate student TA takes primary responsibility for running the class. In many ways this models and mirrors the experience that the trainees will have with their own discussion sections. It is important to get our trainees used to the idea of autonomy and responsibility in their classrooms. We believe that our division of labor conveys this message in a subtle yet powerful way.

It has been our experience (corroborated by feedback from the trainees) that the "climate" of the course has an important impact on the trainees' motivation and the effectiveness of their participation. Thus, we deliberately try to create a warm and informal atmosphere, which emphasizes collegiality and shared experience. The course is held in the late afternoon, after the conclusion of other classes and academic events, and the responsibility of providing refreshments is rotated among the course members (including the instructors, who provide more extensive first and last "meals"). The instructors are also available outside of class, as "on-call" sources of advice and trouble-shooting.

The course addresses such broad issues as professor-TA relations, diversity in student populations, and TA/graduate student life. In addition, it covers more specific topics such as planning sections; preparing exams, quizzes, and TA evaluations; grading exams and papers; delivering lectures; dealing with common classroom problems; and developing effective teaching strategies to optimize students' learning. Trainees observe at least one section taught by an experienced TA at the beginning of the semester; this is extremely valuable in helping inexperienced teachers understand their role as authority figures in groups of undergraduates. For trainees who are teaching their first course concurrently, the class provides opportunities (called "check-ins") to solve immediate problems, to share experiences, and to get support.

What is Microteaching?

It is ironic that the University of California, Berkeley would be indebted to our long-time rival, Stanford University, for building the cornerstone of our teacher training course. Microteaching is a "training concept" that originated in the Stanford Teacher Education Program in 1963. There are many variations on its basic theme but in its essence microteaching is a brief, supervised, practice teaching exercise "in which the normal complexities of the classroom are reduced and in which the teacher receives a great deal of feedback on his [or her] performance" (Allen & Ryan, 1969, p. 2). It is predicated on the assumption that brief samples of teaching behavior may provide a useful window into more enduring, pervasive, and characteristic teaching styles as these might manifest themselves in an actual discussion section or lecture hall (see also McKeachie, 1994).

Classically, microteaching involves a training teacher, a group of four or five actual students, a senior supervising teacher, and a videocamera. The trainee prepares and delivers a five to ten minute lesson to the students while being observed and videotaped by the supervisor. The lesson is typically selected to practice a specific skill or technique (e.g., efficient use of chalkboard space). Immediately following the lesson, the teacher trainee receives written feedback from the students, oral feedback from the supervisor, and objective feedback from the videotape. After synthesizing, integrating, and discussing all of these sources of feedback, the trainee re-teaches the lesson to a new small group of actual students under the same supervisory and monitoring conditions. This process can be repeated as often as necessary or as long as it is deemed productive by the trainee and supervisor.

As we practice it at Berkeley, microteaching retains most of its "classical" features. However, we have made many modifications and innovations over the years to tailor the method to our needs and resource limitations. Among the major changes are: (a) using two supervising teachers, (b) replacing a small group of actual students with a large group of training teachers, (c) manipulating the content of the teaching topic, (d) microteaching in real classrooms, and (e) reteaching new material rather than the same material.

Teachers as students

As mentioned earlier, the Stanford microteaching method typically occurs for a small audience of actual students (e.g., four to five). According to Allen and Ryan (1969), this is part of the process of simplifying the teaching experience. Our Berkeley trainees microteach in front of a large audience of their peers (e.g., fifteen to twenty). We believe that we retain the spirit of the Stanford method in the sense that we simplify the teaching experience. However, we do so by using "pseudo-students" rather than real students. Often our beginning TAs report considerable anxiety about teaching a "real" group of undergraduate students. Many of them were undergraduates themselves just three or four months prior to beginning our training program. These trainees find the experience of teaching in front of a group of peers who are "all in it together" to be quite anxiety-reducing.

We believe that the major advantage of using other trainees as students is that it improves the sophistication of post-microteaching feedback. Immediately following the microteaching episode, the trainee receives an anonymous narrative verdict from a jury of his or her peers. These pseudo-students have the combined advantages of both vast amounts of experience as students (otherwise they would not have been accepted into graduate school) and an investment in learning about teaching (otherwise they would not be in our class). As expert students, they are very articulate about expressing what they need in order to understand the information better. As novice teachers, they are sensitive and constructive in the tone of their feedback. Each and every one knows that his or her time on the hotseat will come.

Our decision to use a large group of pseudo-students rather than a smaller group was borne out of convenience rather than theory. However, a fortuitous side effect of our approach is that the trainee gets a larger sample of feedback. Thus, the well-known problems of drawing inferences from small sample sizes is attenuated. The trainee is given a more representative estimate of his or her performance.

Manipulating the teaching topic

At Berkeley, we have also gained a lot of mileage from being creative about our choice of teaching topic. The Stanford method tends to emphasize the selection of a teaching lesson that gives the trainee an opportunity to practice a specific skill. In our approach, we have tried three different ways of generating lesson content. Rather than emphasizing specific skills *per se*, we have opted to manipulate the lesson content to: (a) de-emphasize content, (b) match medium to message, (c) prepare teachers to handle content outside of their area of expertise.

De-emphasizing content. Beginning TAs are usually simultaneously adjusting to a number of new roles (e.g., scientist, writer). All of our trainees are not only preparing to become teachers in their field but, paradoxically, they are also functioning as students in their field. It is common for beginning TAs in a competitive graduate program to be concerned about whether they have sufficient expertise in their substantive field area to assume the role of teacher. Sometimes this worry is based upon a comparison with peers who all seem much more impressive in the early weeks of graduate school. Sometimes the worry comes from an inappropriate comparison to faculty (either their current advisor or professors from their undergraduate years). Regardless of the source of the anxiety, the point is that sometimes over-concern with the content of the lesson can eclipse attention to the process of delivering the lesson.

One of the points of our training program is that good teaching is a function of skills that are largely independent of the content being taught. This point is easily illustrated by having our trainees teach a relatively benign topic. While any benign topic will serve this purpose, it is helpful to provide a topic that will be of sufficient general interest to the pseudo-students so that "real teaching" can take place. Aside from a shared interest in their discipline, all of our trainees have in common a shared interest in learning how to teach. Thus, our trainees initially microteach about teaching (a process that we sometimes call "meta-teaching"). Meta-teaching involves preparing a five minute lesson based upon a short article from our course reader (each about a different peda-gogical topic). Meta-teaching provides our trainees with non-threatening content to teach during their first time at bat, which is also interesting to the class as a whole.

In addition to solving the threatening content problem, meta-teaching also allows us to kill two more birds with the same stone. One of the mandates of our teaching seminar is to expose our teaching trainees to didactic materials on pedagogy. That is why we assembled a course reader on various pedagogical topics. However, we found that in the initial weeks of our training course the presentation of the didactic material frequently competed with clamors from our trainees for more practicum experience. About half of our trainees take our class in tandem with their first teaching experience. Therefore, we felt that it was our responsibility to provide both didactic and practicum knowledge as soon as possible. The challenge for the instructors was how to cover the didactic material in class and still provide enough time to give the new teachers hands-on experience. Meta-teaching solved this problem by making the didactic material the sub-stance of the practicum experience. Following the meta-teaching exercise, the other trainees provide open-ended, written, anonymous feedback. We typically omit the videocamera and the supervisory feedback in order to make this initial experience as non-threatening as possible.

In sum, meta-teaching is a useful way to solve many problems common with initial teaching training, including: (a) de-emphasizing the content so that the process of teaching may receive greater attention, (b) providing the students with a very early experience practicing presenting information in front of an audience while simultaneously ensur-ing that the didactic pedagoical topics are directly addressed, and (c) encouraging the students to actively work with the didactic material rather than passively read and dis-cuss it.

One drawback to the way that we have practiced meta-teaching is that some train-ees have complained that they find it difficult to simultaneously evaluate the microteaching and learn from the microteaching. This conflict can be resolved by elimi-nating the trainee feedback and depending upon feedback from the supervising instruc-tors.

Matching medium to message. Once our trainees have had an opportunity to practice the basics of presenting a lesson in front of a class, we think that it is important to devote attention to the content of their lessons. Specifically, we want to encourage them to develop thoughtfulness about choosing an appropriate teaching style to convey a particular message. At this point in their training, we encourage them to select a sub-stantive topic from psychology to present in a ten-minute microteaching exercise. Trainees are also asked to identify a particular skill or style that they are trying to improve. We encourage them to try a new style or teaching technique that they have not tried before or one that they find difficult to execute in their real classes. We also tell our trainees that it is not important to present a complete lesson. They can do a fraction of a lesson because some types of teaching tasks are inherently more time-consuming than others. Often students will choose to practice an excerpt from an upcoming discussion section or lecture. Under these circumstances, microteaching provides the opportunity to get early corrective feedback and to re-teach the material more effectively. The ten-minute time limit is strictly adhered to. We believe that it is important for students to foster an inner sense of time and the importance of planning the use of time. Finally, we always introduce videotaping at this stage of the training. The videotapes are not shown in class but the trainees are encouraged to watch the videotape of their work prior to re-teaching the material. The supervising instructors provide direct feedback following the exercise and also make themselves available to provide feedback about the videotape.

Teaching outside one's area of expertise. A common dilemma for the beginning teacher is to be assigned a TA position that is outside of his or her narrow area of expertise. A typical example of this is the situation where a highly specialized graduate student is assigned to teach a broad survey course that spans the entire field. Microteaching can be employed to prepare trainees for this situation by having them randomly assigned to a chapter or subsection of an introductory survey text and to develop a brief lesson on the content. Another version of this approach is to require several trainees to teach the same content using different styles. Alternatively, the instructor may randomly assign teaching style and content. One advantage of these variations is that the trainees will have their attention drawn to the great variety of ways that the same material can be presented. The major goal of these exercises is to provide a brief and relatively non-threatening preparation for a situation that may occur frequently in both their graduate careers and their professional academic careers. Mastery of this skill will certainly put the graduate students in a more competitive position for academic jobs where there is increasing premium put on applicants who can teach outside of their narrow subspecialty.

Microteaching in the real world

As we have said, the Berkeley method differs from the Stanford method in that we tend not to use actual students in our microteaching exercises. We have also argued that in many ways the use of trainees as pseudo-students may be preferable. Nonetheless, there is the danger that our pseudo-students lack the perspective of the average undergraduate. For example, a presentation that may seem "clear" and "brilliant" to the average graduate student trainee may appear "complex" and "intimidating" to the average undergraduate student. Furthermore, our teacher training program would not be complete without testing the trainees' pedagogical prowess against the rapier sharp wits of the average Berkeley undergraduate. Our trainees must eventually leave the relatively "safe" nest of our teaching class and try their wings in an actual classroom.

Our mechanism for meeting this goal is called "guest microteaching." Guest microteaching was originally conceived to provide a practicum experience for those trainees who were not simultaneously teaching a real class of their own. These trainees were paired with a currently working TA. The pair agreed upon an appropriate time and topic for the unemployed trainee to microteach in an actual classroom. Again, the lessons are kept brief (five to ten minutes). Videotaping is typically suspended. Feedback is solicited from the working TA (who acts as a supervisor) and the real undergraduates. We believe that this trial by fire leaves the unemployed TA in an excellent position to assume command of a class of his or her own in the near future.

Reteaching new material

The final major difference between the Berkeley and Stanford methods is that we do not have our trainees "re-teach" the same material under the standard microteaching paradigm (e.g., videotaping and supervision). This is typically due to time constraints related to our large number of trainees. It is simply impractical to have every student teach the same material more than once. Instead, we provide practice in two different ways. First, we emphasize giving our trainees several opportunities to teach new material. The meta-teaching and guest teaching are the mechanisms by which trainees get practice time with novel material. Second, we recommend that our trainees apply the microteaching feedback to their actual classrooms (if applicable). In this sense they do get a chance to re-teach the lesson using the feedback gleaned in our training program. Nonetheless, we would like to build in supervised re-teaching in the future. We believe that such an approach has many merits to recommend it. We hope that in the future sufficient resources become available to realize the potential of this approach.

Incorporating Microteaching Into a Training Program

Microteaching has been an integral part of our teacher training course since its inception, and we have instituted numerous versions of it over the years. In the past, our approach included assigning trainees to teach specific topics and scheduling trainee presentations at the end of each class (after coverage of other basic issues). Neither of these methods was ideal, for various reasons. Assigned topics often result in lowered intrinsic interest and heightened anxiety, and the end of class is a period where there is lowered energy and attention (except for the increasingly impatient and anxious presenters) and where there is the risk of running out of sufficient time for the presentations. Through a rather extended trial and error process, which continues as we receive feedback from new groups of students each year, we have worked out a system which is both pedagogically effective and personally satisfying for all who participate. There are three key principles that have led to our success.

The first key principle is *integration*. From the first day of class each semester, trainees are made aware of the microteaching requirement (see Handout 1). Then, as the course proceeds, they are encouraged to identify issues of both content and style that arise in their own classes, and to use one of these as the focus of their microteaching presentation. Integrating microteaching with their experiences as students and as new teachers allows them to gain experience thinking about pedagogical issues from different perspectives. On a practical level, it also gives them time to accomodate themselves to the idea of teaching in front of their peers and to understand the importance of doing so. (This last point is not a minor consideration. Public presentations are often anxiety-producing for graduate students, whether in their capacity as teachers or as young researchers, and giving them time to prepare themselves psychologically for such events can lower their anxiety levels enough so that they can actually benefit from the experience.)

The second key principle is *flexibility*. Rather than assigning topics, we now permit trainees to choose what they will teach and how they will do so. Trainees are encouraged to choose topics which are of interest to them and to use microteaching as an opportunity to practice pedagogical techniques that may be unfamiliar or difficult for them. As a result, presentations have become extremely varied, ranging from standard lectures about introductory subjects or issues taken from the course's assigned readings, to demonstrations and class discussions about controversial topics central to students' research interests. Most importantly, though, presentations are almost always vibrant and dynamic, owing to the personal pride trainees take in teaching something that is meaningful to them.

The third, and most important, key principle is *evaluation*. One of the disadvantages of scheduling microteaching in the last few minutes of each weekly class meeting had been that this method rarely allowed sufficient time for presenters to receive feedback from their peers and instructors. Trainees often felt that they had no meaningful criteria by which to judge the quality of their presentations, and no methods to help them improve their teaching skills (which, after all, was the objective of the exercise in the first place). There were numerous ways in which this problem might have been solved; our solution was to designate specified class meetings solely for the purpose of microteaching presentations. Presentations now last approximately 10 minutes, followed by a break during which the pseudo-students (peers) fill out the evaluation form and the presenter confers with the instructors. In addition, all presentations are video-taped, and tapes are made available to the trainees so that they may observe and evaluate their own teaching. More will be said about the evaluation portion of the microteaching exercise later in this chapter.

Preparation

It is quite typical for graduate students new to their roles as teachers to be unsure about their function in the classroom. While many different sources might be cited as the reasons for this unease, we have found it to be the case that their questions and fears almost universally center around *what* material they might present to their students, rather than about *how* they might go about doing so. Weekly readings and class discussions therefore emphasize considerations of style as well as content. In addition, the instructors make every effort to utilize a variety of pedagogical techniques and, whenever possible, to bring their own methods to the attention of the class. Trainees are encouraged to view the instructors as role models, and to observe, question, and discuss the various techniques that are utilized in class. Importantly, the instructors are *not* viewed as pedagogical gods. In accord with the principle that even the most experienced teachers can use some improvement, trainees are encouraged to challenge the methods they observe and to provide constructive criticism and helpful input whenever possible.

Trainees are actually more prepared to embark on their new ventures than they realize. Having spent approximately 16 years engaged in formal schooling by the time they enter graduate school, they obviously have an enormous amount of experience of being taught *to*, and it is likely that they have strong ideas about what constitutes "good" and "bad" teaching. Moreover, many of our trainees have had some experience presenting information to others in the form of papers given at professional conferences, or lab reports delivered in small seminars or lab group meetings. Although being the teacher for a classroom of students is quite different from either being one of those students or discussing one's own research with one's colleagues, we encourage trainees to mine their personal experiences for insights and ideas that will help them develop an understanding of the goals and concerns they carry with them as they begin their professional development. Moreover, we emphasize that this process of introspection is an ongoing one — the trainees will constantly need to challenge their own assumptions, examine their strengths and weaknesses, and strive to develop new techniques and fields of expertise if they are to be truly effective in their work as teachers. Microteaching is seen as the first step in this ongoing process.

Preparation for microteaching, then, involves a class segment in which trainees articulate their own philosophy of what is "good" and "bad" teaching, as well as several sessions devoted to problem-solving (e.g. how to maximize student participation) and discussions about technical issues (e.g. the effective use of audiovisual aids). In this sense, microteaching is no different from any other kind of teaching and, indeed, this is the point of the exercise. We want trainees to take the microteaching requirement seriously and to use it as an opportunity to develop their ideas and practice their skills in a way that will allow them to transfer what they have learned to their own work with students.

Thus, we spend a great deal of time exploring conceptual and practical issues related to the overall goal of effective communication in a classroom setting, and we focus on the ways in which teaching may differ from other types of communication. These differences are based on our view of teachers as guides, not demagogues or infallible experts. Citing the psychological and educational literature on such topics as motivation and active learning and, again, drawing from trainees' own experiences as students, we present strong evidence for the necessity of teachers acting as facilitators of students' intellectual and personal development. Successful microteaching (and teaching in general) relies on trainees' willingness to explore the range of issues that will allow them to act in this role effectively.

Feedback

We cannot emphasize strongly enough the value of meaningful feedback to the success of any microteaching program. Receiving constructive criticism and appraisals of their presentations helps trainees not only to evaluate their performance in a single, very specific situation, but it also gives them a taste of how it feels to be evaluated on their teaching in a more general sense. Teaching evaluations will become increasingly important to their professional success as they climb the academic ladder, and it is important that beginning students not fear the process, but that they learn early on how they might use it to their advantage.

Trainees in our teacher training course receive three types of feedback on their microteaching presentations: written evaluations by peers, oral evaluations by instructors, and self-evaluations. The value of providing evaluations in different formats from so many different sources ensures that trainees are exposed to a wide range of perspectives and opinions. This is an extremely valuable facet of microteaching, for it gives trainees an authentic experience of having their performance observed and assessed by people with different interests and experiences, different values with regard to the qualities that a "good" teacher must possess, and different goals with regard to their own teaching and learning. In other words, the experience is very similar to that of receiving feedback from classes of diverse student groups (not to mention the superiors who will one day utilize such assessments to make important hiring, tenure, and promotion decisions).

Written evaluations by peers. The first type of feedback comes in the form of anonymous written evaluations submitted by every member of the class. For each presentation, the pseudo-students in the audience (i.e., the other trainees) complete standard forms that contain space for them to assess the strengths and weaknesses of specific aspects of the presentation, and to add their own questions and comments (see Handout 2). All of the forms are collected and given immediately to the trainee for his or her review.

The other trainees are given instructions to take a dual stance when observing their peers. On the one hand, they are asked to imagine that they are students trying to learn about the topic being presented for the first time. On the other, they are told to make use of their developing expertise as teachers to address important pedagogical issues whenever possible. In addition, pseudo-students are instructed to make their comments as specific as possible, to provide helpful suggestions about how the trainees might improve their teaching effectiveness in the future, and to avoid vague musings and personal critiques.

Oral evaluations by instructors. The second type of feedback consists of oral evaluations provided by the course instructors in a brief, private conversation with each trainee immediately following the microteaching presentation (it takes place while the pseudo-students are completing the written evaluations). This conversation is intended to act as an opportunity for trainees to raise issues of personal concern related to their presentations (or even to their teaching in general) and to receive input from experienced teachers. Topics that are covered range from what the trainee actually said in his/her presentation (e.g., level of expertise required of students being too high or too low, too-frequent use of colloquialisms or jargon, obvious discomfort with controversial issues, etc.) to the ways in which he/she said it (e.g., mechanics of using audiovisual aids, vocal qualities, pacing and speed of presentation, unconscious tics [body language]).

Admittedly, some of these topics can be somewhat sensitive for trainees. Novice teachers can have fragile egos, and we have been faced with how to be honest while also being diplomatic and encouraging. We have found, however, that the give-and-take nature of the conversation (as well as its relative privacy) lessens the possibility that trainees might be offended or upset, and it provides an opportunity to explore issues that might otherwise not be addressed. Moreover, it gives trainees the opportunity to ask questions and clarify misunderstandings directly with the instructors.

The privacy of the oral feedback helps ensure that the experience is neither threatening nor personally intimidating for the trainees. However, the drawback is that the other trainees in the class do not get to hear the instructors' evaluation of the microteaching presentation that they just saw and evaluated themselves. Our experience has been that the private conversations have been more important at the beginning of the microteaching segment of the course, and that as the trainees get more familiar with microteaching, and more comfortable with the evaluation, they begin to request that the instructors' comments be shared publicly with the entire class. We explicitly offer this option at the beginning of the microteaching segment, but allow individual trainees to express their preference in this regard.

Self-evaluations. Finally, trainees are given the opportunity to evaluate themselves — all microteaching presentations are videotaped in their entirety and tapes are made available to the trainees to watch after class hours. Interestingly, this is the one opportunity for feedback that trainees do not seem to make use of to the extent that they might. Those trainees who do take advantage of it, however, find it to be a powerful experience. Watching themselves on tape, they say, is one of the most meaningful ways to assess their strengths and weaknesses in terms of presentation style and to gain perspective on the ways in which their effectiveness might be improved. This positive reaction greatly outweighs the fact that relatively few students choose to watch their videotapes on their own.

To enhance the positive value of this form of self-evaluation, we recommend instituting some sort of course structure that would ensure that the trainees watch their videotaped microteaching and make an assessment of it. Simply asking trainees to watch the tape on their own time (which is very busy) is not enough. One possibility is that the trainee watch the videotape along with one of the instructors; this would be followed by the type of evaluative conversation that we described above. Or the trainee might be asked to watch the videotape and then complete the same written evaluation of it as the pseudo-students did.

Making sense of it all. Having had their presentations assessed on so many different levels, the task for trainees becomes one of trying to make sense of the vast amount of information they have received, and discovering ways to apply it to improve their teaching. Beginning teachers often react in a fairly extreme manner to the input they receive, viewing negative comments as damning evidence of their inherent unfitness in their chosen careers, and positive comments as evidence that they need not try to improve certain aspects of their teaching. Obviously, neither stance is accurate; learning to accept such judgments with equanimity is an ongoing process, and starting it in an atmosphere that is meant to be constructive and nonthreatening can be extremely valuable for the trainees.

Finally, the evaluation portion of the microteaching program carries with it the added benefit of training beginning teachers in how to provide feedback effectively. The development of such a skill is obviously essential in their work with students. What is not so obvious, however, is that it provides a way to gain insight into the qualities one values most in one's own teaching as well as in the work of others. Such insight is essential in the pursuit not only of skill and expertise in teaching, but also of true teaching excellence.

The Value of Microteaching

In our experience, microteaching has a number of virtues to recommend it. First, microteaching is not only "real" teaching, it is also in many ways harder than real teaching. Professional writers have often noted that writing an essay or short story is harder than writing a novel. Public speakers know that preparing a five minute talk is harder to prepare than a forty-five minute talk. Similarly, we believe that in many ways a ten minute lesson is harder to produce than a fifty minute lesson. The microteaching exercise poses a difficult dilemma. How can you create a new understanding or awareness in five to ten minutes? This task enforces an economy of language and brevity of presentation. We are of the philosophy that when a student successfully completes our microteaching training then he or she is well on the way to being able to make longer didactic presentations.

Second, microteaching exposes trainees to a wide variety of teaching styles. Research has shown that teachers tend to quickly settle into patterns of instruction with which they are most comfortable. There is very little motivation to experiment in the classroom. Often teachers are unaware of the range of things that they might try. Microteaching workshops not only present a wide range of options but they also encourage trainees to try out more challenging techniques.

Third, microteaching provides superior corrective feedback than might otherwise be available. Typically, instructors must wait until the end of the term for feedback on their performance. Not only is that feedback too late to be corrective, but it is often too broad to be of use. Microteaching focuses on a specific behavioral episode for which objective data (i.e., videotapes) are also available. The trainee has the unusual opportunity to map feedback onto specific behavioral practices.

Finally, microteaching uses principles that have been known to be very powerful in creating behavior change. One principle is to gradually shape the desired behavior — beginning with the least threatening and working toward the more threatening. For beginning teachers, the most threatening thing is facing actual students. Therefore, we save that part for last. First, trainees get used to presenting information in front of an audience of their peers. The information is rather contextless and intellectually undemanding so that the beginning teacher is freed of handling complex ideas simultaneously with perfecting the demands of their new role. Next, we fill in a little context by letting our beginning teachers select a topic of interest and expertise to prepare in the form of a brief lesson. However, the lesson is only presented in front of "pseudo-students." Last, the trainees are sent to face real students with a brief real lesson and with immediate feedback, as they do their "guest microteaching." The overall effect of this graded set of microteaching experiences is that when the trainees become TAs, they are confident and ready to take on this teaching responsibility.

Conclusion

Microteaching is one of the best ways to ensure that a TA's first regular teaching experience will be a successful one — both for the TA and the students in his or her class. The proof is in the teaching evaluations; we have found that the average scores for first-time TAs have improved markedly since our course, with its emphasis on microteaching, has been implemented on a regular basis. If the intrinsic joy and challenge of teaching are apparent from the beginning, then TAs are more likely to sustain a career of teaching excellence, and that is why it is so important that the first time be a good time.

References

Allen, D. & Ryan, K. (1969). *Microteaching.* Reading, MA: Addison-Wesley.

McKeachie, W.J. (1994). *Teaching tips: Strategies, research, and theory for college and university teachers* (9th ed.). Lexington, MA: DC Heath and Company.

HANDOUT 1: WHAT IS MICROTEACHING?

Microteaching is a supervised, practice teaching exercise that will provide you with a great deal of feedback on your performance. The goal is to help you to develop effective communication skills in the classroom. The microteaching process is designed to provide a supportive environment for skill development and a form of "systematic desensitization" to help reduce the anxiety that many new teachers feel when confronted with teaching classes for the first time. The microteaching experience involves a 10-minute teaching presentation (e.g., the first ten minutes of a lecture, demonstration, class discussion, etc.), followed by written/oral feedback from both your peers and instructors. In addition, your presentation will be videotaped for your private review and critique. Extensive evaluation and multiple teaching opportunities are part of the microteaching process.

For each microteaching presentation, you should choose a substantive topic from your field and identify a particular skill or style to improve. The latter should be one you have not tried before or one that you find difficult to execute in the class you are teaching. It is not important to present a complete lesson. You can do a fraction of a lesson, or choose to practice an excerpt from an upcoming discussion section or lecture. Under these circumstances, microteaching provides the opportunity to get early corrective feedback and to re-teach the material more effectively. The ten-minute time limit will be strictly adhered to, in order to foster an inner sense of time and the importance of planning the use of time. The videotape of the presentation will not be shown in class but you should watch the videotape of your work prior to re-teaching the material.

Immediately following your presentation, your class peers will be asked to give you written feedback. The supervising instructors will provide private oral feedback following the exercise and will also make themselves available to provide feedback about the videotape (if you wish). In all cases, the feedback is intended to be sensitive and constructive — noting what worked well in your presentation, and suggesting how it could be improved. Self-evaluation is also encouraged, along with viewing of the videotape. Watching the videotape can be a powerful learning experience - an important developmental exercise for both becoming a teacher and for becoming a more effective communicator in other areas of your professional life.

HANDOUT 2: MICROTEACHING EVALUATION

TEACHER_____

TOPIC _____

    Please rate the presentation in terms of both SUBSTANCE (this side of the page) and STYLE (reverse side). For each aspect, please circle a number from 1 - 5 , where 1 = weak, 3 = adequate, and 5 = strong. Then explain the basis for your rating. You can put in the margin these notations, and follow with details:

L = Liked; D = Disliked; ? = Questions; R = Recommendations

    SUBSTANCE ASPECTS. Please evaluate the substantive content of the presentation:

How informative was it?	1	2	3	4	5
How clearly were ideas expressed?	1	2	3	4	5
Was it the appropriate level of complexity for the expected audience?	1	2	3	4	5

Additional comments and recommendations:

STYLE ASPECTS: Please evaluate the teaching style of the presentation:
L = Liked;   D = Disliked;   ? = Questions;   R = Recommendations

Voice   1   2   3   4   5

(e.g., volume, rapidity of speech)
Body Language   1   2   3   4   5

(e.g., eye contact, posture, gestures,
relationship to the board or A/V materials)
Mannerisms   1   2   3   4   5

(e.g., anything distracting or effective,
both verbal and nonverbal)

Enthusiasm   1   2   3   4   5
    (both verbal and nonverbal)

Additional comments and recommendations:

The Use of Videotape Feedback in the Training of Instructors

Steven Prentice-Dunn, Ph.D.
University of Alabama
G. Shane Pitts, Ph.D.
Birmingham-Southern College

Note: We thank the graduate students who have completed the Teaching of Psychology Practicum for the benefit of their wisdom. We also appreciate James Flournoy's assistance in the research review.

Overview

Traditionally, new instructors practiced their craft in a vacuum of sorts. They might acquire teaching techniques from reading or from recalling their own teachers; however, they had little feedback on their performance other than student ratings at the end of the term. That situation has changed dramatically in the past decade. There is now an increased emphasis on training new instructors through workshops, seminars, and practica (e.g., Abbott, Wulff, & Szego, 1989; Feldman & Paulsen, 1994). A prominent feature of these more formal methods is feedback that comes from direct observation or videotape.

Despite the increasing use of videotape feedback in teaching assessment, literature regarding precisely how various academic disciplines are using videotape to enhance the training of instructors remains scarce. In this chapter, we attempt to partially fill this void through a detailed description of why and how videotape feedback is used to train instructors in the Department of Psychology at the University of Alabama. However, before embarking on the specifics of using videotape feedback, we first describe the case for using video and briefly review the research on its effects on instructor training. Next, we describe some practical issues in the use of video information as it is employed in our department. Finally, we discuss various consultation models and provide recommendations for videotaping and consultation sessions.

The Case for Videotape Feedback

Prior to the advent of easily accessible video technology, one of the most widely used means of obtaining information about a new instructor's teaching was through direct classroom observation. Often a consultant would attend one or more classes, record observations, and then summarize and report these observations to the instructor.

In comparison to the use of videotape, direct observation does have some advantages. When the video recorder is narrowly focused on the instructor, direct observation may allow the consultant to more fully assess the class environment as a whole. The consultant may more easily see the reactions of students and the interaction among students and between the instructor and the students. This technique, however, suffers from the same dilemma that faces any direct observational strategy. That is, the presence of the observer often affects the behavior of students and the instructor, thereby compromising the validity of the observation. For example, students may be less likely to offer comments or questions or the instructor may focus attention on the observer rather than on the class.

The use of video can overcome this serious shortcoming as well as provide a host of additional advantages. We discuss seven advantages that are unique to the use of videotape feedback in teaching assessment.

One does not have to rely on the memory or the perspective of the observer. Hundreds of studies have documented the susceptibility of human memory to errors and distortions (see Ashcraft, 1994; Schacter, 1990; 1996 for reviews). Using video, in essence, removes the consultant's potential memory distortions from the equation and replaces them with a more objective picture of the instructor's teaching. Likewise, during a structured observation (as is often used), the observer may attend to a particular aspect of teaching at a given time and thus miss valuable information that is occurring during the teaching. Videotaping frees the consultant from the arduous task of attempting to direct close attention to multiple dimensions of a segment of teaching at once.

Video allows for self-evaluation and can heighten awareness of discrepancies. One of the most convincing reasons for using videotape is that, when used in conjunction with feedback, it includes a powerful self-evaluation component that other forms of feedback lack. A potent motivating force to change behaviors or thoughts results from experiencing cognitive dissonance. Cognitive dissonance is an uncomfortable state of psychological tension that occurs when there is an inconsistency between two or more of one's thoughts or between one's thoughts and behavior (Aronson, 1969; Festinger, 1957). This tension is most pronounced when the inconsistencies are central to one's self-concept (Aronson, 1992; Higgins, 1989). Indeed, in a review of instructional feedback practices, Brinko (1993) noted that "feedback is more effective when it creates cognitive dissonance" (p. 580).

A videotape provides an instrumental medium for creating dissonance. It allows for the identification of discrepancies between instructors' self-concept and behavior, or between what they thought they were doing in their teaching and their actual behaviors shown on the tape. When made mindful of moderate discrepancies between ideal and actual teaching performance, instructors are typically motivated to resolve the discrepancies through adjustments in their teaching (Centra, 1973; Fuller & Manning, 1973; Geis, 1991; Paulsen & Feldman, 1995; Perlberg, 1983; Wright, 1995).

The tape can be archived and viewed repeatedly. One of the most common recommendations in the teaching improvement literature is that feedback should be provided in small increments involving multiple instances over a period of time (e.g., Brinko, 1993; Carroll & Goldberg, 1989). That videotape can be archived and viewed repeatedly by the instructor and consultant fits well with most consultation models. The archiving feature of videotape can also be used to vividly demonstrate an instructor's improvement over time which may promote the instructor's sense of accomplishment and hard work. It may also be used to deliver a concrete message to new, apprehensive instructors that teaching well is a skill that develops gradually.

Videotape enables one to focus on the details of teaching more so than any other medium. From a review of research on factors that influence the effectiveness of feedback given to instructors to improve their teaching, Brinko (1993) found that feedback is more effective when it is focused and contains specific data. Because video is a relatively permanent medium that can be replayed, it contains a wealth of specific data from which the consultant can draw. This enables the consultant to offer focused, specific feedback to the instructor. As noted by Brinko, feedback that targets "specific critical incidents help feedback recipients to perform more effectively and to understand better the results of their evaluation" (p. 580). Video offers a tangible view of such critical incidents.

Videotape is arguably the most objective instrument from which to observe behavior. Videotaped analysis of behavior has long been a useful research technique among clinical, developmental, social, and educational psychologists. The primary reason for its use in research is precisely the same reason it is valuable for assessing teaching performance: Video provides a more objective, accurate, detailed picture of the events of interest than does the typical direct observation. Brinko's (1993) review of effective practices for giving feedback to instructors revealed that "feedback is most effective when it contains accurate data and irrefutable evidence" (p. 579). Whether analyses of taped behavior are accurate can certainly be questioned, but that video can provide irrefutable information is a considerable strength of the method.

As a visual medium, videotape is richer in detail and sensory and perceptual attributes than other media. This reason may seem rather obvious, but nonetheless worthy of consideration. When used responsibly, visual media have the power to elicit positive change unlike other media (Perlberg, 1983). Because our attention is directed by vision more readily than other senses, video may have a more powerful impact on an instructor's motivation to change than information gathered from other sensory channels. At the least, it likely serves to direct attention to potential problem areas much quicker than information gathered through other perceptual channels. In the case of teaching assessment, a picture may indeed be worth a thousand words.

Videotape feedback can provide convincing, concrete validation from other sources of feedback. Although disagreement continues regarding the means and interpretation of teaching assessments, researchers and educators are united in stressing the importance of obtaining feedback from a number of sources (e.g., Greenwald, 1997). Overall, feedback is most effective in bringing about change when it comes from multiple sources (Perlberg, 1983). To that end, videotape feedback along with student ratings, peer consultation, and direct observation, can serve as a valuable source of information regarding an instructor's teaching. In circumstances where an instructor has difficulty understanding or interpreting other sources of feedback such as student ratings, video can vividly highlight areas of potential concern that may have previously been unclear to the teacher. Video can help bring to life the numbers obtained from analyses of student ratings.

Most of the advantages listed correspond well with current models of instructional consultation (e.g., Paulsen & Feldman, 1995). Taken together, we think these advantages provide a convincing case for the use of videotape feedback in assessing teaching. However, providing reasonable arguments for the use of videotape feedback is but an initial step in making the complete case for its use. Now, we turn to a review of the research on the effects of providing videotape feedback on instructional quality.

Overview of Research on the Effectiveness of Videotape Feedback

In recent reviews, the effectiveness of videotape feedback has been heralded as one of the most robust findings in the educational research literature (Paulsen & Feldman, 1995; Weimer & Lenze, 1991). Several studies have revealed that feedback from watching oneself on video is associated with improved instruction (Abbott et al.,1989; Dalgaard, 1982; Hendricson at al., 1983; Levinson-Rose & Menges, 1981; McDaniel, 1987; Paulsen & Feldman, 1995; Taylor-Way, 1988).

In one well-designed study, Dalgaard (1982) assessed the impact of a training program on the teaching effectiveness of graduate teaching assistants (TA). The TAs were randomly assigned to a training group or a control group and were videotaped early in the semester teaching their own classes. After the initial taping, participants in the training group attended weekly seminar meetings and individual consultation sessions in which they viewed their tape, engaged in self-evaluation and goal setting, and received feedback from an advisor who had also viewed the tape. At the end of the term, each TA was again videotaped.

Trained and experienced raters independently assessed the two groups using a standardized rating scale. Participants in the training group were rated significantly higher on instructional performance at the end of the term than was the control group. In addition, TAs indicated that the videotape feedback was among the most useful components of the training.

Hendricson et al. (1983) assessed the effectiveness of providing feedback of videotaped teaching episodes to seven pharmacy graduate teaching assistants who taught identical courses across three terms. The TAs were recorded teaching a class both prior to receiving feedback and afterward. Trained raters used a standardized form to independently evaluate the 14 randomly selected taped teaching episodes (seven episodes prior to feedback and seven after feedback). The overall teaching performance of the group was rated significantly higher from pre-feedback to post-feedback. The researchers concluded that providing the video feedback significantly improved the quality of subsequent performance.

Bray and Howard (1980) studied four groups of experienced graduate student teachers. The TAs participated in one of three training groups or in a control group that received no training. The training groups consisted of (a) a training seminar that included instruction on teaching techniques, videotape feedback, and consultation regarding student ratings, (b) videotape consultation only, and (c) student ratings consultation only. Analyses of teaching performance revealed that TAs in the seminar-videotape-student ratings group and those in the videotape-feedback-alone condition benefited compared to those in the control group.

Other research has also found positive effects associated with providing videotape feedback in some form on improvements in teaching activities (e.g., Cassie, Collins, & Daggett, 1977; Melnick & Sheehan, 1976; Rodriguez, 1985). Testimony, personal observation, and attitudinal surveys also corroborate the research findings. For instance, Taylor-Way (1988) indicated that, "in most cases I can see specific improvement even from the very first to the second videotaping and this perception is equally shared by the teacher involved" (p. 187). Surveys conducted at academic institutions in several countries regarding attitudes about the use of various instructional development techniques reveal considerable support for the use and perceived effectiveness of videotape teaching consultation (e.g., Centra, 1979; Erickson, 1986; Konrad, 1983; Wright, 1995).

In summary, studies that have incorporated videotape feedback as a training component suggest that it is effective in improving instructional quality. Nevertheless, research is still needed to help identify the crucial factors that lead to improvements in the videotape feedback process. In reference to the effectiveness of providing videotape and ratings feedback on teaching, Weimer and Lenze (1991) stated that, "the scope, nature, and variables contributing to that impact remain to be discovered" (p. 665).

Practical Issues in the Use of Videotape Feedback

Although more formal experiments are needed to test its effectiveness, the literature suggests that watching oneself on tape can improve instruction, especially when combined with consultation. In this section, we will focus on practical advice for using videos. These comments are gleaned from our experiences with a supervised teaching practicum required of all doctoral students in our department. Readers interested in a course description may consult Prentice-Dunn and Rickard (1994), Prentice-Dunn, Rickard and Lyman (1995), and Rickard, Prentice-Dunn, Rogers, Scogin and Lyman (1991).

Preparing the new instructor for the consultation session. Krupnick (1987) noted that although videotape can be an invaluable asset, it has the potential to do harm. After watching the video, first-time teachers may feel worse about themselves and their students. To increase the likelihood that experience will be positive, the new instructor should not be left with a tape and VCR unless some preparatory steps have first been taken. Foremost among these is to convince instructors to tape a session that is representative of their teaching and not one that has been specifically planned for the benefit of the camera. This is no easy task. Teachers who almost exclusively lecture may spend the entire session conducting a group discussion. Instructors who favor a variety of techniques may revert to a lecture because they assume that the consultant wants to see "traditional" teaching. Thus, establishing that the video is intended as a snapshot of one's daily teaching and not a command performance is a necessary first step.

Another aspect of setting the stage for fruitful interaction is to counter the frequently held belief that teaching is not amenable to more than cosmetic changes. Graduate students often fail to see that the excellence of their favorite professors was primarily due to considerable effort and the wisdom that comes from trying out new strategies that are sometimes unsuccessful. Sviniki (1994) offers a concise rebuttal to the assumption that good teachers are born (not made) and other enduring myths about teaching that may block motivation to improve. Having graduate students read such articles prior to planning their courses helps establish the mindset that instruction is open to change.

Having a representative tape in hand, it is important to forewarn the taped instructor of the tendency to become focused exclusively on one's appearance. Most of us implicitly carry the image of videos as the highly polished, technically sophisticated products that we see on commercial television or on the movie screen. Thus, we are ill-prepared for the cosmetic distortions that come with even the most advanced portable equipment available for college classrooms. One look at the video often reveals a voice that is higher pitched than previously thought, hair that is askew, or eyes that appear to have dark shadows beneath them. Krupnick (1987) calls this phenomenon, "video-induced despair" and says that it must be overcome before meaningful attention can be given to the content of the new teacher's work. Fortunately, a discussion of the distortions beforehand helps substantially as the graduate student comes to realize that such details are less noticeable off camera. Desensitization also comes from repeated viewing and from seeing that the consultant does not dwell on such minutiae.

Forgetting to warn the graduate student ahead of time does have consequences. On those few occasions that we have neglected to do so, the first meeting did not get further than the students' anguished comments about voice, dress, and mannerisms. They noticed very little about their organization, explanations, or the reactions of students to the material.

The first-time teacher can also benefit from some guidance on how to view the tape prior to the consultation session. Although some consultants (e.g., Krupnick, 1987) recommend watching the video with the instructor, we have found that with appropriate forewarning about the tendency to be overly self-critical, new teachers appreciate the privacy of first viewing the tape alone.

Davis (1993) provides several suggestions for viewing tapes of oneself. First, view the video as soon as possible. Thoughts and feelings about the class session are still fresh within a few days of the recording. Second, plan to spend more time analyzing the tape than it took to record. Many consultants suggest that evaluation takes at least twice the time of the class itself. Third, focus on an overview on the initial viewing. Fuhrmann and Grasha (1983) recommend answering the following questions: What specific things did I do well? What did the students appear to enjoy most? If I could do this session over, what three things would I change? How could I go about changing those things? After the first viewing, focus on selected aspects of one's performance. For example, an instructor concerned about communicating enthusiasm might concentrate on her or his voice inflection, whereas a teacher with the goal of involving students might count the students who participate in a discussion. It is important to make note of strengths as well as shortcomings in this process.

Finally, use checklists to focus the analysis. Davis recommends creating lists that reflect one's teaching style or selecting relevant items from established lists. For example, Davis (1993) offers 4-10 questions in each of the following areas: (a) organization and preparation (e.g., Do you state the purpose of the class and its relation to the previous class?); (b) style of presentation (e.g., Do you talk to the class, not to the board or windows?); (c) clarity of presentation (e.g., Do you give examples, illustrations, or applications to clarify abstract concepts?); (d) questioning skills (e.g., Do you ask questions to determine what students know about the topic?); (e) student interest and participation (e.g., Do you provide opportunities for students to practice what they are learning?); (f) classroom climate (e.g., Do you address some students by name?); and, (g) discussion (e.g., Do you draw out quiet students and prevent dominating students from monopolizing the discussion?).

Diamond, Sharp, and Ory (1978) presented a 60-item checklist that taps the dimensions of lectures. Among the covered areas are (a) importance and suitability of content, (b) organization (i.e., introductory portion, body of the lecture, and conclusion), (c) presentation style (i.e., voice characteristics, nonverbal communication), (d) clarity of presentation, (e) establishing and maintaining contact with students, and (f) questioning ability. With each item scored on a three-point scale, the Diamond et al. instrument offers an alternative to the dichotomous evaluations used on the Davis (1993) items.

A third possibility is a form intended to focus the attention of a classroom observer on teacher behaviors (Weimer, Parrett, & Kerns, 1988). However, the actions described can easily be seen in a videotape. Although the instrument appears burdensome at first glance, it provides a compilation from which relevant items for a particular instructor can be selected and then rated on a five-point scale. One advantage of the Weimer et al. list is the additional focus on behaviors involved in active learning techniques.

Consultation models.

After establishing the framework for the new instructor's work with the video, the consultant should watch the tape using the guidelines described in the previous section. Prior to meeting with the graduate student, the adviser must decide among various models of consultation (Paulsen & Feldman, 1995). Five approaches have been identified by Brinko (1990, 1991) based on the nature of the relationship between the instructor and the consultant. These models are similar to ones identified earlier by Dalgaard, Simpson, and Carrier (1982).

In the *prescription* model, the consultant seeks to diagnose problems and recommend solutions for observed deficiencies. The consultant's authority as an expert is apparent in this approach. In the *collaborative/process* model, the consultant joins the instructor as a partner to facilitate improvement. The prescription and collaborative/process models differ in the emphasis applied to the consultant's authority and in the role of the instructor in the problem-solving. In the *product* model, the instructor identifies shortcomings and remedies, hears suggestions from the consultant, and then produces a material product such as a test or lab manual as a solution. The *confrontational* approach involves the consultant challenging the maladaptive assumptions of the teacher that might hinder progress. Finally, consultants who work from the *affiliative* model become counselors who seek to solve the personal problems of the instructor that are affecting teaching.

In practice, the collaborative/process and prescription approaches are used most often by professional consultants, with the other models rarely employed (Brinko, 1990; Paulsen & Feldman, 1995). Many believe that collaborative/process is the model most likely to improve instruction (e.g., Braskamp & Ory, 1994; Geis, 1991), although its success is largely based on testimonials. We also recommend the collaborative role;

however, the consultant must be sensitive to what works best with the individual instructor. For a few graduate students, this involves occasionally prescribing solutions.

Our approach is nicely summarized by Carroll and Goldberg (1989): "We focus on what the instructor already knows about teaching and how this knowledge and experience can be directed and enhanced to help solve the problems at hand. Our primary interest, then, is to develop the individual's ability to diagnose his or her teaching problems, to engage in some creative problem solving, and to become more open to new approaches" (p. 144).

Conducting the consultation session

The meeting between the new instructor and the consultant should always begin with a reminder to the graduate student of the collaborative nature of the work to be done in the session. The student should be assured that whatever issues he or she has brought to the meeting will be addressed. We also find it useful to review the course goals that have been identified by the instructor. (In PY 695, these were developed prior to the semester with the understanding that several strategies (e.g., lectures, small group discussions, student journals, in-class writing assignments) would be used early in the semester and that the individual instructors could then continue the techniques with which they felt comfortable.) Finally, a short review of the content of the taped session and the objectives for that day is beneficial.

Focus on the positive first. Questions such as "What did you see on the tape that worked well?" or "What did you observe that you liked?" force the student to think of strengths and counteract the tendency to be inappropriately self-critical. Although new instructors sometimes appear surprised by this line of inquiry (and may even need assistance in the first session), it is important to establish a balanced approach so that any problems to be discussed later will not be met with defensiveness.

Allow the instructor to take the conversational lead. Krupnick (1987) and Geis (1991) advise that the teacher take the conversational lead from the outset of the meeting. Our experience suggests that such a strategy works best after setting the positive tone for the session. Although the consultant will always have a list of issues to be discussed, it is common to have all of these matters first raised by the instructor.

Give positive feedback in the grammatical second person. Brinko (1993) states that compliments given as "you" statements will enhance self-esteem. For example, feedback phrased as "You really encouraged several of the quieter students to speak" is preferable to "I noticed that several of the quieter students really participated in the discussion". The former statement attributes the behavior to the teacher's effort rather than leaving the cause implied or ambiguous.

Frame negative aspects of the performance in terms of improvement. Hearing about one's shortcomings in any endeavor is unpleasant. Receiving negative information can be especially aversive when the feedback is about a complex set of skills that are practiced in public and are related to one's career aspirations. To the novice instructor, evaluative audiences appear at every turn. Thus, handling negative feedback requires particular care.

The value of first spending considerable time discussing successes should not be underestimated. Indeed, Davies and Jacobs (1985) found that preceding and then following negative feedback with positive information produced the greatest change in targeted behaviors in comparison to other possible orders. Thus, the initial period of the consultation session prepares the instructor for a question such as "What would you like to improve?" Such phrasing accomplishes three things. First, it avoids the sting to self-esteem that comes from using terms such as "wrong" and "incorrect". Second, it appropriately focuses attention on the goal of consultation; that is, improving the instruction rather than reprimanding the instructor. Third, by having the graduate student supply the answer, it reduces the tendency to react with denial or other forms of defensiveness when a problem is identified by someone else.

Brinko (1993) suggests that negative information is more effective when not given in the grammatical second person. Just as a compliment is more powerful when couched as a "you" statement, so too is information about problems with one's presentation. Brinko recommends presenting feedback in the first person or third person. Examples of the latter are "I followed much of the summary, but then found myself expecting more coverage of the last topic of the day" and "The students may have had difficulty following the final part of the summary".

Needless to say, the consultant should take care to avoid needlessly harsh language. Negative comments about the new instructor will be heard loudly and clearly without resorting to strong terms. In addition, the consultant should explicitly distinguish between minor and major issues for the graduate student's attention. For example, remembering to scan the entire classroom when speaking may be seen by the graduate student as equal in importance to providing an organizational scheme for a lecture, unless the consultant makes the distinction.

Combine your reactions with those of students, if available. In our teaching practicum, the first and third consultation meetings are accompanied by narrative and quantitative feedback from the new instructor's students. Geis (1991) observed that "a particular message gains credibility when it is one of a series of similar messages, from a variety of sources" (p.11). The consistency between the students' and consultant's lists of primary strengths and weaknesses is often remarkable and does appear to impress the novice instructor that evaluation is not a haphazard process.

When inconsistencies do arise, the consultant can provide a welcome perspective for the teacher. For example, it is common for our introductory psychology students to complain about the difficulty of the exams, due chiefly to the tremendous amount of material that is covered in a beginning course in our discipline. In addition, our rating scale contains one item about the instructor stimulating the student's curiosity that is habitually rated lower than related items about the teaching style (probably due to the awkward wording of the item). New instructors are comforted to hear that the above responses are normative and do not reflect shortcomings on their part.

Elucidate short-term goals to work toward and end the session on a positive note. Every consultative meeting should end with the identification of a brief list of areas to work on, stated as specifically as possible. These areas will then provide the focus for the next meeting. We also recommend reiterating the instructor's strengths at this point and expressing appreciation for his or her efforts to provide a high-quality experience for the undergraduate students in the course. Virtually all new instructors work extraordinarily hard and yet receive little acknowledgment. A simple expression of appreciation can go far in establishing a relationship that motivates instructors to offer their best.

Above all else, be a listener. Carroll and Goldberg (1989) say that consultation works best for instructors who can identify discrepancies between expected and actual performances. Fortunately, it is rare to find a first-time teacher who has no idea about what can be improved. Indeed, the problem more frequently encountered is getting the instructor to realize that she or he already has many strengths. Much of the consultant's time will be devoted to drawing out the graduate student's concerns and encouraging the student to reflect on the advantages and disadvantages of a particular teaching technique or proposed course of action.

Suggesting that consultants practice restraint does not mean that we have little to offer. Although graduate students teaching their initial course often know what needs changing, they usually need help with how to enact that change. Providing concrete recommendations for how to increase student participation is but one example of using one's expertise to facilitate improvement. We also find that new instructors appreciate hearing about similar obstacles that we have encountered in our own teaching and what worked and what did not. Such disclosure not only creates rapport, it also illustrates that all beginning instructors face adjustments and that roadblocks to effective teaching are present throughout one's career.

Conclusion

Videotape is a wonderful medium for seeing ourselves from the perspective of our students. When combined with consultation, beginning instructors get invaluable information on their success in translating assumptions about teaching, course content, and students into practice. Moreover, consultants usually benefit by reflecting on their own assumptions and learning new techniques from the instructors that can be applied to their own courses. As McDaniel (1987) has observed, there is no need for teaching to be such a solitary activity. Opening the dialogue enriches us all, instructors and students alike.

References

Abbott, R. D., Wulff, D. H., & Szego, C. K. (1989). Review of research on TA training. In J. D. Nyquist, R. D. Abbott, & D. H. Wulff (Eds.), *Teaching assistant training in the 1990s* (pp. 111-123). San Francisco: Jossey-Bass.

Aronson, E. (1969). The theory of cognitive dissonance: A current perspective. In. L. Berkowitz (Ed.), *Advances in experimental social psychology* (Vol. 4, pp. 1-34). New York: Academic Press.

Aronson, E. (1992). The return of the repressed: Dissonance theory makes a comeback. *Psychological Inquiry, 3*, 303-311.

Ashcraft, M. H. (1994). *Human memory and cognition* (2nd ed.). New York: Harper-Collins.

Braskamp, L. A., & Ory, J. C. (1994). *Assessing faculty work*. San Francisco:

Jossey-Bass.

Bray, J. H., & Howard, G. S. (1980). Methodological considerations in the evaluation of a teacher-training program. *Journal of Educational Psychology, 72*, 62-70.

Brinko, K. T. (1990). Instructional consultation with feedback in higher education. *Journal of Higher Education, 61*, 65-83.

Brinko, K. T. (1991). The interactions of teaching improvement. In M. Theall & J. Franklin (Eds.), *Effective practices for improving teaching* (pp. 39-49). San Francisco: Jossey-Bass.

Brinko, K. T. (1993). The practice of giving feedback to improve teaching: What is effective? *Journal of Higher Education, 64*, 574-593.

Carroll, J. G., & Goldberg, S .R. (1989). Teaching consultants: A collegial approach to better teaching. *College Teaching, 37*, 143-154.

Cassie, J. M, Collins, M. B., & Daggett, C. J. (1977). The use of videotapes to improve clinical teaching. *Journal of Medical Education, 52*, 353-354.

Centra, J. A. (1973). Effectiveness of student feedback in modifying college instruction. *Journal of Educational Psychology, 65*, 395-401.

Centra, J. A. (1979). *Determining faculty effectiveness*. San Francisco: Jossey-Bass.

Dalgaard, K. A. (1982). Some effects of training on teaching effectiveness of untrained university teaching assistants. *Research in Higher Education, 17*, 39-50.

Dalgaard, K. A., Simpson, D. E., & Carrier, C. A. (1982). Coordinate status consultation. *Journal of Instructional Development, 5*, 7-14.

Davies, D., & Jacobs, A. (1985). "Sandwiching" complex interpersonal feedback. *Small Group Behavior, 16*, 387-396.

Davis, B. G. (1993). *Tools for teaching*. San Francisco: Jossey-Bass.

Diamond, J., Sharp, G., & Ory, J. C. (1978). *Improving your lecturing*. Urbana, IL: University of Illinois Office of Instructional Resources.

Erickson, G. (1986). A survey of faculty development practices. *To Improve the Academy, 5*, 182-194.

Feldman, K. A., & Paulsen, M .B. (Eds.)(1994). *Teaching and learning in the college classroom*. Needham Heights, MA: Ginn Press.

Festinger, L. (1957). *A theory of cognitive dissonance*. Stanford, CA: Stanford University Press.

Fuhrmann, B. S., & Grasha, A. F. (1983). *Practical handbook for college teachers*. Boston: Little, Brown.

Fuller, F. F., & Manning, B. A. (1973). Self-confrontation reviewed: A conceptualization for video play-back in teacher education. *Review of Educational Research, 43*, 469-528.

Geis, G. L. (1991). The moment of truth: Feeding back information about teaching. In M. Theall & J. Franklin (Eds.), *Effective practices for improving teaching* (pp. 7-19). San Francisco: Jossey-Bass.

Greenwald, A. G. (1997). Validity concerns and usefulness of student ratings of instruction. *American Psychologist, 52*, 1182-1186.

Hendricson, W. D., Hawkins, D. W., Littlefield, J. H., Kleffner, J. H., Hudepohl, N. C., & Herbert, R. (1983). Effects of providing feedback to lecturers via videotape recordings and observer critiques. *American Journal of Pharmaceutical Education*, 47, 239-244.

Higgins, E. T. (1989). Self-discrepancy theory: What patterns of self-beliefs cause people to suffer? In. L. Berkowitz (Ed.), *Advances in experimental social psychology* (Vol. 22, pp. 136-193). New York: Guilford Press.

Konrad, A. C. (1983). Faculty development practices in Canadian universities. Canadian *Journal of Higher Education, 13*, 13-25.

Krupnick, C. G. (1987). The uses of videotape replay. In C. R. Christensen & A. J. Hansen (Eds.), *Teaching and the case method: Text, cases, and readings* (pp. 256-263). Boston: Harvard Business School.

Levinson-Rose, J, & Menges, R. F. (1981). Improving college teaching: A critical review of research. *Review of Educational Research, 51*, 403-434.

McDaniel, E. A. (1987). Faculty collaboration for better teaching: Adult learning principles applied to teaching improvement. *To Improve the Academy, 6*, 94-102.

Melnick, M. A., & Sheehan, D. S. (1976). Clinical supervision elements: The teaching clinic to improve university teaching. *Journal of Research and Development in Education, 9*, 67-75.

Paulsen, M. B., & Feldman, K. A. (1995). *Taking teaching seriously: Meeting the challenge of instructional improvement*. ASHE-ERIC Report No. 2. Washington, DC: George Washington University.

Perlberg. A. (1983). When professors confront themselves: Towards a theoretical conceptualization of video self-confrontation in higher education. *Higher Education, 12*, 633-663.

Prentice-Dunn, S., & Rickard, H. C. (1994). A follow-up note on graduate training in the teaching of introductory psychology. *Teaching of Psychology, 21*, 111-112.

Prentice-Dunn, S., Rickard, H. C., & Lyman, R. D. (1995, January). *The benefits of a graduate course in teaching of psychology: Results of a survey of doctoral graduates*. Paper presented to the National Institute on the Teaching of Psychology, St Petersburg, FL.

Rickard, H. C., Prentice-Dunn, S., Rogers, R. W., Scogin, F. R., & Lyman, R. D. (1991). Teaching of psychology: A required course for all doctoral students. *Teaching of Psychology, 18*, 235-237.

Rodriguez, R. N. (1985). Teaching teaching to teaching assistants. *College Teaching, 33*, 173-176.

Schacter, D. L. (1990). Memory. In M. I. Posner (Ed.), *Foundations of cognitive science*. Cambridge, MA: MIT Press.

Schacter, D. L. (1996). *Searching for memory: The brain, the mind, and the past*. New York: Basic Books.

Sviniki, M. (1994). Seven deadly comments...that block learning about teaching. *National Teaching and Learning Forum, 3*, 4-6.

Taylor-Way, D. (1988). Consultation with video: Memory management through stimulated recall. In K. G. Lewis (Ed.), *Face to face: A sourcebook of individual consultation techniques for faculty/instructional developers* (pp. 159-191) Stillwater, OK: New Forums Press.

Weimer, M., & Lenze, L. F. (1991). Instructional interventions: A review of the literature on efforts to improve instruction. In K. A. Feldman and M. B. Paulsen (Eds.), *Teaching and learning in the college classroom* (pp.653-682). Needham Heights, MA: Ginn Press

Weimer, M., Parrett, J. L., & Kerns, M. (1988). *How am I teaching?: Forms and activities for acquiring instructional input*. Madison, WI: Magna Publications.

Wright, W. A. (Ed.) (1995). *Teaching improvement practices*. Boston, MA: Anker.

The Supervision of Teaching Assistants: Theory, Evidence and Practice

Loreto R. Prieto, Ph.D.
University of Akron

Note: Portions of this chapter first appeared in Supervising graduate teaching assistants: An adaptation of the Integrated Developmental Model. *Journal of Graduate Teaching Assistant Development, 2*, 93-105; and Teaching assistants' preferences for supervisory style: Testing a developmental model of GTA supervision. *Journal of Graduate Teaching Assistant Development, 6*, 1-8. Adapted and used by permission of New Forums Press, Inc.

Overview

Graduate teaching assistants (GTAs) are responsible for a large amount of undergraduate instruction at most major universities in the country. Unfortunately, a significant number of GTAs are ill-prepared to deal with the duties involved, and may receive inadequate guidance to assist them in meeting their responsibilities (Darling & Earhart, 1990; Diamond & Gray, 1987; Yoder & Hugenberg, 1980). Due to increased concern about the quality of undergraduate education, those factors that positively influence GTA effectiveness, such as supervision of their teaching duties, are important to identify.

Although graduate students are often closely supervised in the direct professional practice of their own areas of training (e.g., the practice of psychotherapy by graduate psychology students), these same students are frequently expected to undertake the role of GTA without prior training or without a specified faculty member to supervise their duties and development. In a recent study, Prieto and Altmaier (1994) found that approximately 50% of their GTA sample had received no training prior to undertaking their teaching duties and 25% reported that they were teaching without supervision of any kind. For those GTAs who were receiving supervision, 25% of this group indicated they met only monthly or by appointment with their supervisor. Thus, approximately half of the sample reported having either no or infrequent supervision time to discuss their concerns about teaching. Other studies concerning GTAs have raised similar concerns (e.g., Meyers & Prieto, 2000).

Furthermore, GTAs often teach at the limit of their knowledge as they attempt to disseminate a body of information to their students which they are often just developing themselves (Boehrer & Sarkisian, 1985). This situation is likely to be even more troubling for GTAs teaching outside of their own area of graduate study or expertise. Moreover, the transition from student to teacher is often a difficult one for many GTAs, especially regarding the responsibility and authority associated with the teaching role (Andrews, 1985a). Basic teaching skills, such as lecturing effectively and developing appropriate interpersonal relationships with students, are usually unfamiliar to the novice GTA (Andrews, 1985b). The development of skills to deal with these issues could be addressed within in the context of supervision.

The existing state of affairs concerning inadequate GTA supervision is unfortunate because many graduate students accept GTA positions to prepare for professorial careers (Nyquist, Abbott, & Wulff, 1989; Prieto, 1994). The absence of supervision fails to optimally use the GTA experience as a means to increase knowledge and skills. Without assistance, GTAs who might prove to be good instructors, both during their graduate training and as professionals, may turn away from teaching due to a perceived lack of efficacy. Failing to provide support for GTAs to become effective instructors has even been considered an ethical issue (cf. Smock & Menges, 1985) because universities are mandated to provide undergraduate students with the highest quality instruction possible. Unfortunately, most theory and research in the area of graduate teaching has dealt with training programs (Andrews, 1985a), and relatively little work has addressed supervision. The present model of GTA supervision is a response to this need.

Extant Models of GTA Supervision

Scholars in the TA supervision literature have often applied developmental models of supervision in psychology (e.g., Stoltenberg, 1981) to the supervision of GTAs and student teachers (Kagan, 1988; Sprague & Nyquist, 1989). Research conducted on GTAs to date has also made use of both the theoretical and empirical teacher education literature and has supported the validity of a developmental approach to GTA issues (cf. Prieto & Altmaier, 1994; Prieto & Meyers, 1999; Tollerud, 1990).

For example, Kagan (1988), compared the supervision literatures of teacher education and psychology, and noted similarities between the literatures concerning the supervisory relationship, the various roles of the supervisor, and the fundamental apprenticeship context of supervision for both fields. Kagan also noted that research involving the notion of conceptual level matching (cf., Hunt, 1971) in the supervisory environment of student teachers (e.g., Kagan, 1987; Theis-Sprinthall, 1980; Zeichner &

Liston, 1984) found results similar to the conceptual level investigations concerning psychotherapy trainees (e.g., Holloway & Wampold, 1986; Stoppard & Miller, 1985). Generally speaking, supervisees tend to perform better and are more satisfied with supervision when supervisory environments match their conceptual level. Evidence also suggests that the cognitive complexity of supervisees' conceptualization abilities increases with experience. Student teachers, according to their level of experience, appear to prefer certain supervisor interventions (e.g., Copeland, 1982; Copeland & Atkinson, 1978), similar to psychotherapy trainees (e.g., Worthington, 1984).

In light of these similarities, Kagan asserted that research findings concerning the supervision of student teachers were largely congruent with a popular developmental model of counselor supervision, the Counselor Complexity Model (CCM; Stoltenberg, 1981). Later, Sprague and Nyquist (1989) outlined stages through which GTAs progress in developing as classroom instructors. Again, based upon Stoltenberg's CCM, Sprague and Nyquist focused on the roles of the GTA supervisor (manager, role model, and mentor), and offered descriptions of developmental levels and appropriate supervisory environments for use with GTAs as they grow in skill and experience. Sprague and Nyquist posited a developmental movement of GTAs from anxious, task-oriented, self-focused, novice "learners" to a more advanced stage where as "junior colleagues" GTAs were more skilled, secure, flexible, and student-focused in their teaching.

While these early efforts at conceptualizing GTA supervision (e.g., Kagan, 1988; Nyquist & Wulff, 1996; Sprague & Nyquist, 1989) were based upon Stoltenberg's initial work, a more current and extensive conceptualization of his supervision model exists to guide theoretical and empirical explorations in the area of GTA supervision.

Stoltenberg's Integrated Developmental Model

The most comprehensive model addressing psychotherapy supervision from a developmental perspective is the Integrated Developmental Model (IDM) by Stoltenberg, McNeill, and Delworth (1998). The IDM is largely a synthesis of the constructs postulated in each of these authors' earlier models (Loganbill et al., 1982; Stoltenberg, 1981, Stoltenberg & Delworth, 1987), and continues to incorporate constructs from developmental theory (Chickering, 1969; Erikson, 1968; Hogan, 1964; Loevinger, 1976). Because a full outline of the IDM is beyond the scope of this paper, the reader is referred to Stoltenberg et al. (1998) for a full explication of the IDM. However, a brief synopsis of the model is presented below.

The IDM postulates three stages of development, along three structures, and across eight counseling domains, through which a counselor trainee progresses in mastering the art of counseling and developing an identity as a counselor. These three stages (Levels 1, 2, and 3 Integrated) describe a process in which the trainee characteristics of Autonomy, Motivation, and Self & Other Awareness grow to a point such that trainees move from a highly dependent, anxious, linear-thinking, self-interested and less empathic style of dealing with their patients to a level where trainees rely less on structured supervision, have increased cognitive flexibility, are guided by a broader awareness of themselves and their patients within the counseling process, and find a more stable base of motivation driving their work. The professional counseling domains across which this developmental process occurs are Professional Ethics, Treatment Plans and Goals, Theoretical Orientation, Individual Differences, Client Conceptualization, Interpersonal Assessment, Assessment Techniques, and Intervention Skills Competence.

On the basis of Hunt's (1971) conceptual level matching model, the IDM also outlines optimal supervision environments for use with trainees at each of the stages so as to facilitate their movement from one stage to the next. The IDM also identifies skills necessary for supervisors to possess in order to accurately identify the stages and needs of their trainees, use intervention strategies in supervision, and assess the supervisory relationship and environment. Additionally, the authors incorporated the Piagetian (1970) concepts of accommodation and assimilation, as well as Loevinger's (1977) notion of "ameboid" movement during growth to explain the normal "push and pull" of trainee development. Finally, the authors noted the possibility of differential trainee stage development across domains, the need to recognize idiosyncratic paths of development in individual trainees, the effects of gender and race on supervision, and social psychological influences on trainee development. The IDM and its associated developmental constructs have accumulated solid empirical support (see Stoltenberg, McNeill, & Crethar, 1994; Worthington, 1987 for reviews).

Supervising Graduate Teaching Assistants with the IDM

The adapted IDM used to conceptualize the supervision of GTAs differs from the original psychotherapy supervision IDM in two ways. First, the professional competency domains in the adapted IDM reflect teaching domains as opposed to the counseling domains found in the original IDM. Also, the adapted IDM possesses only seven competency domains as compared to the eight competency domains in the original model. However, this new, adapted model retains the three stages and structures outlined in the original IDM. The adapted model will now be discussed in detail, with attention given to the identified developmental stages, structures, supervisory environments, and teaching domains. See Figure 1 for a graphic representation of the adapted model, the Integrated Developmental Model for Graduate Teaching Assistants (IDM-GTA).

Developmental Structures Within Stages

The adapted IDM-GTA contains three stages; the third stage culminates in an integration (Level Three-Integrated) of developmental structures (Self and Other Awareness, Motivation, and Autonomy) across the identified teaching domains. This portion of the chapter will describe GTAs at each stage of the IDM-GTA, in terms of the three developmental structures.

Structures

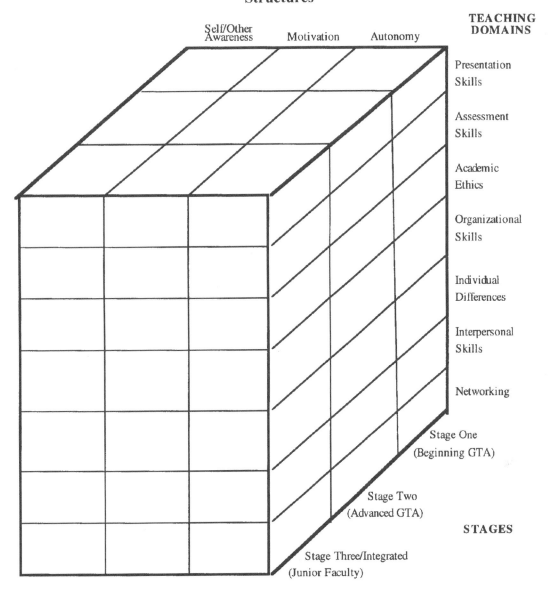

Figure 1.

The Integrated Developmental Model of
Supervision for Graduate Teaching Assistants

Note: Reprinted from "Supervising Graduate teaching Assistants: An Adaptation of the The Integrated Developmemtal Model" by L. R. Prieto, Journal of Graduate Teaching Assistant Development, v.2, p. 97. Copyright 1995 by New Forums Press. Reprinted by permission.

Stage One (Beginning) GTAs are students who have had little or no previous graduate teaching experience. They probably have not had pedagogic course work and may be at the beginning stages of their own graduate programs. Therefore, they are more likely to be similar to than different from the students they are about to instruct. Regarding Self and Other Awareness, Stage One GTAs tend to be more focused on themselves as opposed to their students. This self-focus tends be due to both the anxiety they experience in the classroom and because they are accountable to faculty for their teaching performance. Interestingly, in spite of this self-focus, these GTAs tend not to be highly aware of the weaknesses in their teaching approach or how their personal style affects students or supervisors. In supervision, GTAs at this stage tend to focus more on themselves and their performance in the classroom situation, and less on understanding the learning needs of their students.

The Motivation of Stage One GTAs is usually high; their approach to teaching is excited and optimistic, although they are often anxious. Despite not knowing if the role of teacher suits them well, the combination of limited skills and a desire to excel leads Stage One GTAs to try very hard to be effective instructors. Their determination is often a simple attempt to reduce their anxiety and increase their sense of self-efficacy or the level of confidence one feels in being able to execute a particular behavior intended to bring about a particular outcome (Bandura, 1986).

In supervision, Stage One GTAs tend to believe there is only one "right way" to teach. If they feel confident in their knowledge of course content or have some previous quasi-teaching experience, they may initially appear more efficacious, although this sense of efficacy tends to decline when they deal with the realities of teaching. Research in the teacher education literature suggests that pre-service teachers (those with no experience) tend to report an inflated sense of self-efficacy until they actually encounter the realities of teaching (Dembo & Gibson, 1985; Evans & Tribble, 1986). Also, Stage One GTAs might emulate the teaching style of a favorite professor, in an effort to quell their confusion and anxiety.

Dependency on supervision is the hallmark of the Autonomy structure for Stage One GTAs, who rely heavily on their supervisor for all types of information. In supervision, requests for guidance on all matters of policy and procedure are typical, ranging from "When should I schedule my office hours?" to "How should I deal with John Doe who cheated on the exam?" Training programs that educate Stage One GTAs on concrete, logistic-based skills (e.g., test construction, grading, institutional policies on academic affairs) may be helpful in instilling a foundation of knowledge in GTAs and save supervisors from a relentless barrage of questions. Research suggests that training programs are of benefit to GTAs (see Abbott, Wulff, & Szego, 1989 for a review, and see Meyers; Hainline; Maslach et al.; and Goss in this text for discussions on training GTAs). The major developmental tasks of Stage One GTAs are to (a) acquire an initial sense of confidence, (b) become more independent, (c) begin demonstrating an awareness of student needs, and (d) begin developing an identity as a classroom instructor. Improved effectiveness with basic teaching skills, familiarity with typical classroom processes and situations, and a blossoming sense of "fit" with the role of "educator" are elements that enable the achievement of these tasks. Once these developmental tasks have been addressed, GTAs move on to Stage Two.

Stage Two GTAs (Advanced) typically have had at least a semester or two of teaching experience. On the Self and Other Awareness structure, Stage Two GTAs demonstrate a keener awareness of their students, both individually and as a class, and are developing a stronger appreciation for the complexities of teaching. This includes a recognition of the many factors that influence students in the classroom and can influence student learning. Furthermore, Stage Two GTAs are able to be more empathic and better understand student learning processes. In supervision, Stage Two GTAs often exemplify this newfound awareness of students by extending deadlines for assignments, arguing for exceptions from course policy for certain students, spending too much office time trying to help certain "problem" students, and evidencing a clear loosening of their previous rigid Stage One personal and teaching boundaries. This newfound awareness can be confusing for GTAs as they attempt to sort out appropriate courses of action, especially given their greater empathic appreciation of student perspectives. The Stage One desire to teach the "right" way has yielded in Stage Two to a confusion stemming from the recognition that teaching situations can be effectively handled in many different ways. Due to this confusion, Stage Two GTAs may vacillate between extremes, utilizing either a totally "etic" approach to students (treating everyone the same no matter what the circumstance) or a totally "emic" approach (considering each case individually with no consistency in judgments or actions).

Regarding Motivation, Stage Two is the time when GTAs may reconsider any further involvement in teaching even though they now have a better sense of themselves as instructors. This "ambivalence" toward teaching stems from GTAs' realization of how much energy and work being an effective instructor entails; many graduate students may question their ability or willingness to pay such a price. Depending on their initial reasons for teaching, GTAs may resolve this issue either by deciding against any further teaching or by continuing their employment as a GTA in spite of the pervasive sense of ambivalence they feel toward teaching. Appropriately dealing with this ambivalence is an important task in supervision, and is especially crucial for GTAs who plan on a teaching career. Stage Two is a time when GTAs can fail to genuinely develop further, instead choosing to simply "go through the motions" of teaching. The vulnerability of GTAs to succumb to this outcome is heightened if the institutional or supervisory environment values research or other academic duties over classroom teaching. Care must be taken by supervisors in assisting Stage Two GTAs through this period, so as to ensure that GTAs possess a commitment to excellence in teaching.

A conflicted sense of Autonomy arises in Stage Two GTAs. GTAs are more assertive and self-directed during this stage, but still rely on supervisory advice for difficult issues. Although vestiges of dependence on the supervisor remain, Stage Two GTAs tend to be more reactive or opposed to the supervisor on issues, and tend to disagree with supervisory advice or are quick to offer counterpoints. This reactance is a function, in part, of a growing skill and experience base, but also has to do with a growing sense of independence from the supervisor and a need to further a sense of self as an "educator." In supervision, the "question everything" posture adopted by GTAs in Stage Two is not only a way to gain their independence, but is also an indirect way for GTAs to seek affirmation from their supervisor regarding the appropriateness of their developing sense of autonomy. The developmental tasks of Stage Two GTAs are to (a) appreciate and account for the perspectives of their students, (b) further their sense of autonomy and confidence in their growing knowledge and skill base, and (c) realize and make the commitment necessary to strive for effectiveness and excellence as an educator. When (and if) GTAs successfully negotiate these tasks, they are prepared to move to Stage Three/Integrated.

The overall final stage of development in the IDM-GTA is labeled Stage Three/Integrated (Junior Faculty). Stage Three GTAs have had at least two or three years of teaching experience. At this highest stage of development, GTAs demonstrate an effective and realistic balance of Self and Other Awareness. Through both teaching experience and a less defensive self-appraisal of their own abilities and limits regarding teaching, Stage Three GTAs are now able to identify their strengths and weaknesses as educators. They are able to truly listen to and empathize with student perspectives, yet can still retain an objective viewpoint and act in the best interests of their students. Stage Three GTAs have a much stronger sense of how to use themselves as a tool for student learning, and can tailor their teaching to particular student needs. In supervision, Stage Three GTAs acknowledge, discuss, and learn to prioritize various points of view concerning teaching decisions or procedures, and they value supervisory input as a source of information.

Regarding Motivation, Stage Three GTAs have resolved the Stage Two ambivalence towards teaching. GTAs at this stage feel comfortable and committed in the role of instructor, and have a strong sense of an identity as an educator. They have a more realistic sense of what they can accomplish as a teacher and see their teaching approach as "personalized" and unique to themselves. In supervision, Stage Three GTAs prefer to discuss higher-order or subtle teaching skills, may want to receive mentoring, may want to discuss with supervisors more personal issues surrounding teaching, and may be excellent role models or supervisors for Stage One GTAs.

Stage Three GTAs are autonomous, yet retain and value the option for supervision as necessary. As previously noted, GTAs at this stage are better able to evaluate their areas of competence as well as their limitations, and are better able to seek out information or advice as needed. Stage Three GTAs are more collegial in their approach to supervision, and desire minimal structure or direction from supervisors, realizing instead that they must accept a larger share of responsibility in struggling to resolve complex teaching issues. In supervision, Stage Three GTAs often set the agenda for issues to be covered, are highly self-directed in completing necessary tasks, are cognizant of and well prepared for routine difficulties, and generally function as completely independent classroom instructors.

The Stage Three/Integrated portion of the model serves as a concept to help describe the continuing development of GTAs as they refine and hone their skills within the three developmental structures and across the seven indicated teaching domains. Obviously, employment as a GTA is a time-limited activity, and although assistantships can extend over a period of a few years, no student engages in a "career" of graduate teaching. The IDM-GTA does not seek to outline the development of GTAs beyond their time of graduate training; however, it is reasonable to view GTA employment as the foundation for the professional development of post-secondary faculty. As Nyquist et al. (1989) noted, "not all GTAs will be professors, but almost all professors were once GTAs" (p. 9). Therefore, the final, Integrated stage in the IDM-GTA is theoretically equivalent to the level of functioning found in the teaching of new assistant professors (cf. Sprague & Nyquist, 1989).

Supervisory Environments

Successful GTA supervision depends on the provision of stage appropriate supervision environments. Based on Hunt's (1971) notion of matching student conceptual levels with appropriate teaching environments in order to maximize learning, supervisory environments need to facilitate the development of trainees both within and between stages. These environments are also a part of the IDM-GTA and are outlined below.

It is important to note factors that can affect the supervisory environment. First, there are often differential levels of GTA development across the seven identified teaching domains. In other words, GTAs might be at Stage Two in terms of their Presentation and Assessment Skills, but at Stage One concerning Networking or Academic Ethics. Therefore, the supervisor will need to adjust interventions and the supervision environment accordingly, depending on the manifest developmental level of the GTA within certain teaching domains. Second, although primarily intended to support growth and learning, the supervisory environment also provides an impetus for GTAs to move forward in their development. Operationally, this translates into the supervisor providing an overall "sub-optimal" supervision environment that gives GTAs clear reinforcement for current skills but also maintains (and occasionally fosters) a level of anxiety that encourages GTAs to acquire more complex skills. Finally, as unique individuals, GTAs will display idiosyncratic patterns of development, and variables such as gender, race, age, and life experiences will all affect GTA development and the resultant process of effective supervision.

The supervisory environment most appropriate for use with Stage One GTAs is one in which the supervisor provides high levels of structure and is directive, because Stage One GTAs will often regard their supervisor as an "expert" on teaching matters and will tend to be dependent. Keeping GTAs' performance anxiety at a manageable level and increasing their awareness of students are the chief goals of supervision at this stage. It is important for supervisors to thoroughly explore all classroom situations with GTAs as they arise because GTAs' lower awareness of others may keep them from reliably judging and evaluating students and classroom problems. It is equally important for the supervisor to consistently reinforce the successful efforts of Stage One GTAs when they appropriately handle classroom and other teaching duties, and to consistently offer them constructive criticism when they do not. While this is seemingly an obvious suggestion, some scholars have pointed out that openly (let alone critically) discussing an instructor's teaching methods is traditionally avoided in academia (Wilson & Sterns, 1985).

A helpful tool for Stage One GTAs is to have their lectures videotaped or to have their supervisor observe them while they teach. In this manner, GTAs can be given concrete feedback on their presentation and interaction skills. The use of videotaping as a training tool with GTAs has been successful in promoting the adoption of effective teaching behaviors (Dalgaard, 1982; Sharp, 1981; see Prentice-Dunn & Pitts in this text for a thorough review and suggested procedures). As previously noted, an emerging sense of identity as an educator is an important developmental task for Stage One GTAs. Therefore, socializing GTAs into the role of instructor (cf. Staton & Darling, 1989) is a critical part of this first supervision environment. Orienting GTAs to their role expectations may help them to gain a sense of appropriateness and confidence in their comportment.

Stage Two GTAs are probably the most exciting and challenging graduate students for supervisors to work with. Stage Two GTAs have acquired a good amount of knowledge and skill from their previous teaching experience and are beginning to become more independent. As well, Stage Two GTAs are realizing the complexity of teaching and are becoming more empathic toward students. This represents a confusing change from the rigid perspectives they held in Stage One. The supervisory environment most appropriate for use with Stage Two GTAs is one that fosters autonomy, but still provides stable supervisory advice to assist GTAs in resolving issues. In other words, the supervisor should expect and allow for vacillating periods of confidence, insecurity and unself-awareness in Stage Two GTAs, and respond accordingly. This is not to say that the supervisor should constantly and radically shift the supervisory environment. Quite the contrary, the supervisor and the environment need to be very consistent and stable at this stage so as to both provide GTAs with a dependable source of guidance and to encourage their growing independence. It is against a backdrop of consistent supervisory support and encouragement toward autonomy that GTAs can safely and effectively explore their vacillating perspectives and discover a sense of stability. Moreover, a stable supervisory environment is important because of the fluctuating sense of Motivation that Stage Two GTAs can experience. Supervisors who do not reinforce the efforts of Stage Two GTAs toward excellence in teaching will contribute to GTAs' continued ambivalence, or worse, encourage GTAs an toward disinvestment from their teaching role and duties.

At the highest level of GTA development, the supervisory environment for use with Stage Three GTAs is much more collegial and contains little, if any, supervisor-imposed structure. The supervisor can expect to see in Stage Three GTAs some differential development across teaching domains with occasional regressions to Stage Two functioning, especially when Stage Three GTAs encounter a particularly novel or difficult teaching task. Overall, however, in this final stage of development, Stage Three GTAs are less threatened by either self-exploration or evaluations of their teaching, and the supervisor can be more straightforward in confronting or discussing the viewpoints they hold. Often this is the stage in which supervisors can share with their GTAs some of their own personal reactions to teaching experiences and enjoy watching GTAs function in a truly independent manner when teaching. It is important to mention that supervisors who deal with Stage Three GTAs will often have a difficult time unless they are functioning at a relatively advanced level of teaching skill themselves. For example, it would be difficult for a professor who supervises a Stage Three GTA to provide a less structured and more collegial supervisory environment if the professor has not yet developed a good measure of knowledge, skill, commitment, and security in their own teaching. While this point is pertinent to consider regarding the supervision of GTAs across all developmental levels, it is especially important for supervisors to assess their own level of functioning prior to attempting to supervise Stage Three GTAs.

Teaching Domains Within Stages

In the IDM-GTA, the seven teaching domains represent typical areas of skill involved in graduate teaching (cf. Tollerud, 1990). These domains are outlined below, with a brief mention of developmental stage expectations.

The Presentation Skills domain refers to lecturing and the presentation of educational materials to students. Stage One GTAs tend to stress the importance of content in their classroom teaching, paying much less attention to teaching processes. It is not unusual for beginning GTAs to be highly concerned with "having their facts straight" and making sure that they have more knowledge than their students. As GTAs progress to higher levels of development, they typically attend more to the processes of teaching, have an easier time admitting "I don't know" to their students, and generally feel more effective when conveying course material.

The Assessment Skills domain refers to the ability to develop, design and implement examinations and projects to evaluate student learning. Beginning GTAs can often benefit from having access to a resource that provides item analyses of tests, in order promote their understanding of test construction and measurement issues. Also, beginning GTAs need to become familiar with and confident in administering and evaluating essay type tests and other written materials (e.g., term papers). Resources or information to help them structure or standardize their approach to evaluating such non-objective course materials can also be very helpful. Overall, novice GTAs typically see student performance on exams or course assignments as being unconnected to their teaching methods. Instead, beginning GTAs tend to view student performance solely as a function of the students themselves failing to learn or study. Although learner characteristics are always a factor in academic performance, as GTAs advance in their development they tend to better understand their role in students' learning (or lack thereof). They also learn to utilize test results as a way to adjust their teaching methods, maximize student learning, and foster student achievement.

The Academic Ethics domain refers to understanding the proper conduct required of educators and the responsibilities inherent within this role, as dictated by applicable laws, university policies, and ethical codes (see Prieto, 1998a and Keith Speigel et al. in this text for a discussion of ethics). This domain includes such issues as confidentiality, separating personal issues from teaching issues, and maintaining an educational environment that is conducive to student learning. As well, some research on academic ethics indicates that one of the most troubling violations concerns educators having sexual relationships with their students (Pope, Levenson, & Schover, 1979; Tabachnick, Keith-Spiegel, & Pope, 1991). Because GTAs have been documented as being perpetrators of sexual harassment (Reily, Lott, & Gallogly, 1986), GTAs could benefit from training or information concerning Affirmative Action policies and gender equitable teaching (see Fencl, in this text, for an excellent discussion of gender issues). In addition, GTAs who teach graduate students enrolled within their own academic departments can encounter ethical dilemmas because of dual role or mixed professional/personal relationships. Regardless of the situation, due to their lower level of self-awareness, beginning GTAs may demonstrate an ignorance of ethics or policy in their conduct with students or fail to see how their actions can adversely affect students. Supervisors need to educate GTAs and take definitive steps to ensure the well being of the students they teach. Training and supervision may help to promote GTAs' awareness of their responsibility and power as educators, and perhaps even help to prevent the occurrence of unethical behavior later in their teaching careers.

The Organizational Skills domain refers to the ability to select, develop, and implement course objectives and materials. Beginning GTAs often request that supervisors select reading materials, class activities, and grading policies for their course. As GTAs progress in their development, they gain a sense of efficacy in their own judgment regarding which materials best meet learning objectives, how to plan lessons and structure a course, and how to implement grading systems. Seminars that orient beginning GTAs to these tasks could prove helpful.

The Individual Differences domain refers to the ability to recognize and account for the effects that demographic and other cultural variables have on student learning and the classroom environment. This is especially pertinent for GTAs who teach classes with culturally diverse students. The effective teaching of culturally diverse students necessitates that GTAs possess specific skills and attitudes (Chism, Cano, & Pruitt, 1989). GTAs could receive experiential or didactic training in issues of diversity in order to enhance their understanding of diverse groups and improve their teaching effectiveness with diverse populations.

The Interpersonal Skills domain refers to the ability to communicate effectively with students. Although scholars have often chosen to focus on international GTAs who may use English as a second language (cf. Constantinides, 1989; Fisher, 1985; Sequeira & Costantino, 1989), many US native, English speaking GTAs may lack the facilitative skills necessary to deal with disgruntled, worried, or confused students. Beginning GTAs may be unaware of the effect communication styles have on students, and they may not be receptive to student perspectives. As GTAs progress in their development, they become better able to effectively handle students with difficulties, and better able to communicate an understanding of the problems faced by students.

Finally, the Networking domain refers to the ability to discover and build supportive relationships with various campus offices that can offer services to students in need. Networking with special programs for the learning disabled, student athletes, older or returning students, and students of color is a valuable skill. Beginning GTAs often do not know where on campus to find assistance for students with special needs, and they may not even be able to identify these students in their classrooms. As GTAs progress in their development, they learn to be sensitive to potential student difficulties and anticipate students' needs for additional educational support.

Empirical Support for the IDM-GTA

As aforementioned, the IDM-GTA outlines optimal supervision environments to be used by supervisors to facilitate the movement of GTAs from one developmental stage to the next. According to the IDM-GTA, novice GTAs should prefer a more structured and directive style of supervision (i.e., one that helps them cope with their lack of experience and performance anxiety), whereas more experienced GTAs should prefer course supervisors who assume a more interpersonally-sensitive, mentoring approach in supervision (i.e., help them fine tune their teaching skills and develop a personalized approach to teaching). However, these assumptions are in need of direct empirical tests that examine their validity. Therefore, the following section will present the findings of a study designed to test these assumptions concerning supervisory environments postulated in the IDM-GTA. The study sought to accomplish three goals. First, to determine the frequency and method with which a multi-disciplinary sample of GTAs received supervision of their teaching duties. Second, to determine what overall preferences GTAs have for the supervisory styles employed by their course supervisors. Third, to directly test whether GTAs' preference for supervisory style varied as a function of their level of previous teaching experience, as outlined in the IDM-GTA.

Research materials were distributed to all graduate students at a major southwestern university who held an appointment as a GTA and who were actively engaged in classroom teaching. One hundred GTAs from approximately 40 different fields of study returned usable data and met this above criterion. The sample consisted of 59 women and 41 men with a mean age of 33 years (SD = 10.4). Participants reported their racial/ethnic background as European American (79%); African American (2%), Asian American (3%), American Indian (5%), Latino (5%), and International (3%), Other (3%) racial/ethnic identifications were also reported.

Participants completed the Supervisory Styles Inventory (SSI; Friedlander & Ward, 1984), which consists of 33 adjective stem items characteristic of the three different supervisory dimensions of Attractive (ATT; a collegiality factor), Interpersonally Sensitive (SEN; a mentorship-oriented factor), and Task-Oriented (TASK; a goal-oriented factor). GTAs indicated the extent to which they would prefer each of the 33 characteristics being a part of the supervisory style employed by a course supervisor, using a 7-point Likert scale ranging from 1 (*not very preferred*) to 7 (*very preferred*). On the SSI, there are 7 items measuring Attractiveness (range 7-49 points), 8 items measuring Interpersonal Sensitivity (range 8-56 points), and 10 items measuring Task-Orientedness (range 10-70 points). The SSI also includes 8 neutral, filler items. Subscale totals are divided by the number of subscale items to allow for comparability. The SSI has been shown to effectively discriminate among the supervisory preferences of trainees at different levels of experience (cf. Worthington, 1987) and does so in a manner that would be consistent with the postulations found within the IDM-GTA. Extensive validity and reliability evidence for the SSI, ascertained via five separate validation studies, can be found in Friedlander and Ward (1984).

Internal consistency coefficients for the current SSI subscale data were .85, .80 and .84, for the ATT, SEN and TASK subscales, respectively. The following descriptive statistics were found for the SSI subscales: ATT, M = 5.81, SD = .89; SEN, M = 5.37, SD = .86; and, TASK, M = 5.13, SD = .90. Statistically significant intercorrelations were found among the subscales for SEN and ATT (r = .53, p < .001); SEN and TASK (r = .41, p < .001); and, ATT and TASK (r = .28, p < .005). These observed relations reflected expected differences in magnitude of association, with the SEN and ATT subscales possessing the greatest association, and the TASK subscale having a lesser magnitude association with the other two subscales (cf. Friedlander & Ward, 1984).

GTA Teaching and Supervision Experiences

Participants reported having attended graduate school for a mean of 6.6 semesters ($SD = 4.6$) and reported having taught as a GTA for an average of 4.6 semesters ($SD = 4$). GTAs were hired to teach for a mean of 17.7 hours per week ($SD = 5.9$); however, this distribution was bi-modal and reflected typical quarter-time and half-time appointments, with 73% of the sample holding half-time appointments. Most participants reported being responsible for teaching only one course (74%), although some GTAs taught two or more (26%) different courses. Approximately 81% of the participants reported that their career goal was to become an academician.

The majority of GTAs in the sample reported receiving some kind of ongoing supervision of their GTA duties (70%), although a sizable minority did not receive any supervision (30%). For those who were receiving supervision, 54% reported having one-on-one (individual) supervision only, 39% reported group supervision only, and 7% reported receiving supervision in both formats. Supervision was typically conducted by the professor who was the instructor of record for the course (76%), although several GTAs reported receiving supervision from either some other faculty member in their department (14%) or from some other person or office at the university (10%). Although many GTAs reported attending at least weekly meetings with their supervisor (46%), meeting once a month or by appointment only (54%) was reported as the most common frequency of supervision.

Overall Preferences for Supervisory Style

Bonferroni-corrected t-tests indicated that the mean ATT subscale score was statistically significantly higher than both the mean SEN subscale score, $t(1, 98) = 5.16$, $p < .001$, and the mean TASK subscale score, $t(1, 98) = 6.32$, $p < .001$. Furthermore, the mean SEN subscale score was statistically significantly higher than the mean TASK subscale score, $t(1, 98) = 2.51$, $p < .015$. Overall, GTAs reported preferring a supervisory style that was primarily collegial in nature (e.g., flexible, open), but also included some interpersonally sensitive (e.g., perceptive, intuitive) and, to a lesser extent, task-oriented characteristics (e.g., evaluative, prescriptive).

Preferences for Supervisory Style by Level of Experience

Participants were partitioned into three levels of teaching experience that closely corresponded to the developmental stages outlined in the IDM-GTA and also provided for proportionality across cells. These levels included those GTAs with less than one year (Stage 1 GTA; $n = 33$), one to two years (Stage 2 GTA; $n = 35$), and three or more years of teaching experience (Stage 3 GTA; $n = 32$). Multivariate analysis-of-variance (MANOVA) showed a statistically significant difference in the pattern of SSI subscale across levels of GTA teaching experience (Wilks' Lambda = .87; $F(6, 188) = 2.03$, $p < .036$). Table 1 contains the means and F-values for the follow-up univariate tests conducted, which indicate that the mean TASK subscale scores differed significantly across the three groups. Also, although not to a statistically significant degree, it is relevant to note that the magnitude of mean scores for the SEN subscale increased, between beginning and advanced levels of GTA teaching experience, also consistent with IDM-GTA postulations.

Table 1

Univariate Follow-up Tests on SSI Subscale Means Across Levels of Teaching Experience

Subscale	Stage 1	Stage 2	Stage 3	F-value
ATT	5.89	5.65	5.92	$F(2, 96) = .87$ (not significant)
SEN	5.36	5.26	5.51	$F(2, 96) = .69$ (not significant)
TASK	5.40	5.18	4.81	$F(2, 96) = 3.6$ ($p < .036$)

Results and Discussion

The descriptive findings of the study suggested that approximately one in three GTAs do not receive supervision of their teaching duties. Furthermore, the majority of those GTAs that do receive supervision appear to meet infrequently with their supervisors. This is an unfortunate state of affairs, especially given that an overwhelming number of the participants reported that they are preparing for careers in academia. Indeed, for many of these GTAs, their current teaching experiences may be the only classroom-based preparation they receive before entering the professoriate. Thus, an absence of consistent supervision may represent the loss of a prime opportunity to assist them in developing a sound foundation of teaching skills.

The current sample of GTAs reported preferring an overall collegial style of supervision, in which course supervisors adopt a friendly, supportive and flexible manner in dealing with them. Directly in line with the developmental conceptualizations found in the IDM-GTA, novice GTAs desired greater amounts of structure and direction in their supervision than those GTAs with greater amounts of teaching experience. Furthermore, although not to a statistically significant degree, senior GTAs appeared to prefer more interpersonal sensitivity and mentoring from supervisors as compared to novice GTAs. These findings help to confirm the validity and usefulness of the stage-based supervisory environments proffered in the IDM-GTA; moreover, these findings are also in line with related studies suggesting that the self-efficacy of GTAs increases with their level of previous teaching experience (cf. Prieto & Scheel, 2000, Prieto & Altmaier, 1994; Prieto & Meyers, 1999). In sum, the research to date suggests that novice GTAs have less confidence in their abilities and need more supervisory direction than do senior GTAs, thereby necessitating a more task-oriented approach when supervising beginning GTAs. Conversely, it appears important to emphasize more of a mentoring approach in supervision with GTAs as they gain experience, but additional research is needed to test the robustness of this assumption.

The findings of this study underscore the need for GTA supervisors to encourage their beginning GTAs to participate in formal training programs. Furthermore, GTA supervisors could provide their beginning GTAs with basic information and role-play exercises to help clarify more complex teaching issues (e.g., academic ethics; cf. Prieto, 1998a), and could videotape GTAs to provide more concrete feedback on their teaching skills (see Prentice-Dunn & Pitts in this text). These types of training and supervision activities help to fulfill novice GTA needs for direction, structure, and concrete advice. As well, supervisors would likely want to make time for consistent and frequent supervision meetings; for example, meeting with beginning GTAs on at least a weekly basis. Moreover, supervisors should closely observe the teaching activities of beginning GTAs to ensure that GTAs are clearly delivering course content, assessing student learning in an appropriate fashion, interacting with students and handling teaching issues in a productive and ethical manner, addressing their course objectives in a methodical fashion, being cognizant of the needs of diverse learners, and keeping up to date on resources that can help to maximize their students' in-class performance (e.g., reading/writing labs).

This study offers solid, preliminary evidence that the IDM-GTA is a valid conceptualization of GTA development and supervision. Also, the IDM-GTA appears to be a heuristic model that can guide theory-driven research in the area of GTA supervision, although additional investigations are needed to completely establish the validity of other as yet untested developmental assumptions present in the model. Regardless of the foci of future research efforts, acquiring a better understanding of issues surrounding GTA supervision can only increase the ability of faculty to prepare their graduate students to meet the instructional challenges they will face, not only as GTAs but also as future professors in academia.

Group Supervision of GTAs

The IDM-GTA proffers developmental concepts that are most applicable to the individual supervision of GTAs. However, many GTAs team-teach courses, or professors may be responsible for supervising a large number of GTAs at once, especially teaching high enrollment, multi-section introductory courses. Although the individual supervision of GTAs can be undertaken as an effective method by which to oversee their work, the supervision of GTAs may be more expedient and as effective when carried out within a group format. Furthermore, as the previous study indicated, the group supervision of GTAs is a fairly common practice, and is often utilized either alone or in conjunction with individual supervision. Moreover, group supervision not only enhances GTAs' experiences and growth as educators, but also has the potential to provide unique benefits that may not be available in the individual supervision format.

This section will begin by outlining a conceptual approach to the group supervision of GTAs and then present suggestions and examples for implementing this format of supervision. Similar to the discussion concerning the IDM-GTA, the present discussion will also conceptualize the group supervision of GTAs via extrapolations from the supervision literature in psychology, and will then move toward examining the role of interactive learning processes in supervision groups as they pertain to GTA development and training. Finally, a brief description of a supervision group will be offered to illustrate the conceptual points discussed.

General Processes in Group Supervision

Although few robust empirical studies have been conducted in the area of group supervision, some basic characteristics of this format have become evident through investigations concerning the group supervision of clinical psychology students, which can be reasonably extrapolated to the group supervision of GTAs. Major literature reviews and empirical studies in this area (see Bernard & Goodyear, 1992; Holloway & Johnston, 1985; Prieto, 1996, 1998b; Prieto & Altmaier, 1997) have noted the presence of a stable set of elements in the general practice of group supervision. First, there is a general tendency for group supervisors to adopt a facilitative supervisory style and to create a supportive group environment (e.g., more collegiality, less of a focus on direction and heavy structure regardless of trainees' level of experience). Second, the group format of supervision has been argued to yield unique benefits (as compared to the individual format) with regard to its time-efficient, interactive-learning-based, and anxiety reducing characteristics. For example, in a recent national survey (Prieto, 1997), group supervisors reported this format of supervision as unique in its ability to reduce trainees' anxiety and fear, to allow trainees to learn from one another's perspectives, and to offer the opportunity for trainees to learn skills within a supportive peer environment. Supervisors indicated that the main purposes of group supervision included the improvement of trainees' skills and knowledge bases via peer learning and interaction, and "normalizing" trainees' common learning experiences. Group supervisors reported often adopting the role of facilitator, consultant, and colleague in leading their groups.

Interactive Learning Processes and Group Supervision

In both the psychology and education literatures, there is ample discussion of the benefits that come from peer interactions among students in learning groups; points in this area often focus on the ability of students to "teach" one another, to benefit from observing and learning the problem solving strategies of their peers, and to advance one another's learning and skill building in a catalytic and synergistic fashion that may not otherwise be tapped using traditional didactic methods (e.g., lecture-based or teacher-focused). Although a thorough review of the interactive learning literature is beyond the scope of the present chapter, certain scholars in psychology and educational psychology have discussed interactive learning processes within groups, and these concepts can be applied to the group supervision of GTAs.

In addressing a cognitive-developmental component in supervision, Hillerbrand and associates (Etringer, Hillerbrand, & Claiborn, 1995; Hillerbrand, 1989; Hillerbrand & Claiborn, 1990) applied the constructs of problem representation, pattern recognition, and meta-cognition to the development of psychology trainees abilities to conceptualize clinical problems. By noting the general differences between the functioning of experts and novices with respect to these cognitive abilities, Hillerbrand (1989) suggested that in learning the practice of psychotherapy, trainees should improve over time in their abilities to recognize and organize events in therapy and to self-monitor their reasoning processes. Hillerbrand also asserted that the heterogeneous levels of trainee skill and experience often found in supervision groups, the social interactions inherent in this format, the opportunities for practicing new ways of problem solving, and the reception of feedback on one's performance can all contribute to increasing trainees' cognitive skills. Related, Hillerbrand argued that when novices learn in the presence of other novices, this is likely to increase the skill acquisition of all trainees in the group because novices may communicate with each other more clearly and are more likely to recognize the cues of confusion emitted by other novices. In support of these assertions, with regard to acquiring cognitive skills in conceptualizing and conducting psychotherapy, empirical studies have demonstrated differences in conceptualization processes for novice counselors as compared to veteran counselors (e.g., Cummings, Hallberg, Martin, Slemon, & Hiebert, 1990; Martin, Slemon, Hiebert, Hallberg, & Cummings, 1989).

In the education literature, scholars employing cooperative learning groups in the classroom have identified basic cognitive-developmental processes similar to those discussed by Hillerbrand and associates. As well, education scholars have posited a general developmental process that is consistent with the IDM-GTA. For example, Lyman and Foyle (1990) asserted that effective interactive learning processes with more inexperienced students calls for a group climate that is supportive, fosters an awareness of others, and encourages basic interactive communication skills that strengthen cognitive and verbal abilities. Conversely, interactive learning with more experienced students stresses content that emphasizes higher-order cognitive and communication skills, an appreciation for divergent perspectives, and respecting diverse problem solving methods. Cohen (1986) suggested that interactive group work is an excellent format for fostering intellectual goals such as conceptual learning and creative problem solving. Cohen further stated that group learning can be beneficial in realizing social goals such as enhancing group inter-relations and socializing students into future roles (e.g., colleague). Finally, Cohen stated that individuals in heterogeneous classes composed of novice and advanced students can learn effectively by the method of having advanced students instruct the novices, and pointed out that the varied cognitive and problem solving styles present in the heterogeneous group situation could assist students in achieving gains by increasing the possibility of presenting them with a cognitive style to which they can effectively relate.

Other authors have viewed the presence of heterogeneous trainee skill and experience levels in a supervision group as an optimal situation, because of the potential for modeling effects and advanced trainees' ability to offset the anxiety and confusion usually experienced by beginning level trainees. Furthermore, the interactive-learning based activities in supervision groups help students acclimate to their future roles as supervisor, consultant, or colleague. Last, many scholars identify the necessity of attending to the individual developmental needs of trainees within the context of group supervision (Bernard & Goodyear, 1992; Borders, 1991; Hayes, 1989; Kadushin, 1992.)

These benefits of interactive learning groups can readily be implemented in supervision groups for GTAs, and also demonstrate how the group format (vs. individual) affords unique growth opportunities. In conceptualizing the concrete application of these abstract interactive learning principles, one can consider the idea that honing GTAs' cognitive skills (e.g., problem representation, pattern recognition, meta-cognition) is an important step in helping them understand the processes and techniques associated with effective teaching. For example, a common learning objective for many GTAs is to gain skills in effectively presenting and communicating the course material to their students, in a way that enhances the potential for student learning. Unfortunately, novice GTAs often lack the ability and experience to assess (without supervision or objective feedback) the degree to which they are successful at this task. In addition, novice GTAs are often not "meta-cognizant" of such issues; that is, they are not often able to evaluate the way in which they are approaching and thinking about teaching problems. The IDM-GTA suggests that novice GTAs will tend to stress the content of lectures in classroom teaching, will be overly concerned about "being right," and will be preoccupied with making sure that they have more factual knowledge than their students. As well, novice GTAs will tend to pay less attention to teaching processes and will be less aware of the learning needs of their students. Thus, when a novice GTA's students complain about not understanding the lectures or they do poorly on course examinations, this can cause great concern, confusion, and frustration for the GTA regarding what causal attributions to make concerning this outcome and how to make the situation better. Supervisors who help novice GTAs to acquire ways in which to productively cognitively "represent" or think about these teaching problems, and assist them to learn and recognize a "pattern" of student feedback in class that could signal when the GTA is being ineffective in communicating material, could help GTAs to achieve the cognitive-developmental perspectives necessary to advance their skill level.

Furthermore, within a facilitative supervision group, this novice GTA would be able to feel some sense of support, have her anxiety reduced by discovering that her colleagues currently have or have in the past shared a similar sense of confusion, and could take advantage of colleagues' perspectives on how to deal with these issues. Related, if the GTA supervision group is heterogeneous with regard to teaching experience, the discouraged GTA's concerns will likely resonate with other novice GTAs in the group and serve as an impetus for them to discuss matters from a cognitive perspective that the discouraged GTA can relate to. Furthermore, more veteran GTAs might advise the novice with regard to how they have successfully dealt such issues in the past.

Snapshot of a GTA Supervision Group

The author has supervised teams of doctoral level students who served as GTAs for an undergraduate course. The course was primarily lecture based, although students enrolled in the course also participated in class discussions, small group work, and other activities and exercises. In addition to acquiring a mastery of the course content, the GTAs for this course were expected to acquire and demonstrate knowledge and skills in classroom management, lecture preparation and delivery, test construction and assessment of learning, and effective interpersonal skills with students. The GTAs were largely responsible for the micro-management of their classes and they received evaluations at the end of the semester from their students. There were approximately four to six GTAs each semester in the teaching team for this multi-section course; some co-taught a section whereas others taught sections on their own. Each GTA or pair of GTAs was encouraged to appreciate the sovereignty of their classrooms and the importance of their personal classroom experiences, judgments, and perceptions as a way to build their sense of independence as educators.

Group supervision meetings were held weekly and various teaching issues were covered (e.g., classroom management, teaching techniques, exam development, student issues). The goals of group supervision were to improve GTAs' teaching skills and knowledge bases, to have them collaboratively generate ideas on effectively dealing with their classes and students, and to keep lines of communication open across all instructors with regard to what was happening across the various sections of the course. The meetings were supportive in tone and usually had a specific agenda. However, at each meeting, after logistical and "housekeeping" issues were handled, time was made for each GTA to "check in" with regard to how classes were going and what successes or difficulties they had encountered during the past week in their teaching. Usually, there was a focus on how classroom interactions between GTAs and students were developing, particularly in terms of the strategies that the GTAs used to keep their students motivated in the course. A few "mock" examples of these discussions (based on a synthesis of numerous, typical issues discussed across several supervision groups) will be provided to illustrate how particular issues have been handled in the supervision group.

For example, during one group supervision meeting, a novice GTA noted that he was having a tough time getting his students interested in participating in small group discussions in the class. He had mentioned in a previous supervision meeting that his class appeared to be developing a pattern of being unresponsive to questions and activities. A veteran GTA colleague, who had taught several sections of this course in the past, stated that she had decided to teach that week's material by using characters from a very popular television show that epitomized the points and perspectives she was trying to get across to the students. After explaining her approach in some detail, the GTA team appeared pleased at her suggestions and they quickly began to brainstorm other techniques that could be used to break a teaching impasse with students. In my role as supervisor, I facilitated their collaboration on this issue, and provided the team with an excellent review of small group teaching interventions (Meyers, 1997) to use as a resource to acquire a sense of the theory and research behind this approach. During our next supervision meeting the following week, we took time to evaluate the success of using these suggested teaching techniques in the classroom, and to gain an understanding as to how and why they worked as teaching interventions.

Another time, a novice GTA mentioned that she was having difficulty with a student who was continually missing assignment deadlines and was offering incredible excuses regarding the tardiness of homework; the GTA was unsure if this student should be allowed to make up the work. After reviewing the policies that appeared on the syllabus regarding late assignments, in my role as supervisor, I turned the question over to the team and called for each of their perspectives on the issue. They discussed the pros and cons of several possible positions an instructor could take on the matter, as well as the outcomes associated with similar incidents of this nature that they had dealt with in the past. As a supervisor, I facilitated their consideration of different facets of this issue (e.g., What action would be in the best educational interests of the student in question? To what extent was maintaining a consistent policy in dealing with all of the students in this multi-course an important factor?). This discussion also helped the GTA team address various approaches to classroom discipline and boundary setting, including what methods appeared to work in which situations, and what effects various intervention methods might have on their students.

Although these two vignettes are short, they illustrate the growth and learning potential present in supervision groups for GTAs. As can be seen, within the context of a collegial and collaborative group supervision environment, a GTA supervisor's primary role does not have to be one of handing down decisions for GTAs to implement, but rather can be one where the supervisor encourages GTAs to think through teaching issues on their own and to serve as consultants for one another in collaboratively coming to solutions or strategies. The group supervisor is able to be a guide, a catalyst, an observer of "the big picture," a resource on matters of institutional policy, as well as serving as the "final word" on course issues as needed.

Regarding the interactive learning and cognitive-developmental issues previously discussed, group supervision can offer GTAs a sense of solidarity and support in carrying out their teaching duties. Furthermore, their anxiety can be reduced and concerns normalized, and they can readily benefit from the perspectives of their colleagues. Because the noted examples occurred in a group of GTAs that possessed various levels of teaching experience, they were able to both recognize and genuinely validate their colleagues' concerns as well as offer credible, understandable, and valuable advice as veterans of "the teaching trenches." On a broader scale, group interactions help promote consultation skills in GTAs, an experience that will serve them well regardless of their eventual professional role, but one that will serve them especially well in the world of academia where they will need to work collaboratively and productively with other faculty within their program, department, college and university. Finally, the group format of supervision can also allow for a breadth and depth of discussion on teaching issues that can help GTAs to increase their meta-cognitive abilities, thereby increasing their sense of independence as classroom educators.

Closing Comments

The individual and group supervision of GTAs must be more frequently practiced and better researched; the GTA experience and its appropriate supervision may represent the best form of training for the role of educator that can be offered to graduate students in any academic discipline, especially given the enormous variability in available resources, faculty, and educational missions of academic departments and universities across the nation. Continued research efforts into this area could be informed by extant research in the area of graduate teaching assistant development as well by as those relevant literature bases in psychology and teacher education. Finally, and most importantly, faculty and students in all scholarly disciplines must begin to discuss the best use of the GTA experience as a training tool, thereby maximizing the ability for all university programs and departments to produce well-rounded and capable academicians.

References

Abbott, R., Wulff, D., & Szego, K. (1989). Review of research on TA training. In J. Nyquist, R. Abbott & D. Wulff (Eds.), *Teaching assistant training in the 1990's* (pp. 111-124). San Francisco: Jossey-Bass.

Andrews, J. (1985a). Editor's Notes. In J. D. W. Andrews (Ed.), *Strengthening the teaching assistant faculty* (pp. 1-6). San Francisco: Jossey-Bass.

Andrews, J. (1985b). Why TA training needs instructional innovation. In J. D. W. Andrews (Ed.), *Strengthening the teaching assistant faculty* (pp. 47-62). San Francisco: Jossey-Bass.

Bandura, A. (1986). *Social foundations of thought and action*. New York: Prentice Hall.

Bernard, J., & Goodyear, R. (1992). *Fundamentals of clinical supervision*. Boston: Allyn and Bacon.

Boehrer, J., & Sarkisian, E. (1985). The teaching assistant's point of view. In J. D. W. Andrews (Ed.), *Strengthening the teaching assistant faculty* (pp. 7-20). San Francisco: Jossey-Bass.

Borders, L. (1991). A systematic approach to peer group supervision. *Journal of Counseling and Development, 69,* 248-252.

Chickering, A. (1969). *Education and identity.* San Francisco: Jossey-Bass.

Chism, N., Cano, J., & Pruitt, A. (1989). Teaching in a diverse environment: Knowledge and skills needed by TA's. In J. Nyquist, R. Abbott, & D. Wulff (Eds.), *Teaching assistant training in the 1990's* (pp. 23-36). San Francisco: Jossey-Bass.

Cohen, E. (1986). *Designing groupwork: Strategies for the heterogeneous classroom.* New York: Teachers College Press.

Constantinides, J. (1989). ITA training programs. In J. Nyquist, R. Abbott , & D. Wulff (Eds.), *Teaching assistant training in the 1990's* (pp. 71-78). San Francisco: Jossey-Bass.

Copeland, W., & Atkinson, D. (1978). Student teachers' perceptions of directive and nondirective supervisory behavior. *Journal of Educational Research, 71,* 123-126.

Copeland, W. (1982). Student teachers' preferences for supervisory approach. *Journal of Teacher Education, 33,* 32-36.

Cummings, A., Hallberg, E., Martin, J., Slemon, A., & Hiebert, B. (1990). Implications of counselor conceptualizations for counselor education. *Counselor Education and Supervision, 30,* 120-134.

Dalgaard, K. (1982). Some effects of training on teaching effectiveness of untrained university teaching assistants. *Research in Higher Education, 17,* 39-50.

Darling, C., & Earhart, E. (1990). A model for preparing graduate students as educators. *Family Relations, 39,* 341-348.

Dembo, M., & Gibson, S. (1985). Teacher's sense of efficacy: An important factor in school improvement. *The Elementary School Journal, 86,* 173-184.

Diamond, R., & Gray, P. (November, 1987). *A national study of teaching assistants.* Paper presented at the annual meeting of the Association for the Study of Higher Education, Baltimore, MD.

Erikson, E. (1968). *Identity, youth and crisis.* New York: Norton.

Etringer, B., Hillerbrand, E., & Claiborn, C. (1995). The transition from novice to expert counselor. *Counselor Education and Supervision, 35,* 4-17.

Evans, E., & Tribble, M. (1986). Perceived teaching problems, self efficacy, and commitment to teaching among preservice teachers. *Journal of Educational Research, 80*, 81-85.

Fisher, M. (1985). Rethinking the "foreign TA problem." In J. D. W. Andrews (Ed.), *Strengthening the teaching assistant faculty* (pp. 63-74). San Francisco: Jossey-Bass.

Friedlander, M., & Ward, L. (1984). Development and validation of the Supervisory Styles Inventory. *Journal of Counseling Psychology, 31*, 541-557.

Hayes, R. (1989). Group supervision. In L. Bradley (Ed.), *Counselor supervision: Principles, process, practice* (2nd ed., pp. 399-421). Muncie, IN: Accelerated Development Inc.

Hillerbrand, E. (1989). Cognitive differences between experts and novices: Implications for group supervision. *Journal of Counseling and Development, 67*, 293-296.

Hillerbrand, E., & Claiborn, C. (1990). Examining reasoning skill differences between expert and novice counselors. *Journal of Counseling and Development, 68*, 684-691.

Hogan, R. (1964). Issues and approaches in supervision. *Psychotherapy: Theory, Research, and Practice, 1*, 139-141.

Holloway, E., & Johnston, R. (1985). Group supervision: Widely practiced but poorly understood. *Counselor Education and Supervision, 24*, 332-340.

Holloway, E., & Wampold, B. (1986). Relation between conceptual level and counseling-related tasks: A meta-analysis. *Journal of Counseling Psychology, 33*, 310-319.

Hunt, D. (1971). *Matching models in education: The coordination of teaching methods with student characteristics*. Toronto, ON: Ontario Institute For Studies In Education.

Kadushin, A. (1992). *Supervision in social work* (3rd ed.). New York: Columbia University Press.

Kagan, D. (1987). Cognitive level of student teachers and their perceptions of cooperating teachers. *Alberta Journal of Educational Research, 33*, 180-190.

Kagan, D. (1988). Research on the supervision of counselors- and teachers-in-training: Linking two bodies of literature. *Review of Educational Research, 58*, 1-24.

Loevinger, J. (1976). *Ego development: Conceptions and theories*. San Francisco: Jossey-Bass.

Loevinger, J. (1977). Ego maturity and human development. *Pupil Personnel Services Journal, 6*, 19-24.

Loganbill, C., Hardy, E., & Delworth, U. (1982). Supervision: A conceptual model. *The Counseling Psychologist, 10*, 3-42.

Lyman, L., & Foyle, H. (1990). *Cooperative grouping for interactive learning: Students, teachers and administrators*. Washington, DC: National Education Association.

Martin, J., Slemon, A., Hiebert, B., Hallberg, E., & Cummings, A. (1989). Conceptualizations of novice and experienced counselors. *Journal of Counseling Psychology, 36*, 395-400.

Meyers, S. A. (1997). Increasing student participation and productivity in small-group activities for psychology classes. *Teaching of Psychology, 24*, 105-115.

Meyers, S. A., & Prieto, L. R. (2000). Training in the teaching of psychology: What is done and examining the differences. *Teaching of Psychology, 27,* 258-261.

Nyquist, J., Abbott, R., & Wulff, D. (1989). The challenge of TA training in the 1990's. In J. Nyquist, R. Abbott & D. Wulff (Eds.), *Teaching assistant training in the 1990's* (pp. 7-14). San Francisco: Jossey-Bass.

Nyquist, J. D., & Wulff, D. H. (1996). *Working effectively with graduate assistants.* Thousand Oaks, CA: Sage Publications.

Piaget, J. (1970). *Structuralism.* New York: Basic Books.

Pope, K., Levenson, H., & Schover, L. (1979). Sexual intimacies in psychology training: Results and implications of a national survey. *American Psychologist, 34,* 682-689.

Prieto, L. R. (1994). Psychology students and graduate teaching: Issues of professional development. *Newsletter of the American Psychological Association of Graduate Students, 6,* 10.

Prieto, L. R. (1995). Supervising graduate teaching assistants: An adaptation of the Integrated Developmental Model. *Journal of Graduate Teaching Assistant Development, 2,* 93-105.

Prieto, L. R. (1996). Group supervision: Still widely practiced but poorly understood. *Counselor Education and Supervision, 35,* 295-307.

Prieto, L. R. (1998a). Supervising graduate teaching assistants on the ethics of teaching: A developmental approach. *Journal of Graduate Teaching Assistant Development, 5,* 109-118.

Prieto, L. R. (1998b). Practicum class supervision in CACREP-accredited counselor training programs. *Counselor Education & Supervision, 38,* 113-123.

Prieto, L. R., & Scheel, K. R. (2000). *Teaching assistant training in counseling psychology.* Unpublished manuscript.

Prieto, L. R., & Altmaier, E. M. (1994). The relationship of prior training and previous teaching experience to self-efficacy among graduate teaching assistants. *Research in Higher Education, 35,* 481-497.

Prieto, L. R., & Altmaier, E. M. (1997) Practicum class supervision: General practices and trainee satisfaction. *The Clinical Supervisor, 16,* 89-103.

Prieto, L. R., & Meyers, S. A. (1999). The effects of training and supervision on the self-efficacy of psychology graduate teaching assistants. *Teaching of Psychology, 26,* 264-266.

Reily, M., Lott, B., & Gallogly, S. (1986). Sexual harassment of university students. *Sex Roles, 15,* 333-358.

Sequeira, D. L., & Costantino, M. (1989). Issues in ITA training programs. In J. Nyquist, R. Abbott, & D. Wulff (Eds.), *Teaching assistant training in the 1990's* (pp. 79-88). San Francisco: Jossey-Bass.

Sharp, G. (1981). Acquisition of lecturing skills by university teaching assistants: Some effects of interest, topic relevance, and viewing a model videotape. *American Educational Research Journal, 18,* 491-502.

Smock, R., & Menges, R. (1985). Programs for TAs in the context of campus policies and priorities. In J. D. W. Andrews (Ed.), *Strengthening the teaching assistant faculty* (pp. 21-34). San Francisco: Jossey-Bass.

Sprague, J., & Nyquist, J. D. (1989). TA supervision. In J. Nyquist, R. Abbott & D. Wulff (Eds.), *Teaching assistant training in the 1990's* (pp. 37-56). San Francisco: Jossey-Bass.

Staton, A. & Darling, A. (1989). Socialization of teaching assistants. In J. Nyquist, R. Abbott, & D. Wulff (Eds.), *Teaching assistant training in the 1990's* (pp. 15-22). San Francisco: Jossey-Bass.

Stoltenberg, C. (1981). Approaching supervision from a developmental perspective: The counselor complexity model. *Journal of Counseling Psychology, 28,* 59-65.

Stoltenberg, C., & Delworth, U. (1987). *Supervising counselors and therapists: A developmental approach.* San Francisco: Jossey-Bass.

Stoltenberg, C., McNeill, B., & Delworth, U. (1998). *IDM Supervision: An Integrated Developmental Model for supervising counselors and therapists.* San Francisco: Jossey-Bass Inc.

Stoltenberg, C., McNeill, B., & Crethar, H. (1994). Changes in supervision as counselors and therapists gain experience: A review. *Professional Psychology: Research and Practice, 25,* 416-449.

Stoppard, J., & Miller, A. (1985). Conceptual level matching: A review. *Current Psychological Research and Reviews*, Spring, 46-68.

Tabachnick, B., Keith-Spiegel, P., & Pope, K. (1991). Ethics of teaching: Beliefs and behaviors of psychologists as educators. *American Psychologist, 46,* 506-515.

Theis-Sprinthall, L. (1980). Supervision: An educative or mis-educative process? *Journal of Teacher Education, 31,* 17-20.

Tollerud, T. (1990). The perceived self efficacy of teaching skills of advanced doctoral students and graduates from counselor education programs (Doctoral dissertation, University of Iowa, 1990). *Dissertation Abstracts International, 51,* 12A.

Worthington, E. (1984). Empirical investigation of supervision of counselors as they gain experience. *Journal of Counseling Psychology, 31,* 63-75.

Worthington, E. (1987). Changes in supervision as counselors and supervisors gain experience: A review. *Professional Psychology: Research and Practice, 18,* 189-208.

Yoder, D., & Hugenberg, L. (November, 1980). *A survey of in-service teacher training programs for graduate teaching assistants in basic communications courses.* Paper presented at the annual meeting of the Speech Communication Association, New York, NY.

Zeichner, K., & Liston, D. (April, 1984). *Varieties of discourse in supervisory conferences.* Paper presented at the annual meeting of the American Educational Research Association, New Orleans, LA.

SECTION II

PROFESSIONAL ISSUES IN TEACHING ASSISTANT TRAINING

Ethical Dilemmas Confronting Graduate Teaching Assistants: Issues and Cases

Patricia Keith-Spiegel, Ph.D., Bernard E. Whitley, Jr.,Ph.D.,David .V.Perkins, Ph.D., Deborah Ware Balogh, Ph.D., & Arno Wittig, Ph.D.
Ball State University

Overview

No longer "just students," but not yet recognized as independent educators, graduate teaching assistants (GTAs) occupy an ambiguously delineated territory within higher education. Whenever role boundaries are unclear, GTAs may be unprepared to meet the demands of what is expected of them as educators. Whenever GTAs overestimate the scope of their authority, the potential for committing ethical infractions also increases. Some impact on performance may also result from the recent unrest among GTAs. Protesting the low pay and sub-standard working conditions, GTAs are organizing to achieve increased status, wages, and other benefits (Leatherman, 1998a; Leatherman, 1998b; Perkinson, 1996). Whether this turmoil has any impact on the quality of GTA services and their ethical sensitivity to students and colleagues is not yet known.

Given the pervasive presence of, and reliance on, GTAs in postsecondary educational institutions, serious and consistent consideration of relevant ethical issues is imperative (Folse, 1991). Although a considerable literature exists on the ethical issues facing graduate level interns in fields such as clinical and counseling psychology and medicine, very little has been published about ethical issues confronting graduate students who teach. Similarly, the ethics of supervision of graduate level interns in clinical psychology and medicine has received a fair amount of attention, but the published literature about the ethical obligations of GTA supervisors is sparse. Institutionally generated materials for GTAs provide a natural opportunity to present ethical issues; However, Lowman and Mathie (1993) found that only 50% of their sampling of TA manuals did so. A national survey of TA training faculty was encouraging in that 72%

of the respondents did include instruction in ethical standards of teaching (Mueller, Perlman, McCann, & McFadden, 1997) although how much was not specified.

It is worth remembering that most new GTAs are not far removed from the undergraduate experience. Many may still harbor habits that are counterproductive in their new roles. Prieto (1995) described beginning GTAs as those who have had little teaching experience (and probably no course work on how to teach) and are, therefore, likely to be more similar to than different from their own students. They want to do well, and they try hard. They are excited, but anxious and sometimes more focused on themselves and their performance than on the needs of their students. They are not always clearly aware of their weaknesses or how their personal style affects their students. They may appear to have a high sense of self-efficacy, but this may decrease as the realities of teaching sink in. They may be rigid in their teaching approach, sometimes trying to emulate a favorite undergraduate instructor in an attempt to maintain self-confidence. Prieto's portrait describes a group that is very likely to make some ethical mistakes, albeit usually unintended ones.

In this chapter we emphasize ethical traps and conflicts that may face students new to GTA assignments. Specific risk zones covered include role ambiguities, differing perceptions of what constitutes an ethical dilemma, dual roles and other boundary crossings involving faculty and fellow students, loyalty conflicts, ethical ramifications of inexperience (such as abuse of authority, inappropriate disclosures in the classroom, and breaches of confidentiality), and ethical pitfalls related to relationships with regular faculty (such as dual role and power conflicts, exploitation, and poor role modeling). We also discuss the role that GTA supervisors can play to assist GTAs in developing the level of ethical maturity expected of academics. We make use of cases, based on actual incidents, to illustrate ethically risky predicaments.

This chapter could present many cases of egregiously unethical graduate students, such as the GTA who sold *A* grades to his students for $100 each or another who, upset with departmental policy, burned down the building. However, this approach would not serve our purpose because, thankfully, such extreme cases are rare. Instead, we will focus on more common, everyday situations that can involve and ensnare GTAs (and graduate research assistants as well), even including those who are competent and morally fit. The reader will note that the GTAs' behaviors we describe often are not inherently unethical. Rather, situations that were not correctly perceived led to ethically problematic results. We aspire to alert GTAs and their supervisors to some of these situations so that they can be better prepared to handle them judiciously.

Ethical Danger Zones

Fallout from Ambiguous Roles

Ambiguous role relationships are always potential houses of cards. Only one element need go awry to bring the entire relationship crashing down. But, interestingly, almost nothing has been written about role relationship dilemmas faced by graduate students. The reasoning might be that graduate students are more mature than are undergraduates and in less need of protection from potential role conflicts. However, a strong case can be made that graduate students are even *more* vulnerable to the negative consequences of role conflicts. After undergraduate students leave academia, any problematic experiences they had with their educators typically leave with them. Although undergraduates can certainly be harmed by such experiences, their reputations and career opportunities are very unlikely to be on the line.

Graduate students, in contrast, can suffer indefinitely when role relationships with their educators go sour. The failed relationship may be with the only person who can facilitate the completion of the degree (e.g., the program chair or the sole faculty member in the student's specialty area), and so may hinder the student's professional aspirations. Consider the actual case of a GTA who engendered the wrath of her supervisor for allegedly failing to collect some data in a timely manner. The supervisor fired the GTA, dropped her as an advisee, told other members of the department that the GTA was inept, divulged personal information about the GTA that had been disclosed during supervisory sessions, refused to support her applications for employment, and continued to assail her competence long after she earned her degree. Although we most certainly question the actions of the supervisor on ethical grounds, the fact remains that the harm to the GTA probably would have been less extensive had the role relationship between the two been less complex.

GTAs' ambiguous status of student/educator allows others to define GTAs' roles in whatever ways fit their agendas or needs. One result is that GTAs can get very mixed messages.

Case 1: *Professor Trent asked GTA Suzanne to meet him in the faculty lounge to plan a teaching activity. While waiting for Professor Trent to arrive, Professor Snell entered the lounge and said in a stern tone, "I'm sorry, but students are not allowed in the faculty lounge. You need to leave now."*

The GTA felt belittled and embarrassed and did not know quite what to say. To inform Professor Snell that Professor Trent told her to meet him here might, in some way, reflect poorly on a superior with whom she wanted to maintain a positive relationship.

GTAs can also make easy targets for blame because they stand out. The next case illustrates how a GTA suffered later reprisals simply for carrying out his responsibilities.

Case 2: *GTA Juan agreed to serve as the student representative on the department's Resource Committee. Two groups of faculty members were fiercely scrambling for limited resources. When the vote was taken, one group received considerably more funds by a single vote. The losing group was cool and rejecting toward Juan because he voted for the other group.*

Sometimes awkwardness ensues, even when GTAs made concerted attempts to minimize conflict. The next two cases illustrate how, despite a GTA's best reasoning and efforts, discomfort (rightly or not) was created among the regular faculty.

Case 3 : *GTA Rodney had just started dating an undergraduate student who had already taken the only course he teaches. Furthermore, because the class was not in her major, he would never again be called upon to evaluate her academic performance. He felt fully satisfied that absolutely no conflict of interest existed. Rodney was stunned to hear that a number of the regular faculty in the department were upset that he would be bringing his girlfriend to the annual holiday party. As one confided to him, "You know, we all like to have a few drinks at these functions. The presence of an undergraduate student will spoil the party."*

Case 4: *Sociobiology has fascinated GTA Darwin since his sophomore year in college. He prepared and delivered three lectures devoted to sociobiology in his introductory psychology course. Professor Locke, a well-known proponent of environmental determinism, complained to the department chair that Darwin was polluting his class with bad theory.*

GTAs cannot possibly predict all of the ways others will interpret their actions. To the extent that GTAs may be unjustly viewed as overextending authority or making inappropriate decisions, their professional status may be affected. Will Professor Snell mention to colleagues that GTA Suzanne breaks the rules? Will GTA Rodney's reputation be smirched for ruining the party? Did Darwin spend too much time on a favorite topic, or is Professor Locke making undue trouble for Darwin based on his own biases?

Regular faculty should remain sensitive to the perils of role ambiguity inherent in the GTA status and take them into consideration whenever the actions of GTAs are being evaluated. Often it will be found that GTAs were caught in traps that were difficult to identify in advance or for which consequences might ensue regardless of how the GTA responds.

Differing Perceptions of Ethical Issues

GTAs may become embroiled in ethical dilemmas because their views of what constitutes ethical and unethical behavior may differ from those of regular faculty. Based on an unpublished survey comparing 123 GTAs and 124 regular teaching faculty members (Keith-Spiegel, 1994), graduate assistants found the following behaviors as considerably *less* ethically problematic than did regular faculty:

- Giving easy courses to ensure popularity with students
- Teaching full-time and holding down another job for at least 20 hours a week
- Hugging a student
- Accepting a student's expensive gift
- Selling goods (such as a car or books) to one's students
- Teaching a class without being adequately prepared that day
- Choosing a particular textbook for a class primarily because the publisher would pay a "bonus" to do it
- Choosing a textbook because the publisher would give the department some free films and software
- Privately tutoring students in the department for a fee
- Taking advantage of a student's offer such as getting wholesale prices at a parent's store

Our interpretation of these findings is *not* that GTAs are less ethical than regular faculty members, but that they are less able to see the potential negative consequences of certain actions (such as role blendings) indicating their incomplete socialization into the academy. An interest in generating monetary gain is also apparent, probably reflecting a true need. However, these findings do suggest that GTAs need to be specifically instructed to avoid inappropriate and ethically risky ways of interacting with students or enhancing their financial status.

Dual Role Relationships with Other Students

GTAs (as well as new, younger faculty) often feel a closer kinship to their students than to tenured faculty members, making them vulnerable to dual role relationships with students. Cases 5 and 6 describe situations that illustrate how GTAs can become the victims of inappropriate expectations by their own students.

Case 5: *Gina, one of GTA Marsha's students, engaged in a conversation about clothing fashions as they were walking to class. Gina informed Marsha that her mother owned a dress shop in town. "I can set it up so that you can get a 50% discount on everything," Gina told Marsha. Marsha could not believe her good fortune and purchased a number of outfits at a greatly reduced price. When course grades were issued, Gina was furious with her grade of "C." She stomped into the GTA's office and yelled, "I expected you to give me a break in class like I gave you at my Mom's store. You betrayed me."*

Marsha was shocked by the existence of an implicit *quid pro quo*. She tried to explain the misunderstanding and her ethical commitment to equitable grading, but Gina was clearly agitated. Marsha worried that Gina would cause problems in the department, perhaps by badmouthing her to other faculty members. Marsha also regretted that she did not recognize the potential for conflict when first presented with the alluring offer. We should also note that Marsha may have still faced criticism had Gina earned an A. Classmates who knew of the clothing shop deal might have suspected bribery. Thus, Marsha's acceptance of Gina's offer risked a bad outcome no matter how well or poorly Gina performed in the course.

Although it is impossible to avoid all dual role relationships, especially in smaller college and university towns, more seasoned instructors would have been wary of the type of situation described above. Gifts or the offer of favors from students *currently* enrolled in a class should be politely refused because the potential for misunderstanding or manipulation is ever-present. (Small gifts of appreciation from students after grades are turned in usually pose no problem.) Socializing with students in one's own class is also potentially risky. GTAs are probably wise to restrict socializing with undergraduates to department and campus-sponsored events, except, perhaps, when all students have an equal opportunity of being included.

Sometimes GTAs become closely linked with students who are not in their classes. Case 6 illustrates an awkward circumstance that created some tense times for a GTA and her student.

Case 6: *GTA Robin's student was in a rock band with Robin's boyfriend. The band members were in constant turmoil, taunting each other with threats to quit. Robin had mixed feelings towards her student who, according to Robin's boyfriend, was the main source of the group's dysfunction. Although Robin was not directly involved with the band's problems, she worried that the teacher/student relationship had been compromised. The student was often absent and never came to office hours despite her requests to see every student who was not doing well in her class. Robin worried that the student's grade was in jeopardy for other than academic reasons.*

Robin's supervisor suggested that she speak candidly to the student, informing him that she was not involved in any band matters and that she could separate out her role as academic evaluator from that of a band member's girlfriend. The student responded well to this reassurance.

Finally, students, while still GTAs, may experience their first dual role dilemma during unplanned situations. Case 7 involves possible danger to a third party and the dilemma of how far GTAs should intrude themselves into the situation.

Case 7: *George came to GTA Millie's office hours after a lecture on the physiology of anger. George started by complimenting Millie on her lecture, adding that the subject of anger was very meaningful to him because he and his girlfriend fought a lot. As he talked with Millie about her lecture, George became increasingly edgy and asked tangential questions about acting out anger, such as "How often do couples become violent with each other?" Millie was concerned and asked George several questions* *about his relationship and his behavior toward his girlfriend. George looked extremely uncomfortable, became more evasive, glanced at his watch, and excused himself from the room.*

This difficult case illustrates a sticky dilemma involving balancing concern for the welfare of a student (or third party that the student might harm) and the appropriateness of intruding into students' personal lives. Millie did not learn whether George posed a threat to his girlfriend. We do not know if George left the room because Millie was getting too close to some truth or because he was upset by Millie's interrogation. Millie might have handled this situation better by answering George's question while adding additional information about battering and available resources that might be helpful to George should he and his girlfriend be on the verge of violent interactions. (For more about interactions with students that involve potential physical danger, see Case 16.)

Students often approach GTAs with questions about their personal situations, and GTAs must be careful to remain professional and suggest other resources should a problem require more than just a minor comment (e.g., "I hope you and your roommate can create a plan to share the computer in a way that satisfies both of your needs"). We know of an incident that got very messy when parents became involved after a GTA was asked by a tearful student whether she should get an abortion. The GTA gave his definitive opinion; one that was *not* the one favored by the young woman's parents. Whenever highly personal issues (especially those unrelated in any way to the academic course) would be best worked through with a counselor or other party, GTAs should limit their involvement to encouraging students to take those steps.

Loyalty Conflicts

GTAs can get themselves into situations where loyalties are stretched between regular faculty and their peers. GTAs may have to make ethical decisions that will favor one legitimate loyalty over the other, such as allegiance to friends versus allegiance to the department and its values or policies. The next case illustrates a form that these dilemmas might take.

Case 8: *GTA Fred learned that fellow GTA Marla is dating a student in her class and that GTA Harold is regularly cutting short his classes on Wednesdays so that he can play on a bowling team.*

Both students about whom Fred has knowledge are violating school policies and shirking their professional responsibilities. But, Marla and Harold are Fred's friends. Should Fred try to handle these matters with his peers by himself? Should he tell his supervisor? If he makes a formal complaint, how will other GTAs react? Will they admire his courage or banish him as a snitch? These are hard questions, and ones that regular faculty sometimes face regarding their colleagues as well. At the very least, GTAs should have access to a trusted contact, ideally the supervisor, with whom such dilemmas can be discussed in confidence so that the best plan of action can be formulated.

Mishandling Ethical Matters Due to Inexperience or Ignorance

GTAs are teachers in training and should not be expected to be expert in everything they take on. However, GTAs are expected to do an adequate job, at the very least. Sometimes, however, their inexperience and lack of knowledge can lead to ethical problems.

Gaps in Competence

All college-level teachers struggle to maintain competence, and it is increasingly difficult to do an adequate job of it, even in one's specialty areas. Even the most experienced among us may have the most difficult time keeping up with a literature that is so vast and far removed from our own training. However, for graduate students who are often teaching introductory survey courses, the task of keeping up with an entire field while still in training can feel overwhelming. In addition, most GTAs (and most regular faculty) have not had training in the basics of competent, effective teaching. These include designing lesson plans and course objectives, assessing student performance, and selecting sound pedagogical materials and techniques.

Case 9: *GTA Vance was bright but extremely shy and feeling insecure. Although Vance worked hard on his lecture preparations, he followed the required readings so closely that the students saw coming to class as superfluous. Exams consisted of general questions such as, "Describe the main facts from Chapter 6."*

Vance needed more assistance and direction than his department offered. With adequate training in the techniques of lecturing and test construction, and with proper supervision, it is likely that Vance would have offered his students a far more satisfying and effective experience.

Teaching incompetence can come in other forms besides lack of content mastery. For example, lack of knowledge about the institution's rules and policies can raise questions of competence. In occasional cases, GTA incompetence is expressed as a result of a character or emotional disorder. In general, the program staff should attempt remedial steps, although sometimes it is necessary to remove such students from the program (see Procidano, Busch-Rossnagel, Reznikoff, & Geisinger, 1995). In such instances, institutional procedures must be followed carefully, and the GTA's rights must be protected.

Handling Sensitive Material in the Classroom

There is probably no substitute for classroom experience when it comes to handling sensitive subjects. With such wide diversity in student populations, it is even sometimes difficult for seasoned professors to avoid stepping on tender toes. One way all of us can unintentionally get into trouble is to make a joke, not realizing that it may be viewed as humiliating or a putdown to one or more students in the class. New GTAs may feel confident that they *know* students because they are closer in age and status. However, GTAs may be far more prone to possible censure than they realize. Their students view them as teachers, not peers, and may not be as accepting as GTAs expect them to be. The next case illustrates how an attempt to be clever with an analogy resulted in sexual harassment charges.

Case 10: *A GTA, while teaching students in a human sexuality class how to put on condoms quipped, "Like basketball players, men dribble before they shoot." An offended student argued that by "objectifying the penis" the graduate assistant had created a hostile learning environment* (adapted from Leatherman, 1994).

Whereas a proven way to put people at ease is to use some humor, GTAs should be informed about the danger zones. This is especially true when joking is used as a way of breaking the tension during discussions of touchy issues.

Self Disclosure in the Classroom

Students usually seem to enjoy personal stories told by their educators in class. Assuming the stories are related to the topic at hand, they can be effective pedagogical tools. However, personal disclosures in class must be done with some discretion.

Case 11: *While discussing the unit on substance abuse, GTA Bennie described his adolescent drug use, relaying dramatic stories about his misadventures while under the influence. Most of the students seemed riveted to their seats. Bennie felt good about how he was able to get the class "jamming."*

In general, stories that reveal too much personal information, especially if controversial or illegal behaviors are involved, are not appropriate to share with classes. Bennie's stories spread quickly, and his judgment and fitness to teach were called into question. Bennie was heavily reprimanded for his illegal substance use disclosures.

GTAs' Misuse of New-found Power and Status

For many GTAs, holding a teaching position provides the first taste of prestige and authority. It is a very special type of power because GTAs are now on the other side of a fence that has impounded them for most of their lifetimes. Occasionally, some GTAs get carried away with finally being in charge and overestimate or abuse their position in the process.

Case 12: *A student in the class informed GTA Lester that he saw another student cheat. Lester was outraged that anyone would cheat in his class and assigned the alleged cheater a grade of zero on the exam. When the student came to inquire why he received no points, Lester said, "It's because you cheated. And I have no mercy for cheaters." The student vehemently denied having cheated, but Lester refused to budge. The student went through the formal appeals process, and Lester acted as if he was in a life-and-death struggle. The hearing panel ruled that Lester had not accorded the student due process and found in favor of the student.*

Although no one should fault Lester for his willingness to deal actively with a possible cheating incident, his inexperience led to serious procedural errors. Lester would have fared better had he first carefully reviewed and then followed the academic dishonesty policy. Supervisors should ensure that GTAs know how to confront and manage academic dishonesty.

Teaching to Evaluations

Student evaluations of their instructors' competence and effectiveness can be a source of anxiety, especially for contract and untenured faculty. GTAs may also feel particularly vulnerable, believing that poor student evaluations could derail their longer-term career opportunities. As a defense, GTAs may be tempted to "teach to" evaluations. The next case illustrates how ethical complications can result.

Case 13: *Six members of the class made only half-hearted attempts to hide the fact that they were looking at their neighbors' papers during the exam. GTA Rhonda was shaken, and gave each of them stern looks during eye contact, but this deterred the behavior for only a few minutes. Although Rhonda was upset and angry, she decided to ignore the situation. She feared that if she confronted the students, they would retaliate by giving her negative ratings at the end of the term. She was also concerned that if she told her supervisor or her peers that her students were cheating, they would think that her students did not respect her.*

Because students believe that it is unethical for instructors to ignore obvious cheating (Keith-Spiegel, Tabachnick, & Allen, 1993), Rhonda may get lower ratings anyway from disgruntled honest students. It is also unfortunate that Rhonda did not feel comfortable with discussing the situation with her supervisor. A supervisor or more experienced colleague could have reassured her that this dilemma was hardly unique, and offered her tips on how to control cheating in the classroom.

In a related vein, some GTAs may place being liked by students above their teaching responsibilities. This is most likely to happen among new GTAs when feelings of insecurity are high and socialization into the professional role has not yet taken root.

Confidentiality Breaches and Gossip

Secret-sharing, criticizing instructors, and school-related gossip are normative among undergraduate students. However, once students move into graduate assistant positions, the rules of propriety change markedly. New GTAs may not make the shift gracefully.

Case 14: *GTA Ho was invited to lunch with Professors Green and Cohen. During lunch, the two professors discussed some of the current, sensitive problems related to the departmental curriculum committee's decisions. GTA Ho used this information, completely undisguised, as an example in his next lecture on ineffective problem-solving strategies. Word of Ho's use of this example got back to Professors Green and Cohen, who expressed their dismay to Ho and concern about his professionalism.*

Ho used bad judgment. But, faculty members would do well to explicitly inform new GTAs when certain information is not to be widely shared. A contributing factor to confidentiality and inappropriate secret-sharing among GTAs is their ambiguous role status. The "student" in them may resort to viewing fascinating information as fair game for broadcasting to their peers or students. However, most faculty view GTAs as colleagues-in-training and may make unwarranted assumptions.

Confidentiality requirements are tricky but easily teachable. Confidentiality guidelines should be a part of GTA orientation. Asking GTAs to sign a confidentiality contract helps to formalize a commitment to restrict disclosure of certain types of information. The next case illustrates a common problem, namely sharing information that invades someone's privacy and violates presumed confidentiality.

Case 15: *When Professor Bumpers asked GTA Sandra to take over his classes for a couple of days because he was experiencing serious side-effects from his depression medication, Bumpers assumed that Sandra would hold this disclosure as confidential. Bumpers was shocked when the department chair called him in to inquire about his mental health.*

The next case represents a very difficult situation that arises rarely, but most academics are likely to run into a similar situation at least once or twice during their careers.

Case 16: *When GTA Aaron called Shalia in to discuss her failing test score, he was not prepared for her response. Shalia claimed that she could hardly study or sleep and was failing all of her courses. She then tearfully disclosed that her step-father was raping her when her mother went to work at night and that she wanted to leave home but had nowhere to go. Shalia didn't want to hurt her mother by telling her what was going on. She ended by saying that she wished she had the courage to kill her step-father because he was "no good," and "the family would be better off if he were dead."*

Some students are experiencing severe and deeply troubling difficulties that involve the potential for physical harm to others or to themselves. Students often confide in their teachers, especially those who seem likely to be understanding and sympathetic. GTAs are often closest to undergraduate students in age, thus enhancing their attraction as confidantes. Although conversations between students and GTAs are presumed confidential, there are exceptions whenever threats or knowledge of potential bodily harm are involved. Therefore, it is important that GTAs understand the institution's policy regarding any duty to warn appropriate others of potential bodily harm. GTAs should immediately consult with an advisor whenever such an instance occurs. If danger appears imminent, the GTA should be knowledgeable about the appropriate response, including a duty to warn potential victims. GTAs should always know, in advance, the identity of a back-up for a supervisor who cannot be reached in case of true emergency.

Ethical Pitfalls Related to Relationships with Regular Faculty

Regular faculty, as we have already noted, have complex relationships with GTAs. Problems with potential ethical implications that arise most frequently involve one of two elements: mixing personal and professional roles and power structure issues. Often the two exist simultaneously.

Dual Role Relationships with Faculty Members

One of the significant differences between undergraduate and graduate student status is the nature of interpersonal relationships with faculty. Formalities, such as the use of formal titles rather than first names, often are dropped. Off-campus activities, including pure socializing, increase. GTAs are allowed into previously forbidden territories, such as the mail or coffee room, and are given access to special resources, such as the copy machine. They get keys. In the department's inner sanctum, GTAs become privy to more inside information. Activities planned specifically to promote graduate/staff interaction are commonplace. This enhanced status is usually welcomed by graduate students, especially those weary of feeling like little more than a line in a grade book for so many years.

The relaxation of role boundaries also gradually socializes GTAs into academic culture, a critically important aspect of their graduate school experience. When all goes well, everyone is satisfied and enriched; however, blended roles involving one group with more power than another always carry risks. The next three cases illustrate how faculty/GTA relationships can go awry.

Case 17: *Professor Love and GTA Jimmy discovered that they are both avid tennis players and decided to play each other. Jimmy turned out to be a very aggressive player, beating Love virtually all of the time and teasing Love about being "an old man." When their paths crossed in the department, Love became more distant. He was*

---

not so sure that he liked this young man. Love began canceling tennis games and eventually told Jimmy that he didn't want to play any more. Love also refused Jimmy's request to borrow some teaching aids.

Maybe Jimmy is not the type of person Love wants as a tennis partner (or a friend), but it is also possible that Love is punishing Jimmy-the-student because Jimmy-the-tennis-player humiliated Love on the courts. Love has every right to discontinue the more personal relationship, but he may be misusing his power to the detriment of Jimmy's academic and professional development.

Case 18: *At a department reception, GTA Richard and Professor Delaney's wife got into a rather heated argument about a political candidate's fitness for office. Both felt passionately about their positions which were completely opposite. The intense conversation culminated with Delaney's wife telling her husband, who had wandered over to see what the problem was, "How could you let this ignorant person into your program?" Although Professor Delany was uncomfortably stuck in the middle, he never again mentioned the matter to Richard. However, the relationship between Delaney and Richard felt strained to both parties. Richard had hoped to work with Delaney during the following year, but decided to abandon that plan.*

Richard might have been wiser to avoid charged conversations with his educators (and their partners) regardless of his level of passion. Yet, the fact remains that the same conversation, replacing Richard with a colleague equal in status to Professor Delany, would have probably resulted in uneventful sequelae. We believe that Professor Delaney should have initiated a discussion with Richard shortly after the incident, perhaps reassuring him that his choice of political candidates was not an issue in their professional relationship.

Case 19: *GTA Gary was running off quizzes on the duplicating machine for his next class. Professor Wait came in with a short article that she wanted to copy. Gary continued running off his exams, informing Professor Wait that he would be finished in just a few minutes. Wait later told the secretary, with colleagues within ear shot, "Gary is a very insensitive young man."*

Although it is not uncommon for people to allow others to cut in when a duplicating job will take a great deal of time, Professor Wait apparently believed that Gary should have, in deference, abruptly interrupted his job to allow her to copy her article. We take the position that Wait was not entitled to break in, but her place in the power structure allowed her to interpret the situation in a way that not only supported her position but justified a negative attribution to a person of lower status.

To our knowledge no research has been done on this topic, but there probably is a rather sturdy "glass wall" with regard to GTA (and, perhaps, contract faculty) status. At some point that might not be entirely explicit or visible, a GTA may overstep his or her bounds in the eyes of one or more regular faculty members. This phenomenon probably varies from campus to campus, and certainly among individual faculty members. GTAs can easily be confused when the power hierarchy is not understood, as the next case illustrates.

Case 20: *GTA Eric enjoyed discussing his career and impending marriage to a fellow student with Professor Tork. After the first few conversations, Eric felt that he was being selfish because the conversations centered exclusively on him. He overheard Tork telling a colleague about moving to a new apartment after her husband left her for a secretary in the Provost's office. He decided to disclose to her that he knew about the situation and expressed his sympathy, expecting that Tork would welcome a two-way rather than a one-way personal relationship. Tork, however, dismissed the comment, and remained cool toward Eric for the remainder of his graduate career.*

Eric did not commit an ethical offense, but in an attempt to equalize the relationship he clearly overstepped Tork's tolerance for intrusion into her personal life. Tork apparently perceived this as a serious boundary violation. What Eric did not understand is that professors are used to one-way conversations with students, and to keeping their private lives to themselves. Given the ambiguity inherent in individual GTA and faculty member relationships, GTAs would do well to move into closer relationships with faculty with caution.

We would not want to leave the impression that we are advocating a position that GTAs need to accept their lower status and remain hyper-vigilant lest they offend regular faculty. Indeed, we believe that the regular faculty can be the ones who are ethically insensitive. However, we do mean to portray a realistic picture of what can happen so that GTAs can try to avoid situations that may work to their disadvantage.

Exploitation of Graduate Teaching Assistants

Occasionally, faculty members intentionally manipulate and exploit graduate students. However, professors may also misuse their influence and power without full awareness. Even so, exploitation is still at issue, as the next case illustrates.

Case 21: *GTA Hillman taught the four one-credit laboratory classes that accompanied Professor Dillard's two lecture courses. His required duties, as described by the department, were to supervise the students' lab work, grade their lab reports, and write and grade lab exams. However, Professor Dillard also required Hillman to collect articles for Dillard's lectures, create slides, arrange for films (including picking up and returning them), create and grade the lecture section exams, tutor students who were having problems with the lecture material, and keep attendance and grade books current for both the lecture and laboratory components. Dillard explained, "It will be a good experience for you to oversee the total picture." In the meantime, Hillman is having trouble keeping up with his own studies and the progress on his thesis is falling behind schedule.*

It appears that Professor Dillard is using his GTA to play a major role in teaching his own courses, although Hillman's formal job description (and pay rate) is only for lab course supervision. Sometimes it is difficult to differentiate between offering a GTA an enriching opportunity and exploitation, and sometimes the difference is in the eye of the beholder. However, if Hillman is overworked with duties or believes he is doing too much, he might approach Professor Dillard with a request for a modification in his assignments. GTAs do, however, risk receiving a negative reaction which is why departmental guidelines for GTA duties, stated as specifically as possible, are highly recommended.

More subtle situations are rarely openly discussed. For example, graduate students are often the *only* people their educators know well who are both trusted *and* possibly available to perform certain non-academic tasks. Thus, hiring GTAs as house and baby-sitters, gardeners, private secretaries, dog walkers, and the like appears to be common-place. In the absence of empirical evidence, it appears that such situations usually work out to the benefit of both faculty and students, and no one feels exploited in the process.

When faculty members, who have great power over the present and the future careers of graduate students, misuse their powerful advantage, GTAs may feel that compliance to any requests is the only option. Some GTAs, however, have sued their advisors for what they describe as academic hazing (Leatherman, 1997). In some cases it appeared that the faculty member became too informal, paying a GTA with a bottle of whiskey for example. In more serious instances, it looked as though professors treated graduate students as all-around servants.

We believe that it is important for GTAs to have someone to confide in when exploitation and other difficult matters arise. The GTA supervisor is the ideal confidante. It is unfortunate, however, that it can be the supervisor who is the exploiter, as we illustrate in the next section.

GTA Relationships with Supervisors

Many GTAs are not supervised at all, or are supervised only superficially and sporadically. Instead, they are left to their own resources which renders them very vulnerable. In this section, we discuss the role that GTA supervisors can play in developing the ethical and professional fitness of GTAs.

Role Modeling

First and foremost, supervisors must remember that they are role models for GTAs. Supervisor's conduct, problem solving strategies, and responses to ethical dilemmas will be duly noted and absorbed. On the other hand, sexually predatory, unethical, unavailable, uncivil, or exploitative supervisors create appalling role models for graduate students (Fly, van Bark, Weinman, Kitchener, & Lang, 1997; Glaser & Thorpe, 1986; Pope, Levenson, & Schover, 1980). The next case is somewhat ambiguous but illustrative of our point:

Case 22: *As soon as GTA Melanie arrived for her weekly supervisory session, Professor Fox would evaluate what she was wearing (e.g., "That color doesn't do anything for you" or "That sweater is absolutely gorgeous"). He often lost track or interrupted the flow of her attempts to focus on her lesson plans with remarks such as, "Have you gone to the new jazz bar on 4th street yet?"*

Fox appears to be using his supervisee as a source of personal enjoyment. Supervisors who use their status and power for their own gratification are exploiting those who have entrusted their professional development to them. Even though the above case may not have involved intentional abuse, the supervisor has abandoned the professional role in favor his own personal agenda. Although we cannot be sure about Dr. Fox's motives, he is flirting with sexual harassment. Unfortunately, supervisees who are devalued, humiliated, ignored or criticized in nonconstructive ways may be unlikely to protest, especially if the supervisor is well-liked and respected in the work setting (Jacobs, 1991).

Role Complexities Between Graduate Teaching Assistants and Their Supervisors

It must be recognized that the formalized roles between GTAs and their educators are no less complex than the informal ones. Regardless of what supervised role graduate students hold, inherent role complexities require special attention from the standpoint of ethical management.

The roles that a GTA's supervisor hold include some (if not all) of the following:
• Mentor
• Confidante
• Teacher
• Quasi-therapist or counselor on personal matters
• Academic and career advisor
• Performance evaluator
• Evaluator of personal fitness for the profession
• Role model

These supervisory roles, when held by a single individual, are not always compatible. It may be difficult to confide in the person who is also responsible for evaluating your performance (Brown & Krager, 1985; Koocher & Keith-Spiegel, 1998; Pope, Keith-Spiegel, & Tabachnick, 1986; Sullivan & Ogloff, 1998). Consider these possible conflicts:

Should I tell Dr. Smith that I am having trouble relating to two of my students who are becoming openly hostile toward me? She might be able to give me some pointers, but she may also think that I am incompetent and put that in my record.

If I tell Dr. Jones that I am having trouble concentrating on my lecture because I am so sexually attracted and distracted by a young woman in the front row, will he assume that I have a serious problem and am not fit to teach?

I just don't understand this chapter in the textbook. But, if I admit that in my supervision group the department may think that they made a mistake in hiring me.

It may also be difficult for the supervisor to switch from being critical some of the time and listening empathically at other times (Whiston & Emerson, 1989). The GTA supervisor, however, can contribute a great deal to GTAs' professional development and ethical sensitivity. With the guidance of the GTA supervisor, many ethical dilemmas can be prevented, defused, or minimized. We conclude with some practical tips for supervisors.

Some Recommendations for Supervisors

1. **Roles to avoid.** Some elective roles between graduate students and their educators should be avoided altogether because the risk of harm to one or both parties is high (and such relationships are often considered unethical). These include sexual liaisons or other role complications that are incompatible with the role of educator, any role that unnecessarily accentuates the power differential between the supervisor and the GTA, or any role that exploits a GTA (Kitchener, 1988; Sullivan & Ogloff, 1998).

It is the supervisor's responsibility to first recognize that the risk of such complications is present (e.g., supervisory sessions are becoming mildly flirtatious, the supervisor is becoming dependent on the GTA, favors from the GTA are expected, viewing a GTA as a central person in one's life, or finding rationalizations for treating a certain GTA differently than is the norm). It is also the supervisor's responsibility to take the lead in limiting roles with GTAs to those that preserve and promote the GTA's academic and professional socialization. In less formal settings, the task of turning down a person's interest or offer can be difficult because most of us do not want to hurt another person's feelings. However, in a formal, supervisory relationship one can gently yet firmly restate the nature of their professional relationship.

In our experience, the best way to prevent problems from ever beginning is to have an open group discussion regarding the dilemmas that the complex roles of supervisor and supervisee can cause. Although such discussions can be held in individual sessions, group sessions are recommended because discomfort may be more easily diffused. Role play exercises, such as having a GTA present a "mistake" to the "supervisor," can enhance understanding and open candid discussions.

Another suggestion to help prevent the occurrence of role conflicts is to discuss role complexities in the context of GTA rights. For example, it can be explicitly stated that GTAs have the right to a strictly professional relationship with their supervisors, free from sexual harassment or other forms of exploitation. (This also helps to remind supervisors of their responsibilities.)

2. **Early conversations about role conflicts between GTAs and their students.** Role complications that can easily arise between GTAs and their students should be discussed soon after supervisory sessions begin. GTAs need to be reminded that role conflicts are likely to develop with other students (and sometimes other faculty). Discussing cases, such as the ones we have provided, is an especially useful way of educating students about such dilemmas. Using a case study method allows GTAs to explore the range of "what-ifs?" that can occur in teaching environments as well as the range of techniques for managing various scenarios.

Maintaining professional boundaries with GTAs assists in preventing such rationalizations. Supervisors must keep in mind that although many GTAs may understand, on an intellectual level, that role conflicts are to be avoided, they (as well as fully-trained professionals) have a tendency to rationalize situations. They may say to themselves something like, "this will work out fine because it is different ," or, "it's OK to do just this one time."

Sometimes risky behavior has no negative fallout. However, it is critical that GTAs understand that when incompatible roles create complications, as they do often enough, people can be harmed and their own careers can be terminated even when barely started. We know of several cases where graduate students were forced out of a program for engaging in unethical role relationships that turned out badly.

3. **Ease the difficulties GTAs may have about discussing ethical conflicts.** Graduate students should be made to feel comfortable to state honestly any concerns related to their roles with their educators. They should not fear adverse evaluations for disclosures of mistakes. GTAs are still very "evaluation sensitive" and do not relish revealing a weakness or problem that could suggest lack of fitness.

One way to facilitate discussion in a group supervisory session is to invite GTAs to submit their ethical concerns or problems anonymously. This technique allows GTAs to be frank without having to fear censure. In most cases, the entire group benefits from such a discussion because most of the problems will be ones that many GTAs may face. These types of problems include coping with sexual attraction to students, feeling too depressed or stressed to do one's best work, not knowing what to do with a student's highly personal disclosure, and dealing with a conflict with another faculty or staff member.

We suggest adapting Bosk's (1979) model for dealing with supervisee errors. In Bosk's view, errors in technique are forgivable and inevitable during training. However, normative errors (i.e., those that occur when GTAs fail to do what is expected of them or fail to act conscientiously) are moral failures. Covering up technical errors can lead to a normative error. The two types of errors call for different reactions by supervisors.

First, explain the two types of errors to students. When teaching and teaching-related activities do not work out as anticipated, all GTAs must accept that this no cause for shame. Indeed, were such problems not expected, supervision would not be necessary. Errors in technique must not be hidden. They should be identified and openly discussed as a competence and as an <u>ethical</u> obligation.

When GTAs commit normative errors, a more serious discussion is called for. The GTA should be confronted as soon as possible. The matter should be described, and the GTA given an opportunity to respond. (Sometimes what appears as a normative error has another, less problematic explanation.) Normative errors call for closer monitoring, and if the problem is systemic and not amenable to rehabilitation, more serious action—including termination—must be considered.

Most types of problems that GTAs will disclose usually create chances to help the GTA as well as to assist in ensuring the future integrity of the profession. Many conflicts and difficulties GTAs face can be framed in a positive context. That is, the issues can be cast as opportunities to explore, learn, understand, re-frame, and project into how to best handle similar situations in the future.

Supervisors must keep in mind that GTAs are likely to someday ask their supervisors to provide employment references, and want to be perceived as solid and competent. Supervisors may have to reassure their GTAs that they do not expect perfection and that now is the time to learn from any type of mistake. Supervisors can provide reassurance by informing GTAs that the ability to take constructive criticism and act upon it is a highly desirable trait.

It has been found that even when graduate students understand ethical standards, they often react by doing far less that they believe they should (Bernard & Jara, 1986). On one survey (Mearns & Allen, 1991), almost all of the graduate student respondents had known about ethical transgressions committed by one of their peers. Supervisors can help empower GTAs to engage themselves in helping to resolve ethical problems on their own.

4. **Remaining alert to power differentials.** Supervisors should remain alert to the fact that GTAs may have a difficult time refusing requests or advice, fearing that the entire supervisory relationship could collapse. The power differential between GTAs and their supervisors (or other faculty members) is great, and special care must be taken to ensure that no undue coercion is being placed on GTAs.

We have found that an early discussion wherein GTAs are empowered to speak out if they feel uncomfortable helps minimize such conflicts. For example, one might say, "Let me know whenever you feel overwhelmed or under too much pressure. We can work together to see what can be done." We also advise asking GTAs informally and on a regular basis how things are going. One can pick up clues that might not be shared during a group or formal supervisory session that a GTA needs additional support.

Including *advanced* GTAs in discussions with novices can be very helpful because this normalizes mistakes and also models improvement. New GTAs can see how quickly they will develop with guidance at a time when they may be worrying that they will never have the skills that they see in their supervisors. Directly observing skill development in their more experienced peers can be reassuring.

5. **Keeping ethical issues active.** Instruction and discussions about ethical issues common to the academy should be held (perhaps in group supervision sessions) on a regular basis. We hear often of "one shot ethics sessions" after which the subject is closed. Ethical awareness and sensitivity grows and matures over time and requires consistent nurturing.

GTAs should be taught ethical decision-making skills because the correct course of action is not always apparent. Resources exist that provide relevant discussion materials (e.g., Keith-Spiegel, Wittig, Balogh, Perkins, & Whitley, 1993, currently in revision). Ideally, ethics discussions should occur before GTAs set foot in the classroom.

6. **Confidentiality limitations.** GTAs may assume that whatever they disclose to their supervisors will be held in strictest confidence. However, that is not—nor should it be—necessarily true. Assuring the GTA that *almost* everything that is discussed will be held in strict confidence is appropriate. Supervisors should clearly inform GTAs of any limits placed on disclosing information during supervisory sessions. Issues could arise that reveal a serious violation of policy, professional ethics codes, or state evidence codes. For example, if a GTA becomes depressed and threatens to commit suicide, a supervisor may be required to report this information to appropriate third parties. If a GTA reveals a plan to physically harm another or to commit a crime, the supervisor may need to seek outside assistance.

If GTAs clearly understand the nature of the limitations, disclosure of relevant information is unlikely to be hampered. For example, a GTA said to one of us, "I am bummed out because my girlfriend called it quits, so I could use a little cheering up. But, don't worry, I'm not going to do anything rash!"

7. **When personalities collide.** If the supervisor and a GTA appear to be a poor match, we advise first attempting to work things out. Successful conflict resolution is, in itself, a positive process for the GTA to experience and even models for the GTA how conflicts with his or her students can be resolved. Here is a chance for the supervisor to also teach a skill by acknowledging the problem without becoming defensive or angry. An approach might start with something like this: "You know, Bill, there is tension between us and we need to discuss this. Let's consider what we can try to do differently that might work better for both of us."

If an active attempt to work through differences is unsuccessful, the supervisor should discuss the impasse openly and honestly with the GTA and, if possible, mutually terminate the relationship. Dysfunctional mentoring relationships can be extremely harmful to students (see Scandura, 1998). Assisting in the identification of a new supervisor would be a constructive and perhaps appreciated gesture.

We are not suggesting that this process turn into a therapy session or that the purpose be to try to make the GTA more to the supervisor's own liking. As professionals, we know that not everyone clicks with us, and vice-versa!

8. **The need for formal policy.** Supervisors should be fully aware of their department and institutional policies for dealing with impaired or unethical GTAs. If no such policies exist, we advise that departments generate a mechanism for dealing with graduate students who pose difficult problems for the program and the institution. Because due process and other legal issues may pertain, the institution's legal counsel should be consulted.

9. **Helping GTAs get the lay of the land.** GTAs should be encouraged to learn the rules and policies that govern undergraduate as well as graduate students, especially if they did not attend the institution as an undergraduate student. Supervisors should provide (or loan) their GTAs the faculty handbook and the undergraduate catalog and encourage them to review these as well as the institution's web page. Ethical problems can arise from ignorance or misunderstanding formal policy.

Candidly, but prudently, supervisors also should inform their GTAs about the structure of the department, the hierarchy within it, and any tips for avoiding trouble. This usually can be done *without* resorting to negative characterizations of colleagues. For example, you might say, "Dr. Trim is in charge of the laboratory, and he has high standards of cleanliness, so look around before you leave to make sure the bench is cleaned off and no supplies are left out" rather than, "Watch out for Trim. That neat-freak will turn purple and hit the ceiling unless the lab is spotless." (But, also remember that using GTAs as a dumping ground by inflicting one's own gripes is not appropriate.)

10. **Finally, never forget yourself back when!** Supervisors should never let the image of themselves at the GTA's stage of professional development be very far back in their minds. This recollection often aids in supervisors' ability to empathize and understand how GTAs are handling their duties. Indeed, a supervisor's appropriate use of disclosure about his or her own experiences as a graduate student can help put GTAs at ease and serve as proof that it is possible to become fully competent, mature, and successful in academia.

References

Bernard, J. L., & Jara, C. S. (1986). The failure of clinical psychology graduate students to apply understood ethical principles. *Professional Psychology: Research & Practice, 17*, 313-315.

Bosk, C. L. (1979). *Forgive and remember*. Chicago: University of Chicago Press.

Brown, R. G., & Krager, L. (1985) Ethical issues in graduate education. *Journal of Higher Education, 56*, 403-418.

Fly, B. J., van Bark, W. P., Weinman, L., Kitchener, K. S., & Lang, P. R. (1997). Ethical transgressions of psychology graduate students: Critical incidents with implications for training. *Professional Psychology: Research and Practice, 28,* 492-495.

Folse, K. A. (1991). Ethics and the profession: Graduate student training. *Teaching Sociology, 19,* 344-350.

Glaser, R. D., & Thorpe, J. S. (1986). Unethical intimacy: A survey of sexual contact and advances between psychology educators and female graduate students. *American Psychologist, 41,* 43-51.

Jacobs, C. (1991). Violations of the supervisory relationship: An ethical and educational blind spot. *Social Work, 36,* 130-135.

Keith-Spiegel, P. (1994). *Ratings of ethical issues by graduate assistants and professors: A comparison.* Paper delivered to the Graduate Student Forum, Ball State University, Muncie, IN.

Keith-Spiegel, P., Tabachnick, B. G., & Allen, M. (1993) . Students' perceptions of the ethicality of professors' actions. *Ethics and Behavior,* 149-162.

Keith-Spiegel, P., Wittig, A. F., Perkins, D. V., Balogh, D. W., & Whitley, B. E. (1993). *The ethics of teaching: A casebook.* Muncie, IN: Ball State University Office of Academic Research and Sponsored Projects.

Kitchener, K. S. (1988). Dual role relationships: What makes them so problematic? *Journal of Counseling and Development, 67,* 217-221.

Koocher, G. P., & Keith-Spiegel, P. (1998). Ethics in Psychology (2nd ed.). New York: Oxford University Press.

Leatherman, C. (March 16, 1994). Fighting back. *Chronicle of Higher Education,* A17-18.

Leatherman, C. (July 18, 1997). Should dog walking and house sitting be required for a Ph.D.? *Chronicle of Higher Education,* A10-11.

Leatherman, C. (August 14, 1998a) Graduate students gather to learn 'Organization 101.' *Chronicle of Higher Education,* A10-11.

Leatherman, C. (December 4, 1998b) Graduate students push for reform. *Chronicle of Higher Education,* A12-13.

Lowman, J. & Mathie, V. A. (1993). What should graduate teaching assistants know about teaching? *Teaching of Psychology, 20,* 84-88.

Mearns, J., & Allen, G. J. (1991). Graduate students' experiences in dealing with impaired peers compared with faculty predictions: An exploratory study. *Ethics & Behavior, 1,* 191-202.

Mueller, A., Perlman, B., McCann, L. I., & McFadden, S. H. (1997). A faculty perspective on teaching assistant training. *Teaching of Psychology, 24,* 167-171.

Perkinson, R. (1996). Bad marks for Yale's labor policies: Rights of graduate student teachers at Yale University. *The Progressive, 60,* 20.

Pope, K. S., Keith-Spiegel, P., & Tabachnick, B. G. (1986). Sexual attraction to clients: The human therapist and the (sometimes) inhuman training system. *American Psychologist, 34,* 682-689.

Pope, K. S., Levenson, H., & Schover, L. R. (1980). Sexual behavior between clinical supervisors and trainees: Implications for professional standards. *Professional Psychology: Research, Theory and Practice, 11,* 157-162.

Prieto, L. R. (1995). Supervising graduate teaching assistants: An adaptation of the integrated developmental model. *Journal of Graduate Teaching Assistant Development, 2,* 93-105.

Procidano, M. E., Busch-Rossnagel, N. A., Reznikoff, M., & Geisinger, K. F. (1995). Responding to graduate students' professional deficiencies: A national survey. *Journal of Clinical Psychology, 51,* 426-433.

Scandura, T. A. (1998). Dysfunctional mentoring relationships and outcomes. *Journal of Management, 24,* 449-467.

Sullivan, L. E., & Ogloff, J. R. (1998). Appropriate supervisor-graduate student relationships. *Ethics & Behavior, 8,* 229-248.

Whiston, S. C., & Emerson, S. (1989). Ethical implications for supervisors in counseling of trainees. *Counselor Education and Supervision, 28,* 318-325.

Overview of Gender-Conscious Teaching

Heidi S. Fencl, Ph.D.
University of Wisconsin-Oshkosh

Overview

I recently attended a Ph.D. graduation ceremony with my eight-year old daughter. Part way through the hooding ceremony, she leaned over and asked why there were so many men and almost no women. The answers are so many and so varied that they cannot be packaged into a tidy set of reasons for adults to understand, let alone into a satisfying answer for an eight-year old. (Which is not to say I did not try.) It is abundantly clear, however, that how we teach, from kindergarten through graduate school, is a significant part of the answer. Though this chapter addresses only a small subset of those years, it is an extremely important subset. In 1987, for example, the National Science Foundation found that over half of all students entering college with an intended major in mathematics or the natural sciences left those fields after a single year of introductory courses. What happens in introductory courses, a typical teaching responsibility for many teaching assistants, makes a significant difference in the lives of students.

Unfortunately, course policies aimed at retention of students, and especially at retention of women students, sometimes raise concerns that they come at the expense of others in the course. That simply is not true. Gender-conscious teaching is student-conscious teaching, or, as a male colleague of mine once said, "It's just good teaching." Educators are increasingly taking the view that teaching should be evaluated according to what students learn, not by what the instructor says. And the two are not always the same. Students' prior knowledge, varied learning styles, and acceptance in a course all affect the way in which they learn. When educators focus on who students are, and when they design learning opportunities around that knowledge, the depth at which all students understand course material increases.

Part of understanding students is understanding gender norms which affect communication and interactions. Cultural norms do not get left at the classroom door, and they have a significant impact on how students behave and learn in educational settings. In the following section, "The Need for Gender Conscious Teaching," I first examine the importance of diversity in academic disciplines, then briefly highlight some of the climate and communication issues which affect women in the classroom. This provides a theoretical basis for the section on gender-conscious teaching. Subsections titled "Tips for TAs" provide an overview of material which can be presented to teaching assistants. In the "Teaching TAs" subsection, I suggest exercises and resources to use for exploring climate issues in training sessions. References for further reading are provided throughout.

The Need for Gender-Conscious Teaching

Background: Statistics on the Representation of Women in Higher Education

Women are increasingly present in college and university classrooms, accounting for half or more of the undergraduate population at most institutions. That alone is reason to care about the dynamics in our classrooms. A brief look at some statistics about where women are, and are not, sheds additional light onto the importance of climate. For example, according to National Science Foundation data, women received 46.5% of science (agricultural, biological, computer, physical, and social sciences), mathematics, and engineering bachelor's degrees awarded in the United States in 1995. In fields such as the biological and social sciences, undergraduate degrees were awarded to men and women in approximately equal numbers, and 73% of the psychology degrees were awarded to women. On the other hand, in physics and engineering women received only 17% of the bachelor's degrees granted in 1995, and they earned less than 30% of the computer science degrees.

Snapshot statistics such as these tell only part of the story. In some disciplines, such as computer science, the representation of women is decreasing, and in all areas the percentage of women in a discipline decreases through advanced degrees and academic ranks. (Additional statistics, including those for advanced degrees, are available through the National Science Foundation web site, http://www.nsf.gov/sbe/srs/stats.htm.).

Background: Why Is Diversity Important?

The need to consider gender diversity in academic discussions goes much deeper than numbers and statistics. Important questions include: "Why are women under-represented in some fields and at advanced ranks?"; "What price do women pay to participate in academic life?"; and "Why is it important to strive for racial and gender diversity in all disciplines?" Though related to climate issues discussed throughout the bulk of this chapter, the first two questions are beyond the scope of TA training. Interested readers are referred to a summary of the Project Access study (Sonnert & Holton, 1996) for an overview.

The third question, that of the importance of diversity, is very relevant when teaching TAs about teaching. It provides a framework and a motivation for making positive changes in classroom climate, and it increases the respect that instructors give to multiple voices in their sections. A frequent argument for diversity rests simply on the changing demographics of the workforce, and the need to have women and people of color to fill job openings at all levels. I argue, however, that there are deeper reasons to strive for diversity.

Equity for individuals is one such reason. Education, especially education which includes some scientific training, is tied to power: power to be heard in political dialogues; power to move into decision making positions in the business world; power to affect medical decisions which impact us directly. Practices that discourage women in the classroom have a negative impact far beyond their grade in the course or their choice of major. By systematically removing them from sciences, women are effectively removed from upper levels of discourse in government and the private sector, and their voices in environmental and medical decisions become even easier to discount. Women's voices matter to women's lives, and education is a key to gaining a stronger voice.

Women's voices also matter to their academic disciplines, at introductory levels as well as through research. In any academic discipline, the questions that are asked, and the follow-up results that are pursued, are chosen according to the interests of researchers. Literature is full of examples of women who have chosen to pursue different questions and who have radically changed our view of the world as a result. The work of Ellen Swallow Richards and Rachel Carson, and the recent growth in the area of women's medicine, are only several examples. By promoting greater diversity among researchers, we allow a greater range of questions to be asked and we grow to a wider understanding of our world than is possible when practitioners in a field are narrowly defined.

Social studies of the ways in which we practice research demonstrate that our cultures, our backgrounds, and our unrecognized assumptions do affect the way we interpret results. Sandra Harding (e.g., Harding, 1991) is but one researcher who has specifically looked at the importance of women's voices in scientific discourse.

When courses are taught in such a way that they address only one voice, when knowledge is presented as a set of "laws" rather than models, and when stories of discovery and dissension are left out of the discussion, students learn that there is only one way to view a discipline, and that their questions might not be the right questions. The situation is complicated when instructors are uncomfortable with their own grasp of the content being taught. An example from my early teaching career comes to mind. I assigned a problem in which students were to assume the force of wind on the sail of an ice boat remained constant. One student, a hockey player, had the physical experience of being on the ice on a windy day. His experience told him that the assumption was not true. I explained that the intent of the problem was to assume a constant wind speed and moved on to other questions. In retrospect, I realize that his own experience was much more powerful than an (incorrect) assumption and it completely changed the way that he viewed the problem. I also realize that he presented a perfect opportunity to explore modeling, its role in my discipline (physics), and the nature of scientific inquiry. I have since changed both the way I approach my courses and they way I consider student questions. My drop rate has gone down, and women and students with poor math backgrounds especially find more ways to successfully connect with course material.

As part of their training, teaching assistants need to understand that diversity of life experiences and of learning styles play an important role in disciplinary discourse, and to further recognize that those differences have a huge impact on the ability of students to connect with material. Specific teaching strategies for opening a classroom to a diverse student body are discussed in the "Practical Suggestions" section, following a discussion of another factor which affects a student's ability to connect with a course: classroom climate.

Classroom Climate

Regardless of discipline, the classroom climate is not always hospitable to women and girls. Bernice Sandler et al. (1996) discuss alarming aspects of education which create a very different educational experience for female students than for male students. For example, men and boys are asked questions in class more frequently than are women and girls, and the nature of the questions also shows a variation based on sex. Male students are more likely to be asked questions involving higher-order thought, and to be given more time and encouragement for their answers. Female students tend to be asked questions requiring memorization rather than analysis. This is so deeply a part of our culture, as well as of our educational experience, that it generally goes unnoticed. In fact, it is not uncommon for men in a classroom without such an imbalance to express concern that the women are receiving preferential treatment.

Relatedly, communication norms exert a powerful influence on how students interact in a classroom. Deborah Tannen, in her popular book, *You Just Don't Understand: Women and Men in Conversation*, highlights ways in which men and women use language differently. On average, women are more likely to be comfortable contributing to a discussion among a small group of people than in a large group and to use language to seek consensus. Men, on average, participate more in large group conversations than do women, and are more likely to use language to establish their place in a hierarchy. Comfort level in small vs. large groups, as well as both cultural and gender differences in determining pause time between speakers, have obvious ramifications in the degree to which students participate in class discussions. Students who are used to striving for consensus face additional barriers in class structures which are based on competition.

Communication differences also affect the weight which a student's contributions are given. Tannen points out that women are more likely to end their statements with tag questions ("all right?") or to precede them with qualifiers ("I've been wondering" or "this might not be important"). I recommend her book for a fascinating analysis of how such differences arise. The important point for this discussion, however, is that such qualifiers are used as conversation fillers. They do not indicate the lack of knowledge that they suggest if interpreted at face value. Peers, as well as instructors, can undervalue a student's contributions due to her conversational style. Polly Fassinger and collaborators (1995) studied classroom interactions at a Midwestern liberal arts college, and found that the climate created by fellow students was more important than the instructor in determining classroom dynamics.

Communication patterns of both instructors and students do not, of course, account for all differences in classroom experience. Students arrive at college after years of expectations from friends, family, teachers, media, and society as a whole. Their goals and confidence in their abilities to succeed are a cumulative result of such influences. Women tend to under-rate their competence; studies in mathematics and computer science show that both women and men underpredict the grades of women in a course and overpredict those of male students, and further show that the scores of women who drop scientific majors are significantly higher than those of men who drop such majors. It has also been my experience that first generation college students have a lower confidence level than their abilities would merit.

Whatever the reason, when students do not have confidence in their abilities to succeed in a field of study, they are more likely to be discouraged by poor teaching or competitive pedagogies. Analyses of scientific research questions chosen by women and men find that women are more likely to be engaged by material connected to real world experiences. Presentation of material as a set of disconnected ideas is discouraging to students of both sexes (e.g., Tobias, 1990), and a hierarchical and competitive (e.g., grading on a curve) teaching style is especially discouraging to women.

Practical Suggestions for Gender-Conscious Teaching

The above summary suggests that there are two components involved in providing an equitable educational climate for women. One is creating an inclusive classroom (and departmental) experience that values all students; the other is using a variety of pedagogies to engage students around course material. Parker Palmer (1993) provides strong arguments for a class model of students and teachers engaged together around a subject, in contrast to a model of the teacher as an authority who dispenses knowledge to students. In the first model, learning is active; in the second, students are passive participants and active engagement is required only of the instructor.

Actual teaching situations for teaching assistants vary greatly. With some assignments, they might have the freedom to determine course structure and content, and to incorporate a wide variety of pedagogies. In others, lesson plans and teaching strategies might be determined by a course coordinator. However, in all cases, TAs can impact the climate of their sections. A variety of suggestions, both large and small, are included in the "Tips" section below. Suggestions for TA training activities which highlight climate follow. An excellent and easy to use resource to distribute at training activities is Achieving Gender Equity in Science Classrooms (available on the web at *http://www.brown.edu/ Administration/Dean_of_the_College/homepginfo/equity/ Equity_handbook.html*).

Tips for TAs: Ideas for Creating a Gender Friendly Classroom Climate

Setting the Tone. As indicated by the work of Fassinger et al. (1995), students are at least as important as the instructor in influencing classroom dynamics. It is much easier to set expectations during the first class meeting than to deal with inappropriate behavior later in the term. One first day exercise, especially useful for courses involving a great deal of participation, is to divide the class into small groups and to ask each group to list behaviors that discourage them from participating in class discussions. The lists are used by the class as a whole to establish courtesies that will be the norm for upcoming sessions. I discuss both communication and learning styles on the first day of my course, although I do not focus explicitly on gender differences, and I explicitly tell my students what teaching strategies I will use to include them all in learning opportunities.

Other strategies can be used if students create, by words or actions, a cold climate for their peers. One is for the instructor to intervene, which is particularly applicable if the behavior is subtle. For example, a student who interrupts another can be reminded of the discussion guidelines allowing speakers to finish their thoughts. Students who frown, turn away, or use other body language to devalue a speaker's contributions can be asked to articulate and support their objections. The important point is that many actions which create an inhospitable climate go unnoticed and unchallenged by both teachers and students. Noticing and discouraging inappropriate behaviors has a powerful impact on the classroom environment, and on allowing women to participate equally in classroom discussions.

In some cases, students might make comments or arguments that are blatantly sexist or racist. These can be awkward and harder to address, especially if the student is antagonistic. One approach is to turn to the class and ask if anyone would like to reply. A peer comment in this case can be much more effective than an instructor response.

Even if no one chooses to comment, waiting for an answer gives the instructor a moment to collect her/his thoughts and decide how to respond.

Encouraging Equitable Participation. Even when an inclusive classroom structure is established, it takes initial effort on the part of the instructor to elicit participation from more than a core group of students. The good news is that after an initial period of careful attention, a class will generally function very well and require less effort from the teacher in the long run. Several very simple ways to encourage broadly-based participation are to wait longer before calling on students, to give students a minute to think about a question before calling for an answer, or to allow students to discuss questions with their neighbor.

I emphasize that it is very hard to be equitable when calling on students. If a teaching assistant (or any other instructor) is not completely comfortable in front of a class, it comes as such a relief to have anyone answer that the boldest few will generally be allowed to respond. A false impression by some students that the instructor is favoring women can also be very damaging on evaluations. Two ways to address both of these issues share the common theme of being explicit in demonstrating fairness. Once the instructor has learned students' names (and it is well worth the effort!), an attendance sheet can be used to visibly keep track of student responses. It is then easy to thank vocal students for their responses, but to ask that someone (by name) who has not yet spoken contribute. For lecture-oriented discussions, instructors can use note cards, with students' names listed either individually or in small groups and shuffled for random order. The student(s) on the top card are asked to respond when a question is posed to the class, and the card is then moved to the back of the stack. Both of these methods increase participation of women and other students who do not initially volunteer to speak in large groups.

In my experience, the initial hurdle to speaking up in class is the greatest. Once students are drawn into participation, they are more vocal and active throughout the course. For this reason, a first day activity involving students can be extremely useful, even if it means not addressing the course syllabus until the second meeting. If a teaching assistant does not have the flexibility to schedule course content, a simple first day activity which does not require any additional time is to ask students to respond to the attendance call with their favorite movie or with a good book they have read lately. Another way to encourage participation from a broad group of people is to recognize that students who are intimidated by speaking up in a large group are often more willing to participate when the class is divided into smaller units. Including a variety of activities will engage a variety of students!

Increasing Student Confidence. Establishing a classroom climate that encourages participation from all students goes hand in hand with building student confidence, especially for students who under-rate their abilities. It is likely that some students will come to teaching assistants after class or during office hours with questions that they chose not to ask in front of the entire group. Beginning the following period with, "A student came to me yesterday with an excellent question I think we should discuss" validates their status as good learners. Seeing that the rest of the class is also interested in the question helps to break the "everyone knows this but me" barrier.

"Muddiest Waters" is one of many excellent techniques for staying in touch with students which can be found in *Classroom Assessment Techniques*, by Angelo and Cross (1993). In this assessment, note cards are distributed to students at the end of each class period and students are asked to write down the one thing they least understood that day. Several of the questions can be used to generate discussion at the beginning of the next class period, again validating the worth of student questions.

One important consideration when addressing lack of confidence for women students is that inappropriate praise can do more harm than good. Instructors who praise men for performance, and women for effort, for example, send a very clear picture of their expectations for student achievement. Useful praise is specific ("you did an excellent job analyzing....") and gender-equitable. Within those constraints, even in very large classes it is possible to show an interest in students. Comments like "excellent job" or "great analysis on problem 3" take little time to write on exams or homework, but show students that their instructor takes an interest in their performance.

General Words on Gender-Equitable Climate. The above sections address large-scale influences on the classroom. Small details, too, are important for the overall climate in a course. Use of inclusive language, avoiding stereotypes in essay or story problems, and avoiding jokes which play on stereotypes are mandatory in setting an equitable classroom experience. Instructors need to take care not to comment on the appearance of female students or to use different modes of address for men and women. Many inequitable behaviors are subtle and are pervasive outside the classroom. This makes them hard to notice, even by instructors who consciously monitor their interactions. It can be useful to videotape or invite an observer to a class in order to get an accurate picture of subtle variations in how students are received.

Teaching TAs About Climate: Tried and True Exercises

An important part of training for gender-equitable teaching requires giving TAs a chance to think critically about the nature of inquiry in their disciplines, to explore their own interaction norms, and to observe and practice good teaching. These can be hard issues to raise, and especially hard to raise in a way that students feel open rather than defensive. The exercises below are a few ideas to start training in gender-conscious teaching on a positive note.

Reflecting on one's discipline. Catherine Hurt Middlecamp and Anne-Marie Nickel (2000) provide a wonderful first day activity for classes and teaching assistant training alike. (For brevity, I will use "students" to refer to students, TAs, or any other audience, "instructor" to refer to any leader, and "class" to refer to a class or other group situation.) On the surface, this activity introduces students to each other. The instructor asks the class to think of questions that they would like to ask about each other. Each question goes on the blackboard along with multiple choice answers which the students suggest. Students also determine the rules: does everyone have to answer every question, are students only allowed one answer per question, etc. Instructor guidance is needed, just as for any other situation which impacts classroom climate. For example, if even one student votes that not all questions must be answered, that vote should determine the rule.

Once blackboards are full and rules are established, the class is turned loose to answer the questions (each student making a hash mark by the best answers). After answers are tabulated, the exercise can be used to open a reflective discussion on disciplinary inquiry. Students are likely to have noticed that there were questions they wished they had asked, or which did not have the right answer for them. These observations lead to a discussion of how what we learn in research depends not only on what we ask but on how we ask it. The impact of diversity among researchers can be illustrated by comparing the questions asked to those asked in other situations (e.g., a group of all faculty members). Instructors can address many other aspects about the nature of research or the discipline being studied by drawing out other parallels with this exercise.

The importance of using the exercise for TA training is that it is likely to be the first time many teaching assistants have considered their discipline as a fluid body of knowledge, heavily influenced by who practices in the field. Issues relating to diversity are raised in a way unlikely to make anyone feel defensive, and the ensuing discussion can be used to highlight the importance of valuing both students' questions and the life experiences they bring to the classroom.

Exploring interaction norms. One of the best instructive situations I encountered in TA training was being videotaped while giving a presentation, and later having the chance to view my tape. Watching oneself in this way makes habits such as pacing and overuse of conversational fillers very obvious. Tapes can also provide an objective way of recording gender-related behaviors: how many times women and men were called on; if high order questions were posed to women, if language was gender neutral. However, use of videotape can raise a defensive response to the message of gender equity. Even if viewed privately, it is hard not to take a tape personally — few professions require putting forward as much of yourself as does teaching. Video also does not provide a motivation for changing behavior; it merely records what behaviors took place.

One exercise which can be used to highlight that qualities such as gender, race and age do matter in classroom dynamics is described in *Female Friendly Science* (Rosser, 1990). In the example described, Dr. Rosser suggests that six to eight chairs are placed in an inner circle, with the rest of the group observing from seats around the outside. Six to eight participants are selected for role playing, and each wears a label which she/he is not allowed to see. Suggested labels include "Female untenured professor. Ignore me." and "Male department head. Tell me I'm right." The exercise is suggested for a mixed sex/status group of participants, with each given a label as far as possible from his/her actual status. Role players are given 15 minutes to discuss a question such as a sexual harassment policy. The effectiveness of this exercise comes from the surprise of participants who experience a different type of treatment from that which they generally expect. The discussion, of course, can be applied directly to classroom dynamics, and especially to how reactions of other students can set the tone of the classroom.

Observing good teaching. A video produced by Purdue University (Keehner & Wadsworth, 1996) is a resource I highly recommend for TA training. The video provides three short scenes, centered around a chemistry lab lead by a teaching assistant. The first scene is optional and intended as an introduction. In the second scene, a series of small behaviors take place which provide a discouraging experience for a female student in the section. The third scene replays the second exactly, except for small changes on the part of the teaching assistant which lead to a very different classroom climate.

There are several reasons I enthusiastically recommend this video. The first is that I find it to be optimistic. It effectively demonstrates that small changes (especially in communication norms) make a large positive difference in overall classroom dynamics.

A second positive aspect of the video is that it uses only examples of behaviors that actually took place on the Purdue campus. Because of the condensed nature of the program (each scene runs about ten minutes) it is easy for viewers to expect that behaviors are exaggerated or contrived for their effect. The fact that all are real makes the scenes more powerful; the fact that they take place on a different campus makes them less personal.

Finally, I like the Purdue tape because it is well moderated. Introductory information is provided at the beginning and between scenes, and the tape comes with a user-friendly facilitator's guide. In addition to producing the tape, Purdue has an acting troupe which is available to travel. It is fully moderated, and has additional impact because the actors remain in character between scenes. Teaching assistants are free to ask questions of the characters, and the actors do an excellent job of retaining their roles. If your budget allows it, the live troupe experience is well worth the effort of arranging it.

Practicing good teaching. The final exercise I include in this chapter allows teaching assistants a chance to practice good teaching. It is used by Dr. Claudia Barreto of University of Wisconsin-Milwaukee in her TA training sessions (and also for faculty development seminars.) In this exercise, teaching assistants act out skits based on a variety of teaching situations. Situations can be chosen which might arise in a given discipline (e.g., a student who has personal experience with a sensitive topic being discussed in class) or to bring out particular climate issues. Each skit is stopped just before the instructor in the "class" is required to respond.

As the skit is stopped, small groups of participants are given questions to discuss and answer about the situation and how it could be handled. Each group puts their suggestions on an overhead, and the training leader uses them to generate large group discussion.

A number of positive results appear from using skits to think about teaching. First, teaching assistants get positive feedback for their suggestions and gain confidence in their ability to handle awkward situations. As importantly, the skits cause teaching assistants to think about potential situations ahead of time. They are therefore more prepared to handle, for example, a student who is derogatory towards women in class. Finally, Dr. Barreto points out that students begin to see each other as resources, and spend time with their peers focusing on teaching as well as on research.

Tips for TAs: Using Gender Conscious Content and Pedagogies

While teaching assistants are likely to have more control over climate than other course areas, an even greater impact to a class can come through pedagogies and content. Middlecamp and Subramaniam (1999) provide an overview of using such pedagogies in a chemistry course. The material is written in such a way as to make the article an excellent reference for a wide variety of disciplines.

Put simply, pedagogies shown to be beneficial to women (and men) are those which involve the learner as an active part of the educational process, and which value the contributions that learners bring to the study. Problem Based Learning (PBL), Cooperative or Collaborative Learning, Peer Instruction/Concep Testing, and Discovery Based Laboratories are all examples of such teaching techniques. Though not a "technique," per se, including contributions made by women and people of color explicitly in course material is also important to the gender-friendly classroom.

Problem-Based Learning. PBL (see *http://www.pbli.org/bibliography* for a bibliography) is a teaching strategy in which a problem or question is taken as the focal point for study. Information presented in class and gathered by students outside of class is included because it is needed to understand the problem. Psychological or medical case studies, political questions, and environmental issues are all natural ways to include PBL in a course. Educators who use Problem Based Learning have found that putting a face to the material to be learned increases student interest in the subject and results in more effort on the part of students. Another benefit to approaching learning in this way is that students must use analytic and critical thinking skills to integrate diverse information around one topic.

While growth in higher-order thinking skills is important to most instructors, the integration aspect of PBL is especially important for women. Studies of research patterns between men and women scientists have found that on average women are more likely than men to choose problems which have immediate benefit to society or which include interactions between several areas. Women also tend to view the world more in terms of connections than do men (Tannen, 1990). A pedagogical approach which connects course material to real world situations speaks to the strengths and interests of students who learn best by making connections.

Cooperative and Collaborative Learning. Cooperative and collaborative learning opportunities are other ways to engage students around course content, rather than in competition. Such learning opportunities can take many forms, but all share the advantages of encouraging students to learn from each other and of requiring students to participate actively in their own learning. They share additional climate advantages of providing smaller group sizes (which allows voices from a variety of conversational styles to be heard), and of turning peer interactions from competition to collaboration.

Successful cooperative learning experiences require planning on the part of the instructor. The benefits of working together need to be made clear to the students, either by the nature of the work itself or by the structure of the assignment. However, this does not mean that all groups need to be formally structured or that all projects need to be large in scope. Synthesis questions, either as review or over current material, are a wonderful opportunity to use cooperative learning. When students work in groups, it is possible to give them more difficult questions than otherwise might be assigned.

If an instructor is tentative about trying collaborative pedagogies, a simple first activity is to reserve a slot of time (say the first 15 minutes of class each Friday) for small group activities. Students can be allowed to choose their own groups, and given one or two questions somewhat more difficult than what would otherwise be on an assignment. Ideally, questions should require synthesis, analysis, and evaluation. This allows class standards to be set higher than they otherwise would, and instructors will find that students look forward to those class periods. Gaining experience in teaching via collaboration in this way helps instructors gain confidence to develop other collaborative exercises which directly address learning goals that they have for their own sections. The world wide web is also an excellent source for finding collaborative learning activities which are discipline-specific.

Concep Testing/Peer Instruction. ConcepTesting (New Traditions Project, University of Wisconsin-Madison, *http://www.chem.wisc.edu/%7Econcept/index.htm*), or Peer Instruction (Eric Mazur, Harvard University, *http://mazur-www.harvard.edu/*), is a variation of collaborative learning that works especially well for encouraging student interaction in large sections. In this case, students are required to review material before class and lecture is used only to address material which requires extra attention. Throughout the period, students are asked to answer multiple choice questions which the instructor puts on the overhead. Each student answers the question for her/himself, and includes a confidence level with the answer. Students are then given a few minutes to discuss the question with a neighbor, and to again provide an answer and confidence level.

In order for the method to be a success, attention must be given to the preparation of the questions: if all students get them right the first time, there is no benefit to collaboration. If no students have the correct answer, discussion does not progress towards a good understanding. *Peer Instruction* (Mazur, 1997) discusses question development and use of this teaching method in the context of introductory physics courses, although the material is written in such a way that it is applicable across disciplines. Sample questions and even lesson plans for physics and other natural sciences are available on both the New Traditions and Peer Instruction web sites.

I have high praise for using concept tests and peer interactions in courses of all sizes, and find that it is an especially effective technique for instructors who have not previously included a great deal of student interaction in their courses. For example, the entire course period does not need to be designed around concept questions; one or two can be inserted into each session to engage students. My main enthusiasm, however, comes from the fact that for well chosen questions students show an increase in confidence as well as in understanding. It is especially important that women be given learning opportunities which develop confidence: not only are they more likely to under-rate their abilities than are men, but a wide body of research relating to mathematical and scientific majors (e.g., Hackett et al., 1992) indicates that a woman's self-efficacy in a given field is one of the most important factors in her scholastic success in that major. Finally, of course, pedagogies using one-on-one peer interaction effectively address communication barriers known to reduce classroom participation by women and therefore open active-learning opportunities across the class.

Course Content. The above pedagogies combine active student participation with changing classroom culture. All provide better learning for students in general while specifically addressing barriers faced by women. A further modification important to affirming the place of women in higher education is attention to course content. Just as for books and movies, students are more likely to connect to a field and to view themselves as part of that field when they are able to connect to the characters involved. Taking the time to tell the stories of discovery, highlighting mistakes as well as successes, and crediting by name the work of a diverse group of researchers all add the flavor of a field into even introductory classes. Our disciplines are not all facts and theories; they are processes of discovery and evolving understanding. Teaching something of that process is the best thing we can do for our students. Searching out contributions made by women and people of color affirms that our body of knowledge benefits from the contributions of all.

Conclusion

As stated in the introduction, gender-conscious teaching is about establishing climate and learning opportunities that allow all students access to a good education. In principle, there should be nothing controversial about it, especially because pedagogies which benefit women also encourage better learning for men. In practice, however, change is uncomfortable and is sometimes challenged. It is easier for students to challenge the authority of a TA than it is to challenge that of a professor, and female TAs often have to work harder to earn authority than do their male counterparts. Teaching is as much about selling as it is about content, and so while TAs sell their subjects, they cannot forget to sell themselves.

TA coordinators must also recognize their role in supporting graduate teaching assistants. Graduate students are in an extremely vulnerable position, and are overwhelmed by teaching, course, and research responsibilities. TA coordinators have a responsibility to take the challenge of gender equity on themselves: to train TAs in gender conscious teaching; to defend such practices to the department when required; and to support teaching assistants when students challenge course structure. They also need to be aware of challenges faced by female teaching assistants. Yes, female TAs are still asked by students when the "real" TA will appear, they are still evaluated on their looks and style of dress, and they are still physically intimidated by male students. TA coordinators need to recognize that these behaviors are all too common, and provide a departmental approach for dealing with them.

The benefits of leading a gender-friendly course come to an instructor in satisfaction as a teacher, and to students in their enjoyment of the class. However, they also impact our disciplines. Research is done by humans, who choose the problems that they wish to study, who choose the results they wish to pursue, and who interpret the observations they make. By encouraging a diverse group of people to participate in a field, we strive for a more rounded understanding of our content areas.

References

Angelo, T. A., & Cross, K. P. (1993). *Classroom assessment techniques: A handbook for college teachers*. San Francisco: Jossey-Bass.

Fassinger, P., Brunsberg, M., & Matvick, T. (1995). How students and professors shape classroom interactions at Concordia. *Teaching at Concordia, 17*, 1-6.

Hackett, G., Betz., N., Casas, J. M., & Rocha-Singh, I. (1992). Gender, ethnicity, and social cognitive factors predicting the academic achievement of students in engineering. *Journal of Counseling Psychology, 39*, 527-538.

Harding, S. (1991). *Whose science? Whose knowledge?* Ithaca, NY: Cornell University Press.

Keehner, M., & Wadsworth, E. M. (1996). *Classroom climate workshops: Gender equity video and facilitation guide*. Purdue, IN: Purdue University.

Mazur, E. (1997). *Peer instruction*. Upper Saddle River, NJ: Prentice Hall.

Middlecamp, C. H., & Nickel, A. L. (2000). Doing science and asking questions: An interactive exercise. *Journal of Chemical Education, 77*, 50-52

Middlecamp, C. H., & Subramaniam, B. (1999). What is feminist pedagogy? Useful ideas for teaching chemistry. *Journal of Chemical Education, 76,* 520-525.

Palmer, P. J. (1993). Good talk about good teaching. *Change,* Nov./Dec, 8-13.

Rosser, S. V. (1990). *Female friendly science: Applying women's studies methods and theories to attract students.* New York: Pergamon Press.

Sandler, B. R., Silverberg, L. A., & Hall, R. M. (1996). *The chilly classroom climate: A guide to improving the education of women.* Washington, DC: National Association for Women in Education.

Sonnert, G., & Holton, G. (1996). Career patterns of women and men in the sciences.

American Scientist, 74, 63-71.

Tannen, D. (1990). *You just don't understand: Women and men in conversation.* New York: Ballantine.

Tobias, S. (1990). *They're not dumb, they're different: Stalking the second tier.* Tucson, AZ: Research Corporation.

University of Wisconsin System Women and Science Program Resources, *http://www. uwosh.edu/wis.*

The Teaching Assistant Training Handbook

Preparing for Diversity in College Teaching

Pamela Trotman Reid, Ph.D.
University of Michigan

Linwood J. Lewis, Ph.D.
Sarah Lawrence College

Roseanne Flores, Ph.D.
Hunter College

Overview

The new millennium is here. We can no longer point to a changing demographic base for colleges and universities. It has already changed. The fact is that more change will continue, but it is now that we are least prepared and most in need of making changes in our approach to diversity. The academy, once exclusively White and predominantly male, is increasingly multi-ethnic and female. Assumptions of Judeo-Christian philosophy, as well as of heterosexual orientation, must be suspended. Students vary widely in terms of age and economic background. A number will have a disability and others need remedial education. These demographic changes are particularly true of students at less selective institutions, community colleges, as well as at the urban and public institutions. But do not be misled, in even the most elite institutions, students are markedly different from just a decade ago.

As we note the shifts in our student community, we must recognize that many other dimensions of the academy have also changed. Technology, once the purview of the sciences, has become a pervasive force in both social sciences and the humanities. More and more institutions are developing global perspectives along with international campus experiences. In addition, the curriculum now includes interdisciplinary areas and newly emerging specialties. As we note the many areas of change, we must acknowledge the need to change our strategies, some policies, and also our demands.

Clearly we cannot be successful in our efforts if we approach teaching in the new academy in the same way that we have used for decades.

To prepare for this new level of diversity, we offer some suggestions to department chairs and others directly to teaching assistants. In this chapter we will focus primarily, but not exclusively, on issues of ethnic and cultural diversity. Changing our perspectives in these areas may offer the most resistance because they may affect our established expectations and assumptions about the world. In the U.S., de facto segregation occurs in housing and through school in many communities. Many people, including faculty and graduate students, have not been exposed to individuals unlike themselves or their family members. Thus, working with and incorporating diverse groups into the classroom or into the departmental community may instill a level of discomfort. The discomfort may be on both sides, thus, there is a real need to acknowledge the issue and confront the manifestations in concrete and deliberate ways.

We will address a number of areas and make suggestions for both department chairs and graduate teaching assistants, however, the first step for everyone is to conduct an honest self-examination. Each person must try to acknowledge and overcome personal biases and underlying fears based on ignorance of the "other." An important strategy is making explicit our own assumptions, discovering how these assumptions came to exist, and recognizing which parts are true and which are not. A basic goal should be to try to accept each person as an individual while simultaneously giving respect and understanding to the background, culture, and experiential differences that that individual brings to the exchange.

In addition to discussing how the department may make itself a welcoming community for diverse groups of students, including graduate teaching assistants (GTAs), we wish also to address the need for preparing GTAs to teach diverse students. This will require attention to the influence of cultural background, learning styles, preparation and expectations. Finally, we will discuss the need for diversity in the curriculum. By diversity in the curriculum, we primarily refer to the content and scope of courses and the scholarship of the discipline. Curricular issues need to be examined, particularly in light of the dearth of materials on people of color/ethnic minority populations. Clearly we cannot hope to address every disciplinary area, so we will be necessarily broad in the attempt to provide an overview of some issues and a general rationale for our suggestions. For each area of concern, we will also list some suggestions to help faculty in their preparations for diversity.

Department Chairs: Diversity Through Recruitment and Retention

Department chairs are the first line administrators responsible for several levels of diversity. They are often required to report on their success in establishing a certain level of diversity in undergraduate and graduate student enrollment, as well as in faculty ranks. Issues of recruitment and retention have been found to be distinctly related across these three areas. By this we suggest that greater diversity among faculty will typically result in greater diversity among students. Conversely, diversity at all levels often translates into a community that will offer some mutual support, affirmation, and result in greater retention.

For the above reasons, there is a need to attend to diversity in the selection of graduate teaching assistants (GTAs). The selection process may appear straight-forward, even formulaic, but the reality is that some students are selected based on several subjective criteria. Attention should be given to (a) how and whose recommendations count, (b) what criteria are really relevant for success as a GTA, and finally, (c) what provisions for training opportunities are made for those students who are interested in GTA positions.

As departments try to expand their pool of underrepresented groups (e.g., women and ethnic minorities) attention must be paid to preparing these new students for all aspects of a future career in academia. Thus, research departments should take care to be equitable in distributing and rotating both research and teaching assistantships. Demographic data should be viewed to determine if students of color and women are given assignments in the same proportion as majority male students. Stipends should also be compared on demographic bases to ensure that insidious inequities do not creep into the process. An analysis of departments recently conducted by senior faculty at the Massachusetts Institute of Technology dramatically revealed how subtle distinctions can amount to blatant discrimination (Women Faculty in Science, 1999).

It should be underscored that recruitment alone is not sufficient to ensure meaningful diversity; an active plan for retention of GTAs is also needed. Department chairs must lead faculty in discussions of the goals and advantages in having GTAs and in having diversity. Just as thoughtful policies are needed to guide appropriate GTA responsibilities, assignments, and work loads, forethought should be given to the development of a department environment that respects ethnic, religious and cultural differences. The department chair must consider what skills GTAs will need to provide adequate service to the department, to the faculty, and to students; similarly, the chair must provide the model and guidance needed for all members of the department to value diversity.

Some Suggestions

- The valuing of diversity will be seen in the roster of invited colloquium speakers, in department curriculum, in full-time faculty appointments, as well as in daily informal conversations.
- Respect for all faculty members, staff and students should be cultivated to ensure that it is a normal and expected part of the department's culture.
- Monitor disbursement of awards and appointments and review for trends over several years.
- Evaluate student performance and need for using multiple criteria.

GTAs: Managing Classroom Diversity

There have been long held negative beliefs and attitudes towards minority groups, women, and disabled people. In the social sciences these attitudes have led to the portrayal of some groups as deficient in desirable characteristics. In psychology, for example, these deficit models were tied to the assumption that White, middle class, heterosexual male subjects could and should appropriately serve as the normative group to which others would be compared (Graham, 1994). These theories of group deficiency fit well with some a priori beliefs in the inferiority of minorities and led to a self-sustaining system of discrimination and underrepresentation.

Recognize Existing Biases

We start by laying out these beliefs because they are so ingrained in our society that we have all learned and accepted them to varying degrees. To prepare to teach a diverse group of students, new instructors should recognize their own biases, as well as the prejudices that exist in their discipline. Since researchers have demonstrated the power of self-fulfilling prophecy and lowered/raised expectations, we encourage the recognition that the instructor to some extent sets the stage on which the students will play out their success or failure. If each student is to have the maximum opportunity for success, the instructor must begin with an acceptance of him/her and a sincere belief that each is capable of success.

Meeting Varied Needs

In recognizing the diversity of today's students, the greatest challenge is in understanding that no prescribed method for dealing with this diversity exists. Those instructors who deal with students as if they were a homogeneous group may in fact be ignoring some important issues. For example, Roberts (1994) pointed to the variety of needs that adults who have returned to college have. The needs range from increased financial support to weekend and evening class times. More students than ever before are self-supporting or work at least to support their attendance at the university. Many students are parents and have the added consideration of child care. Increasingly students come from other countries, are non-native speakers of English, have a disability that needs accommodation or are under-prepared by the public school system.

It would take considerably more space and time than we have available to consider the many needs and differences which may present themselves in today's classrooms. Happily there are publications dealing with each; some are even discipline specific (e.g., Banks & Banks, 1993, Rosenthal, 1996). There are some general principles that we can offer to assist faculty in preparing and managing this experience. The key is to approach each student with respect and to convey that respect throughout the term. Casual and/or sarcastic remarks about a student's performance may seem innocuous or even amusing, but the humiliation and discouragement that could result is not worth the instructor's fleeting experience of feeling clever. The goal is to invite and encourage everyone to participate and contribute to the class efforts. Instructors should definitely seek to avoid students' marginalization and take active steps to draw all students fully into the class.

In her autobiography, *Black Ice*, Lorene Cary (1991) describes her experience as one of very few African American students attending a prestigious prep school. Through most of the first year, she feels as if she is a visitor while the other students appear to her to belong. Incorporating diversity into the course materials is only the beginning; helping students from a variety of backgrounds to feel that they have a rightful place in each classroom is the ultimate goal. To establish a healthy classroom climate for open discussion and honest feedback, the instructor must set the tone by example. Giving preference to some students or allowing a few to dominate sends a signal that some students are more valued than others.

Some Suggestions

- Begin the semester by learning something about the students in your class. Ask about their reasons for taking this course and consider how best to shape the course to maximize their interest and commitment.
- Check with the Student Affairs Office for institution-wide programs on diversity that will be offered during the academic year. These might provide some useful information for you and your students.
- Check the library and the Internet for resources in your discipline to learn more about the students in your class. Plan to incorporate students' perspectives and cultural experiences in the class discussion if possible.
- Remember that no one student represents his or her entire group, any more than one GTA represents the entire department. It is not the student's responsibility to be an apologist on all issues dealing with ethnic minorities, for example. Take care not to put a student on the spot or under unwarranted pressure.
- For students with different skill levels, provide information about clinics, labs or

tutorial services available at your institution. The Student Affairs Office will be able to advise you on how to accommodate students with disabilities.

- Monitor your attention and feedback to male and female students, and to majority and minority students, to be certain that you have been equitable in your treatment of all. (Some institutions provide services to allow you to videotape your class. Try this, you might be surprised by what you see.) For classes dealing with controversial topics the use of a student journal may provide less outspoken students a venue for expression. Journals can be structured to collect reactions to readings and class discussions.

Department Chairs: Defending Diversity

Diversity, as a core ideal for higher education, is under fire and department chairs may need to reinforce the commitment of a program to opening opportunities to minority students. Recent legislation in California and in Washington has caused race-based policies across the nation to be questioned by public universities. In this climate, we wish to make clear that this chapter is presented with the assumption that racial and ethnic diversity in the teaching staff, in the student body, as well as in the curriculum, is a desirable goal and a valuable outcome. Still, we realize that some will raise the issue: "Why is diversity necessary?" A rich and complex discussion of possible answers to this question has generated an extensive literature and many powerful responses. We suggest that a compelling argument can be made on the basis of "good science" or more broadly "good scholarship." In response, then, to "why seek diversity", we suggest a side trip into the philosophy of science. We note that in addition to the arguments of fairness and equity, the ultimate goal of educators is the progression of scientific knowledge and the importance of the competition of opposing research programs (Lakatos, 1978). Thus, new knowledge is borne from change and difference.

We find that Kuhn's (1970) work on the structure of scientific revolutions provides a model to advance the "Good Science/Scholarship" argument. Kuhn posited the existence of paradigms, or scientific worldviews, which set the agenda for appropriate research questions and the preferred methods for answering these questions. Most research in a scientific domain is set within the dominant paradigm of that domain. Most scientists are engaged in "normal science" which is charged with the refining and enlarging the dominant view. For Kuhn, the process of normal science continues until the accretion of disconfirming or anomalous evidence overwhelms the ability of the paradigm to account for such anomalous data. A crisis ensues within the field, and the response to this crisis can be: (a) readjusting the dominant or pre-existing paradigm; (b) setting aside the crisis until further refinements in the paradigm can account for the data; or (c) creating a new world view.

When the novel paradigm, which is a fundamentally new approach, competes with and ultimately supplants the pre-existing paradigm, we believe that "good science" has been achieved. The novel paradigm causes a dramatic shift in the way scientists interpret data. Appropriate research questions within the dominant or pre-existing paradigm are reevaluated, reformulated and sometimes discarded within the novel paradigm and new methodologies are created to answer the reformed questions.

Good Science Theory and Diversity

Kuhn's meta-theory was based on the "hard" physical sciences, but much of his theory has relevance for how scholars in other fields evaluate competing sets of evidence. Does there exist a single, dominant paradigm within any discipline? Or do many competing paradigms or explanations exist? It is apparent from Kuhn's proposals that the progression of a discipline is based on the ability to discern anomalous evidence and invent new perspectives.

How can researchers discern anomalies if they have been trained to accept as doctrine the existing belief system? It is clearly a difficult feat; it has often been found that contrary explanations are most likely to arise from those whose backgrounds (scientific, social, and/or cultural) differ from the predominant mode. So it is no surprise that models of African American fatherhood led African Americans to challenge the deficit models and to propose new explanations; similarly, female scholars reexamined the notion that girls and women are necessarily debilitated by their hormonal fluctuations.

New pedagogical strategies can also be credited to the women and minority scholars who have challenged notions of patriarchy, dominance and the existing theories (see Alexander, Estrada, Heller, & Reid, 1997; Clark, 1993; Maher, 1994). These new strategies focus more on assumptions that the faculty role is to support and encourage student success, not to "weed out the weak links" as one colleague interpreted his role. As these new theories and methods emerge, faculty are challenged to evaluate them for inclusion in courses and consider how such changes may impact their own beliefs, as well as their students perception of the materials study being presented.

Some Suggestions

- When preparing graduate students as teaching assistants, make explicit for them what the implicit assumptions of the discipline are and consider how the discipline would be different if these givens were not accepted.
- Become aware of the issues and positions that have been discussed by minority and/ or female scholars in your discipline.
- Avoid stereotyping groups in discussions of concepts and theories. If in doubt of the impact, try substituting another group in the discussion to see how the substitution affects the perception of the group.

- Recognize how and why certain standards in each discipline have become accepted and discuss with GTAs how those norms were developed.

GTAs: Diversifying Your Teaching

Good teaching forces the instructor to examine course material and the supporting literature in ways that being a good student does not. Instructors are required to engage the material in a deeper way in order to present it to students effectively. GTAs must be prepared for students who may approach materials irreverently (remember your own student days!), and who may force the instructor to defend the material and, by extension, the dominant paradigm. For some GTAs the expectation that they may have to defend the inclusion of issues of diversity may inhibit them from trying. We hope the discussion above directed at department chairs will be useful in this regard.

How can diversity be infused in your curriculum? Again the answer may be to help students to recognize and challenge the dominant assumptions. Lead them to question the hypotheses and to critically assess the methodology. In every discipline, from Art History to Zoology, we can simply accept the status quo or we can push the margins of the discipline into the middle of our thinking. In many disciplines, issues dealing with ethnic minorities, gender, disabilities and sexual orientation are at the margins.

An anecdote may illustrate this point with respect to minorities: The first class taught by one of the authors (Lewis) was an Introduction to Psychology class at Bronx Community College in the City University of New York. His class was largely made up of non-traditional students, mostly African Americans and Latinos/as. As his lecture on Cognitive Psychology progressed according to the text, the students were enchanted with the notion of implicit memory and the explanation of implicit learning (learning without conscious, phenomenological awareness). When one student asked, "Does everyone, Black, White, everyone learn without knowing it?," Lewis' immediate standard answer was, "Yes, of course." This student interrupted again and asked, "Were there any Black folks in the study?" The students had been taught to question sampling bias, but they took it further by calling into question a fundamental premise of the long-accepted research. (Parenthetically, the answer to the student's initial question still cannot be answered affirmatively, because no one has evaluated it.)

Even in science courses, which may seem acultural, there are opportunities to dispel the notion that scientists are all White males. Encouraging awareness of the contributions of ethnic minority and female scholars can motivate students of color and increase their aspirations for success. These same strategies can provide majority students with an understanding of the values and contributions that are the benefits of diversity.

There still is a dearth of information about diversity in most disciplines; however, the assistance of the Internet as a research tool promises to help remedy this situation. Increasingly more web sites provide information that may relieve some pressure for faculty members who want to include new information in their classes. In some disciplines there are also books and journals that may provide an new instructor with concrete examples. A standard in this genre is a book edited by Bronstein and Quina (1988) which contains resources and strategies for helping to make courses more inclusive.

Some Suggestions

- Review your textbook and course materials to determine how sensitive they are to ethnic diversity, gender, sexual orientation, and issues of disability.
- Provide supplementary materials or invite an outside expert to cover gaps in information about underrepresented groups.
- Assume that your students are capable and that you can interest them in learning more about your subject. Recall why you became interested in your discipline and try to determine what relevance the subject has to the lives or aspirations of your students.
- Seek out innovative materials in the library and on the Internet to enrich your own knowledge about persons of color in your field and the contributions they have made in your discipline.
- Develop alternatives to traditional lectures. Simulations, collaborations, and small group discussions encourage participation by all students.
- Learn how portfolio assessment might be used as a comprehensive measure of student performance (see Roberts, 1994 for further discussion of this approach).

Department Chairs: Training Diverse GTAs

The impact of diversifying graduate teaching assistants will be to encourage new perspectives in the academy. This should result because there is an expectation that scholars may engage the dominant paradigm in different ways depending on their background. (Please note, minority and/or women scholars are not required to focus on issues relevant to their status or background and some do not.) We have observed that explanations in social sciences developed by persons from the dominant culture, i.e., White, middle class, and male, have focused on their own experiences, strengths and high status. We might expect that similar demand effects are likely from others.

Recognize, however, that students and scholars from different backgrounds typically have to negotiate two cultures (home culture and majority culture). This means that they potentially respond differently to the effects of cultural forces (LaFromboise, Coleman, & Gerton, 1993). Department chairs should be alert to such conflicts and provide opportunities to address these in non-threatening ways. The areas which should be of concern are training GTAs to teach, understanding their status as role models, and the pitfalls of ignoring diversity issues.

Some Suggestions

- Departments can host outside scholars of color and provide opportunities for them to meet with students privately to allow an honest airing of needs and difficulties.
- Departments expect research assistants to develop their skills by taking more courses in methodologies and theory. Teaching assistants can also be encouraged to attend workshops and conferences that address issues of teaching and diversity.
- Journals, books and other teaching materials can be provided to further the ability of students to teach diverse groups of students.

Role Models for Students

Besides advancing departmental goals, a diverse pool of teaching assistants allows the department to reflect the population of the national and local community from which it may draw students and supporters. Diversity in GTAs sends a message to minority students that teaching is a possible career choice for students. This may validate the choice of seeking a college education for some students. Many students have never had an African American or Mexican American professor or have never even seen one. For students of color, an encounter with an ethnic minority faculty member may open for them the possibility of an academic career choice. For White students, having faculty of color may challenge and displace their untested assumptions and biases. When faculty and teaching assistants of color are involved in department activities, students of all races recognize their value and authority.

Pitfalls

We would be remiss if we did not point out some possible dangers. Many minority GTAs feel compelled to teach classes on minority issues due to departmental need, personal philosophy, or the belief of others that they must be an "expert" in cultural areas. The assumption, however, that the one ethnic minority GTA will teach the course on their ethnic group could present problems if, indeed, that student does not feel prepared to do this.

There are also occasions when a GTA of color is assigned multiple roles outside of teaching. In addition to teaching, he or she may have advisement duties and committee assignments. Although these may be useful opportunities for having an impact on the department, they also take a sizable commitment of time. Institutions and departments committed to the retention and success of GTAs must set realistic limits on these duties. If no outside limits are in place, a GTA may remain unaware of the extent to which these responsibilities limit their scholarship.

Some Suggestions

- GTAs will usually benefit from having a senior faculty as a mentor who will guide them and provide support in teaching and career decisions.
- Serving as a role model for students may lead to extensive involvement to the neglect of other responsibilities. The department chairperson should monitor the progress of GTAs towards their degree completion.

Next Steps

Achieving diversity in colleges and university is a goal that many espouse. Obviously the academic department holds the key to accomplishing this goal. We know that women and men of color are more successful academically and more likely to pursue advanced degrees when they have the encouragement of role models already in the professoriate. The dilemma we face is like the "chicken and egg" problem; which comes first? How can we recruit a more diverse faculty if we do not have more doctoral students from a variety of background and of varying ethnicity? And more undergraduates who desire to advance? How can we train more doctoral students if we do not have sufficient numbers of faculty to train and inspire them?

Numerous institutions have demonstrated that when the motivation exists to accomplish a change in faculty and/or student demographics, it happens. However, it does not happen without planning or without supporters and support systems. Confronting the status quo will continue to be a challenge. However, with arguments for good science and good pedagogical practice, we should find that the resulting diversity will benefit all.

Models for Institutional Success

Mentoring programs. To develop the talent pool of minority students and faculty, departments might consider creating a peer-mentoring program using advanced students to encourage those who are less experienced. Minority alumni who have been successful in advancing through the program could be invited to return and give advice on how to succeed.

Visiting professorships and regular speakers. Professional progress of visiting minority scholars (both within and from other institutions) may provide some additional inspiration and guidance. This could be done within the department as well as university wide.

Minority student programs. Careful and thoughtfully developed programs of support addressing both financial and academic needs often encourage and enrich the pool of undergraduate students and GTAs for departments and institutions.

References

Alexander, P., Estrada, I., Heller, B. R., & Reid, P. T. (1997). *Before the class: A handbook for the novice college instructor*. New York, NY: City University of New York Graduate Center.

Banks, J. A., & Banks, C. A. (1993). *Multicultural education: Issues and perspectives* (2nd ed.). Boston: Allyn and Bacon.

Bronstein, P. A., & Quina, K. (1988). *Teaching a psychology of people : Resources for gender and socio-cultural awareness*. Washington, DC: American Psychological Association.

Cary, L. (1991). *Black ice*. New York: Knopf.

Clark, L. W. (1993). *Faculty and student challenges in facing cultural and linguistic diversity*. Springfield, IL: Charles C. Thomas.

Flores, R. (1999). Teaching psychology from a cross-cultural perspective. In B. Perlman, L. I. McCann, & S. H. McFadden (Eds.). *Lessons learned: Practical advice for teaching psychology* (pp. 159-163). Washington, DC: American Psychological Association.

Graham, S. (1994). Most of the subjects were White and middle class:Trends in published research on African Americans in selected APA journals, 1970-1989. *American Psychologist, 47,* 629-638

Kuhn, T. S. (1970). *The structure of scientific revolutions* (2nd ed.). Chicago: University of Chicago Press.

LaFromboise, T., Coleman, H. L., & Gerton, J. (1993). Psychological impact of biculturalism: Evidence and theory. *Psychological Bulletin, 114,* 395-412.

Lakatos, I. (1978). *Mathematics, science and epistemology*. New York: Cambridge University Press.

Maher, F. A. (1994). *The feminist classroom*. New York : Basic Books.

Roberts, H. R. et al. (Eds.) (1994). *Teaching from a multicultural perspective*. Thousand Oaks, CA: Sage.

Rosenthal, J. W. (1996). *Teaching science to language minority students: Theory and practice*. Philadelphia, PA: Multilingual Matters.

Women Faculty in Science. (1999). *A study on the status of women faculty in science at MIT*. The MIT Faculty Newsletter (Special Edition), XI (4).

Annotated Bibliography on College Teaching Sources

Julie Feldman, Ph.D.
University of Arizona

Richard Coughlan, M.S., MBA
University of Richmond

Overview

This is a truly exhilarating time for college teaching. Advances in research and technology have helped promote exciting new methods of teaching and learning. Training instructors at the college level has finally become recognized as a valuable and rewarding endeavor worthy of effort and energy. We believe that teachers are made rather than born, and that the process of teaching is a learning experience that continues throughout a teaching career. We have selected the following references based on what we thought might be useful to faculty or administrators interested in designing or implementing their own departmental TA training program. This is far from an exhaustive list. Rather we hope to provide you with a foundation from which to begin.

Resources for this bibliography were selected on the basis of perceived usefulness to teachers of higher education. Searches were made of databases such as ERIC, PsychInfo, and other education-related databases and search engines for materials related to higher education, with a focus on aspects of teaching especially relevant to university instruction. Topics included text selection, generating writing assignments, active learning strategies, leading discussion, test construction and grading, teaching philosophy, and diversity among others. These resources were screened to exclude outdated, overly general, vague, or philosophical cites. The remaining resources were covered in detail, and inclusion was based on perceived applicability to the college classroom with an emphasis on (1) specific strategies and tips and (2) good organization and understandability, and (3) favorable evaluation by students in a course on the teaching of psychology.

Course Development

Text Selection

Bartlett, L. E., & Morgan, J. A. (1991). *Choosing the college textbook: A textbook selection checklist for instructor use.* Curriculum and program planning. (ERIC Document Reproduction Service No. ED 365 197). This report provides the details of a project designed to develop a checklist for textbook selection. Main contributions of this work are the inclusion of both instructor and student perspectives on what comprises a "good" textbook as well as a comprehensive textbook selection checklist.

Kellough, R. D. (1990). How do I know what content to teach? In *A resource guide for effective teaching in postsecondary education* (pp. 97-107). Lanham, MD: University Press of America, Inc. This chapter includes checklists for determining textbook reading level and selecting a textbook.

First Class Meeting

Northeastern University. (1988). *Handbook for teachers.* Boston, MA: Office of Instructional Development and Evaluation: Author. This is a wonderful resource for thinking through teaching in the college classroom. It contains a great section on implementation that includes numerous useful tips on surviving the first class meeting, skills that make a "good teacher", improving communication, classroom management, and using multimedia. It also contains a helpful section on lecturing that discusses many key ingredients of generating an effective lecture.

Syllabus Development

Erickson, B. L., & Strommer, D. W. (1991). Preparing a syllabus and meeting the first class. In **Teaching college freshmen** (pp. 81-92). San Francisco: Jossey-Bass. This chapter contains helpful suggestions about what to include in a syllabus and what to do when meeting a class for the first time.

Lowther, M. A., Stark, J., & Martens, G. G. (1989). *Preparing course syllabi for improved communication.* University of Michigan, Ann Arbor, MI: The National Center for Research to Improve Postsecondary Teaching and Learning. This article offers helpful examples, strategies, and checklists that are useful when developing or modifying syllabi.

Testing and Grading

Buchanan, R. W., & Rogers, M. (1990). Innovative assessment in large classes. *College Teaching, 38,* 69-73. This article contains helpful suggestions and strategies for developing and administering exams, especially to large classes.

Cameron, B. J. (1991). Using tests to teach. *College Teaching, 39,* 154-155. This article contains suggestions for developing multiple-choice exams that teach students to think more critically about the material.

Cross, L. H., Frary, R. B., & Weber, L. J. (1993). College grading: Achievement, attitudes, and effort. *College Teaching, 41,* 143-148. This article describes and discusses survey results from 365 faculty members regarding their grading practices. Recommendations are included.

Kellough, R. D. (1990). How do I evaluate student achievement? In *A resource guide for effective teaching in postsecondary education* (pp. 263-289). Lanham, MD: University Press of America, Inc. This chapter contains guidelines for developing a grading system; tips for administering exams, avoiding cheating, dealing with angry students; and discusses advantages and disadvantages of twelve types of exam items.

Goals of Education

Teaching Philosophy

Austin, A. E., & Baldwin, R. G. (1991). *Faculty collaboration: Enhancing the quality of scholarship and teaching.* ASHE-ERIC Higher Education Report No. 7. George Washington University: Washington, DC. This report provides a discussion regarding the growing trend of collaborating with colleagues and includes a chapter on team teaching, which describes the advantages and limitations associated with faculty collaboration.

Beidler, P. G. (Ed.). (1986). *Distinguished teachers on effective teaching.* San Francisco: Jossey-Bass. This resource consists of a series of interviews with CASE Professor of the Year finalists who provide advice on teaching for the first time, and balancing teaching with research and professional responsibilities.

Lowman, J. (1984). What constitutes masterful teaching? In *Mastering the techniques of teaching* (pp. 1-22). San Francisco: Jossey-Bass. Lowman proposes a well-developed two-dimensional model of effective college teaching. He includes tables describing teachers who fall in the low, moderate, and high ranges of the dimensions of intellectual excitement and interpersonal rapport, as well as providing a detailed table resulting from the combination of both dimensions.

Effective Teaching

Bender, E., Dunn, M., Kendall, B., Larson, C., & Wilkes, P. (1994). *Quick hits: Successful strategies by award winning teachers*. Bloomington, IN: Indiana University Press. A collection of more than 100 very useful ideas from faculty at Indiana University is provided. Each idea is one page or less and can be put to use immediately. Contributors come from a variety of disciplines, but their suggestions are generic enough to be applicable anywhere.

Eble, K. E. (1972). Teaching effectively. In *Professors as teachers* (pp. 36-53). San Francisco: Jossey-Bass. This chapter discusses qualities of "good" teachers including such areas as discipline, generosity, energy, variety, use of examples and illustrations, enthusiasm, clarity and organization, and honesty.

Eble, K. E. (1983). Seven deadly sins of teaching. In *The aims of college teaching* (pp. 103-119). San Francisco: Jossey-Bass. This chapter provides a very thoughtful discussion of seven teaching "sins" including arrogance, dullness, rigidity, insensitivity, vanity, self-indulgence, and hypocrisy that are easy to overlook in one's own teaching. Eble uses these sins to illustrate what to avoid when teaching.

Fink, L. D. (1984). *The first year of college teaching*. San Francisco: Jossey-Bass. Based on a study of 97 new teachers, this text offers suggestions designed to enhance the satisfaction and effectiveness of first-year instructors.

Flood, B., & Moll, J. K. (1990). Classroom presentation. In *The professor business: A teaching primer for faculty* (pp. 43-84). Medford, NJ: Learned Information. This chapter is a great resource for ideas on enhancing and adding to your classroom methods. It discusses the advantages and disadvantages of more than 20 approaches to classroom presentations such as team teaching; leading discussions; utilizing invited speakers; incorporating simulations and games; and using media and technology.

Weston, C., & Cranton, P. A. (1986). Selecting instructional strategies. *Journal of Higher Education, 57*, 259-288. Part of the challenge for instructors is deciding what approach to teaching to use when. This article contains research-based suggestions for integrating various approaches and strategies at different times.

Student Diversity Issues

Border, L. L. B., & Chism, N. V. N. (Eds.). (1992). *Teaching for diversity*. San Francisco: Jossey-Bass. This book includes an annotated bibliography of diversity resources and describes diversity programs at eight universities. It also contains an excellent chapter on ensuring equitable participation in the classroom.

Chism, N. V., Cano, J., & Pruitt, A. S. (1989). Teaching in a diverse environment: Knowledge and skills needed by TAs. In J. D. Nyquist, R. D. Abbott, & D. H. Wulff (Eds.), *Teaching assistant training in the 1990's*. San Francisco: Jossey-Bass. This is a straightforward account of issues that can arise in an increasingly diverse student body.

It provides suggestions and strategies for handling student diversity in an effort to increase responsiveness to nontraditional students.

Davis, B. G. (1993). *Tools for teaching* (pp. 39-51). San Francisco: Jossey-Bass. This chapter contains ideas and strategies for teaching to a diverse set of students and includes a variety of areas in which diversity issues are likely to come up such as course content, class discussion, exams and assignments, advising, and overcoming biases.

McIntosh, P. (1992). White privilege and male privilege: A personal account of coming to see correspondences through work in women's studies. In M. L. Anderson & P. H. Collins (Eds.), *Race, class, and gender: An anthology* (pp. 70-81). Belmont, CA: Wadsworth. This is an extraordinary analysis of what it is like to have "male privilege" from the perspective of a woman recognizing and acknowledging her own "white privilege". McIntosh succeeds in raising awareness not only about racism, but its corresponding corollary regarding the often overlooked, and sometimes denied, advantages associated with privileges inherent to males and Whites in today's society.

Suzuki, B. H. (1989). Asian Americans as the "model minority": Outdoing whites or media hype? *Change, 21*, 13-19. A thoughtful discussion of diversity issues specific to Asian Americans is provided. It helps to dispel popular myths about this minority group, especially regarding socioeconomic status, and describes the problems that Asian Americans face in higher education.

Styles of Teaching and Learning

Fuhrmann, B. S., & Grasha, A. F. (1983). Designing classroom experiences based on student styles and teaching styles. In *A practical handbook for college teachers* (pp. 101-134). Boston, MA: Little, Brown and Company. This chapter contains descriptions of models that explain different learning and teaching styles. It provides insight into individual differences within students and teachers, and makes suggestions about approaches to teaching given these differences.

Brookfield, S. D. (1995). *Becoming a critically reflective teacher*. San Francisco, Jossey-Bass. This book is a thoughtful guide for instructors interested in reflecting on and (hopefully) improving their teaching. It provides suggestions for obtaining peer and student feedback and facilitates the use of this information to modify teaching philosophy and practice.

Classroom Tools and Strategies

Leading Discussion

Brookfield, S. D., & Preskill, S. (1999). *Discussion as a way of teaching: Tools and techniques for democratic classrooms*. San Francisco: Jossey-Bass. This book is a good general resource for using discussion in higher education. It provides a rationale for using discussion as a method for teaching and learning as well as approaches to using discussion in the classroom, especially with respect to maintaining interest and participation. In addition, there are several chapters regarding how to manage diversity and maintain balance by both the students and the teacher. Finally, and very helpfully, there are suggestions and tips regarding evaluation of participation, often a very difficult task for instructors.

Clarke, J. H. (1988). Designing discussions as group inquiry. *College Teaching, 36*, 140-143. Clarke proposes a four-phase model for developing an effective discussion. Phases include (1) concept development, (2) concept clarification, (3) factual verification, and (4) interpretation and analysis. He provides clear descriptions in addition to useful suggestions, and offers examples specific to each phase of the cycle.

Frederick, P. (1990). The dreaded discussion: Ten ways to start. In R. A. Neff & M. Weimer (Eds.), *Classroom communication: Collected readings for effective discussion and questioning* (pp. 9-16). Madison, WI: Magna Publications. This chapter is one of the best resources for leading discussions we have come across. It contains detailed descriptions of ten specific approaches to leading a discussion and offers suggestions for matching discussion strategy with type of material.

Welty, W. M. (1989). Discussion method teaching: How to make it work. *Change, 22*, 41-49. This article describes a method of teaching based almost solely on discussion. It contains fundamental, but often overlooked, recommendations for preparation including modifying the physical setting to maximize effectiveness, and what to do before, during, and after the discussion.

Active and Cooperative Learning

Bonwell, C. C., & Eison, J. A. (1991). *Active learning: Creating excitement in the classroom.* ASHE-ERIC Higher Education Report No. 1. Washington, DC: The George Washington University. This text includes suggestions for enhancing student involvement in classroom activities. Short discussions of cooperative learning and role playing are well presented. It also provides alternative classroom formats to lectures.

Finkel, D. L., & Monk, G. S. (1983). Teachers and learning groups: Dissolution of the Atlas Complex. In C. Bouton & R. Y. Garth (Eds.), *Learning in groups: New directions for teaching and learning* (pp. 83-97). San Francisco: Jossey-Bass. This is a phenomenal article that addresses weaknesses in the traditional role of teacher as expert/group leader and student as novice learner, while promoting the less conventional notion of teacher "functions" that facilitate and enhance student learning. Examples are offered illustrating both conceptualizations, and a thoroughly enlightening discussion follows.

Meyers, C., & Jones, T. B. (1993). *Promoting active learning: Strategies for the college classroom.* San Francisco: Jossey-Bass. This is a wonderful resource for anyone interested in incorporating active learning in the classroom. It contains a section describing four major active learning strategies including informal small groups, cooperative student projects, simulation and role play, and the case study method. Another section discusses ways of actively using reading assignments, outside resources, and media.

Nyquist, J., & Wulff, D. (1990). Selected active learning strategies. In J. Daly, G. Friedrich, & A. Vangelisti (Eds.), Teaching communication: Theory, research, and methods (pp. 337-361). Hillsdale, NJ: Lawrence Erlbaum Associates. This chapter describes and offers structural suggestions for several active learning strategies including writing; oral presentations; small groups; case study method; games, simulations and role plays; and field study methods.

Billson, J. M., & Tiberius, R. G. (1991). Effective social arrangements for teaching and learning. In R. J. Menges & M. D. Svinicki (Eds.), *College teaching: From theory to practice* (pp. 87-109). San Francisco: Jossey-Bass. Basic principles and specific guidelines for designing and implementing cooperative learning strategies are described. It includes several examples of activities that instructors will find useful.

Teaching Critical Thinking and Learning Through Writing

Brent, R., & Felder, R. M. (1992). Writing assignments: Pathways to connections, clarity, and creativity. *College Teaching, 40*, 43-47. This article is a wonderful resource for designing writing assignments effectively. It contains examples and rationales for different types of assignments.

Ericksen, S. E. (1984). *The essence of good teaching*. San Francisco: Jossey-Bass.

Practical tips from an educator with more than forty years of experience are offered. This book also provides suggestions for generating enthusiasm and teaching students to think independently.

Keim, M. C. (1991). Creative alternatives to the term paper. *College Teaching, 39*, 105-107. This article contains detailed descriptions of four alternatives to the traditional term paper that are basically equal in student effort and energy.

Meyers, C. (1986). Designing effective written assignments. In *Teaching students to think critically* (pp. 69-89). San Francisco: Jossey-Bass. This chapter provides a guide for developing written assignments that maximize critical thinking. The author begins with a discussion of the term paper as an illustration of what does NOT teach critical thinking, followed by characteristics, descriptions, and examples of five written assignments that do.

Simon, L. (1988). The papers we want to read. *College Teaching, 36*, 6-8. This article discusses the very important issue of identifying clear expectations in written assignments. It contains guidelines helpful for instructors who hope to elicit what they expect from students.

Sorcinelli, M. D., & Elbow, P. (1997). *Writing to learn: Strategies for assigning and responding to writing across the disciplines*. San Francisco, CA: Jossey-Bass. This text is a great general reference to teaching and learning through writing. Several chapters provide unique approaches to facilitating both graded and ungraded writing. Responding and providing feedback to student writing is covered in depth, including on-line responding.

Lecturing Effectively

Clarke, J. H. (1987). Building a lecture that works. *College Teaching, 35*, 56-58. This is a comprehensive reference to use when generating a lecture. It contains step-by-step instructions detailing the process of both lecture development and delivery.

Evensky, J. (1996). The lecture. In L. M. Lambert, S. L. Tice, & P. H. Featherstone (Eds.), *University teaching: A guide for graduate students*. Syracuse, NY: Syracuse University Press. This chapter offers many practical and helpful suggestions and tips for generating effective lectures, especially for the novice.

Lowman, J. (1984). *Mastering the techniques of teaching* (pp. 96-117). San Francisco: Jossey-Bass. A highly useful and well-written chapter that describes the process of creating and delivering a lecture. A must, especially for the novice instructor.

Penner, J. G. (1984). *Why many college teachers cannot lecture: How to avoid communication breakdown in the classroom*. Springfield, IL: Charles C. Thomas. A professor of speech offers suggestions for planning, organizing, and delivering lectures that motivate students. Special emphasis is placed on verbal and nonverbal communication skills.

Using Technology in the Classroom

Davis, B. G. (1993). In *Tools for teaching* (pp. 313-341). San Francisco: Jossey-Bass. This chapter is helpful when developing computer-generated teaching materials. This reference is especially appropriate for the novice.

Fuhrmann, B. S. & Grasha, A. F. (1983). Using media in the clasroom. *A practical handbook for college teachers*. Boston: Little, Brown and Company. This chapter contains guidelines for selecting and using media to enhance teaching, and discusses in detail the advantages and disadvantages of different types of instructional media. Additionally, it includes tips on how to maximize use of media technology.

General Teaching Resources

Teaching Portfolio

Doolittle, P. (1994). *Teacher portfolio assessment*. Washington, DC: ERIC Clearinghouse on Assessment and Evaluation (ERIC/AE Digest No. ED 385 608). This report outlines what a teaching portfolio is, and how and why it is used. Two especially useful sections delineate what to include and the steps to take when developing a teaching portfolio.

Seldin, P. (1997). *The teaching portfolio: A practical guide to improved performance and promotion/tenure decisions* (2nd ed.). Bolton, MA: Anker Publishing. This book contains research-based information regarding all aspects of teaching portfolio development and utilization including (a) suggestions for incorporating technology into the teaching portfolio, (b) step-by-step instructions for selecting what to include and what to exclude, and (c) helpful tips for using the portfolio as a means to improving teaching.

Seldin, P. et al. (1993). *Successful uses of the teaching portfolio* (pp. 101-209). Bolton, MA: Anker Publishing. This chapter contains outstanding models of teaching portfolios developed in different departments.

Urbach, F. (1992). Developing a teaching portfolio. *College Teaching, 40*, 71-74. This article describes seven dimensions of documenting a teaching portfolio including: (a) what you teach, (b) how you teach, (c) changes in your teaching, (d) your academic standards, (e) student impressions, (f) developing your teaching skills, and (g) assessment by colleagues. Questions are posed for consideration regarding each dimension.

Feedback and Evaluation

Katz, J., & Henry, M. (1988). *Turning professors into teachers: A new approach to faculty development and student learning.* New York: Macmillan Publishing. The authors describe the benefits associated with having faculty members observe one another in the classroom. The importance of student feedback in improving teaching is also emphasized. Data is predominantly in the form of student and faculty unstructured interviews. Interview format is provided as well.

Weimer, M. E. (1990). *Improving college teaching: Strategies for developing instructor effectiveness.* San Francisco: Jossey-Bass. This book contains a chapter delineating a five-step process for systematically improving teaching based on student and peer evaluation and observation. Another helpful chapter provides brief descriptions of teaching improvement programs at 11 colleges and universities.

Wulff, D. H., Staton-Spicer, A. Q., Hess, C. W., & Nyquist, J. D. (1985). The student perspective on evaluating teaching effectiveness. *Association for Communication Administration Bulletin, 53*, 39-47. This report compares more traditional anonymous methods of student evaluation to an innovative mid-semester small group approach and discusses student perceptions of the evaluation process.

Training Teaching Assistants and Teachers

General Resources for TA Training

Allen, R. R., & Rueter, T. (1990). *Teaching assistant strategies: An introduction to college teaching.* Dubuque, IA: Kendall/Hunt. This book offers a thorough introduction to college teaching geared primarily to the new teaching assistant. Contents include both basic and applied information pertaining to most aspects of the teaching assistant process. It also contains an informative chapter about relationships between TAs, professors, and students.

Cross, K. P., & Steadman, M. H. (1996). *Classroom research: Implementing the scholarship of teaching.* San Francisco: Jossey-Bass. Four separate case studies are presented, each dealing with a specific classroom challenge. The format encourages discussion of cases. Educational research relevant to the important issues is described and suggestions for handling these challenges are offered.

Downs, J. R. (1992). Dealing with hostile and oppositional students. *College Teaching, 40*, 106-108. Here is a practical resource for dealing with problem situations involving students. It includes helpful tips for de-escalating difficult situations.

Grieve, D. (Ed.). (1989). *Teaching in college: A resource for college teachers.* Cleveland, OH: Info-Tec. The author provides excellent descriptions of teaching situations at various types of institutions, from small liberal arts schools to large research universities. A chapter written by Bill Frye outlines goals and objectives for college courses. Also, the book contains a theoretical chapter on teaching older students; planning student evaluation, testing, and grading; and student motivation.

McKeachie, W. J. (1999). *Teaching tips: Strategies, research, and theory for college and university teachers* (10th ed.). Boston: Houghton Mifflin. We use this text in a graduate course on teaching. It is a practical reference that contains sections on most aspects of college teaching including course development; basic skills such as leading discussions, testing and grading, and lecturing; teaching techniques and tools; teaching large vs. small classes; and other practical and theoretical issues that can arise in teaching. We recommend it highly, especially if you are looking for a single resource on teaching.

Pica, T., Barnes, G. A., & Finger, A. G. (1990). *Teaching matters: Skills and strategies for international teaching assistants.* New York: Newbury House. This text is an excellent resource for teaching assistants who are from outside the United States, developed by faculty members involved with the Drexel University Program in Teacher Preparation for International Graduate Assistants.

Whitman, N. A. (1988). *Peer teaching: To teach is to learn twice.* ASHE-ERIC Higher Education Report No. 4. Washington, DC: Association for the Study of Higher

Education. This report highlights the benefits of using partnerships and work groups in the classroom, and provides suggestions for implementing peer teaching.

TA Training Program Development

Haworth, J. G., & Conrad, C. F. (1997). *Emblems of quality in higher education: Developing and sustaining high-quality programs.* Needham Heights, MA: Allyn and Bacon. This book focuses on program quality and is applicable to undergraduate through doctoral level programs. Chapters emphasize approaches to developing and sustaining high-quality educational programs based on "Engagement Theory." According to this theory, five separate clusters of program attributes contribute to enhancing teaching and learning including (a) diverse and engaged participants, (b) participatory cultures, (c) interactive teaching and learning, (d) connected program requirements, and (e) adequate resources.

Lewis, K. G. (Ed.). (1991). *The TA experience: Preparing for multiple roles.* Stillwater, OK: New Forums Press. This compilation of readings is selected from the 3rd National Conference on the Training and Employment of Graduate Teaching Assistants and covers TA training. Topics include enlightening research studies; descriptions of campus-wide and discipline-specific programs; the role of mentoring, diversity, and evaluation in TA training programs; and a section on International TA training, among others.

Nyquist, J. D., Abbott, R. D., Wulff, D. H., & Sprague, J. (Eds.). (1991). *Preparing the professoriate of tomorrow to teach: Selected readings in TA training.* Dubuque, IA: Kendall/Hunt. This compilation of readings is selected from essays presented at the 2nd National Conference on TA Training and is a comprehensive selection of important issues related to TA training. It includes suggestions for designing effective programs that provide TAs with appropriate resources and tools, and discusses the role of TA supervision, with an emphasis on accomplishing goals in the context of increased student diversity. Issues specific to international TA training are also addressed.

Nyquist, J. D., & Wulff, D. H. (1996). *Working effectively with graduate assistants.* Thousand Oaks, CA: Sage Publications. This book emphasizes the role of teacher/advisor in preparing graduate teaching and research assistants for their instructional roles, research responsibilities, and special challenges in teaching, among others. One chapter covers special considerations when working with international teaching assistants. An insightful model of the stages of TA and RA development with regard to indicators and implications for supervision is provided. An annotated bibliography of resources specific to supervision of graduate students is provided.

About the Editors

Loreto R. Prieto received his doctoral degree in Counseling Psychology from the University of Iowa in 1996. He is currently an Assistant Professor of Counseling Psychology at the University of Akron. Dr. Prieto has supervised graduate teaching assistants, has written and published several articles concerning teaching assistant development, and during his graduate training taught as a teaching assistant at the University of Iowa for over two years. In addition to his interest in issues concerning teaching assistant development, Dr. Prieto's clinical training focused upon psychological testing and assessment as well as multicultural psychology and diversity issues. Dr. Prieto is active in Division 2 of the American Psychological Association, the Society for the Teaching of Psychology. He serves as the Chair of the Division 2 Task Force on Diversity, is a member of the Division 2 Long Range Planning Committee, has served as a Liaison to APA for Division 2 on projects concerning diversity issues, and has been an active reviewer for the Division 2 journal *Teaching of Psychology*. In addition, he serves as Chair of the Diversity Working Group for APA's Psychology Partnerships Project (P3), an Education Directorate initiative involving scholars and educators from various specialty areas from across the nation who, in an effort to meet the demands of the new millennium, are seeking to update and enhance current teaching and training practices in the discipline of psychology.

Steven A. Meyers received his doctoral degree in Clinical Psychology from Michigan State University in 1995. Currently, he is an Assistant Professor and Coordinator of the Instructor Development Program in the School of Psychology at Roosevelt University in Chicago. Dr. Meyers conducts orientation programs, workshops, and seminars to prepare psychology graduate students and faculty for their teaching responsibilities. He has written numerous articles that have documented the amount and kinds of training that graduate students receive for their teaching responsibilities, how training and supervision contribute to the success of teaching assistants, and ways to improve TA training. His other research interests include examining how family relationships develop within their social contexts. Dr. Meyers' teaching skills have been nationally recognized. He was the 1994 recipient of the McKeachie Early Career Teaching Award that is given by the Society for the Teaching of Psychology. He has also received the Excellence-in-Teaching Citation from Michigan State University. Dr. Meyers has actively participated in the Society for the Teaching of Psychology and recently led an executive committee and a task force that have examined the preparation that graduate students in psychology receive for careers in academia.

About the Contributors

Deborah Ware Balogh is Dean of the Graduate School and Professor of Psychological Science at Ball State University. After completing her doctorate in clinical psychology at Bowling Green State University in 1981, she joined the faculty at BSU, specializing in adult psychopathology. A Fellow of the Society for Personality Assessment, her research focuses on personality disorders. She formerly served as Director of the Graduate Student Development Project, a BSU program aimed at enhancing the professional skills of graduate students, including those serving as GAs.

Richard Coughlan is Assistant Professor of Management at the University of Richmond, where he teaches courses on business ethics and organizational behavior to undergraduates and MBA students. He holds a Ph.D. from the University of Arizona, where he was named Outstanding Teaching Associate in Management. His research on decision-making has appeared in leading academic journals including *Organizational Behavior and Human Decision Processes* and the *Journal of Behavioral Decision Making*. A member of the Organizational Behavior Teaching Society, he is currently involved in the development of course portfolios for undergraduate and graduate courses in management.

Julie Feldman earned a Ph.D. in cognitive psychology from the University of Washington in June, 1995. She completed a Post-Doctoral Respecialization Program in clinical psychology at the University of Arizona and a clinical psychology internship at the Tucson VA Medical Center in August. 1999. Dr. Feldman has extensive experience in teaching psychology. During graduate school, she was a Teaching Assistant Fellow (Head TA) for Introductory Psychology for three years and the lead Departmental TA during the 1994-1995 academic year. In her last year at the University of Washington, she modified and co-taught a graduate course on the teaching of psychology. She had full teaching responsibility for courses in research methods and introductory statistics as a graduate student. At the University of Arizona, she has taught introductory statistics, research methods, and a graduate course on the Teaching of Psychology. Additionally, she presented a Participant Idea Exchange entitled "Teaching the Teaching of Psychology" at the 19th Annual National Institute on the Teaching of Psychology in January of 1997. In June of 1999, she presented a Participant Idea Exchange with Jake Jacobs and Jill Booker entitled, "A Cognitive-Behavioral Approach to University Teaching." She enjoys working with students very much, and is strongly committed to improving undergraduate education.

Heidi S. Fencl received her PhD in theoretical astrophysics from The Ohio State University. She taught physics at Ohio State - Mansfield and was assistant professor of physics and astronomy at Concordia College, Moorhead, MN before coming to the University of Wisconsin System. Fencl currently holds a joint appointment as director of the University of Wisconsin System Women & Science Program and coordinator of the University of Wisconsin Oshkosh Office of Science Outreach. Through the Women & Science Program, she provides faculty development opportunities in gender conscious teaching to educators in science, mathematics and engineering from colleges and universities throughout the country. Through the Science Outreach Office, she offers hands-on science workshops to Wisconsin elementary and middle school teachers each summer, and coordinates a wide variety of science programs for students throughout the academic year. Fencl's current research interests include the interaction between teaching pedagogies and student performance in the context of social-cognitive theories. She is also pursuing an interest in gender conscious distance education.

Roseanne Flores received her doctorate from the Graduate Center of the City University of New York in Developmental Psychology in 1993. Dr. Flores is an assistant professor of psychology at Hunter College of the City University of New York. She has lectured doctoral students on issues of classroom management and class preparation. Her research has explored issues of poverty and its impact on children's cognitive development and daily functioning.

Louise Hainline received her Ph.D. from Harvard University in 1973. She is Professor of Psychology at Brooklyn College and the Graduate School of CUNY. She recently served as Acting Dean for Graduate Studies and Research and previously was the head of the Experimental Psychology Subprogram of the CUNY Graduate Center. About 12 years ago, Dr. Hainline and a colleague first taught a non-credit course on teaching for doctoral students. Since that time, the course has been offered on a two to three year cycle taken by almost all doctoral students in the program. Dr. Hainline's research focuses on the development of vision and the assessment of visual problems in infants and populations with perceptual problems, such as dyslexics. She continues to be very interested in helping students through the process of becoming a professor. Dr. Hainline can be reached at the Department of Psychology, Brooklyn College of CUNY, 2900 Bedford Avenue, Brooklyn, NY 11210. E-mail may be sent to louiseh@brooklyn.cuny.edu.

Sandra Goss Lucas received her Ph.D. from Indiana University, Department of Counseling and Educational Psychology, in 1984. Her Ph.D. minor was in psychology and women's studies. She taught introductory psychology in high school and two community colleges prior to joining the University of Illinois. She is currently the Director of Introductory Psychology at the University of Illinois. She has been involved in writing the instructor's manual and testbank to accompany the Bernstein, Clarke-Stewart, Roy, and Wickens' Psychology text. Her research interests include college teaching, academic dishonesty, and student achievement in college. Dr. Goss Lucas can be contacted through e-mail: *gossluca@uiuc.edu* or through regular mail at 633 Psychology Building, 603 East Daniel, Champaign, IL 61820

Linwood J. Lewis received his doctorate from the City University of New York Graduate School, and has taught psychology at the College of New Jersey and at Bronx Community College. He is now an assistant professor of psychology at Sarah Lawrence College in New York. His research interests include the developmental aspects of implicit learning as well as applications of psychology to health issues.

Christina Maslach is Professor of Psychology at the University of California at Berkeley. She received her A.B., magna cum laude, in Social Relations from Harvard-Radcliffe College in 1967, and her Ph.D. in Psychology from Stanford University in 1971. She has conducted research in a number of areas within social and health psychology, but is best known as one of the pioneering researchers on job burnout. She is recognized as an outstanding teacher, having won a national award as "Professor of the Year" in 1997, and the Distinguished Teaching Award from the University of California at Berkeley.

Emily J. Ozer received her doctorate in clinical psychology at the University of California at Berkeley with over three years of experience as a TA. Her research interests include school-based interventions for adolescents, community violence, and post-traumatic stress disorder. Prior to entering graduate school, she was a program developer for a community-based social service agency in East Palo Alto, CA.

David V. Perkins is Professor of Psychological Science at Ball State University. His research concerns community-based supports and services for persons with serious mental illness and their families, and among his current projects is a study of ethical decisions made by providers of community mental health services. He is co-author of

Principles of Community Psychology: Perspectives and Applications (2nd edition; New York: Oxford University Press, 1997). Dr. Perkins received a B.A. with Honors in Psychology from Oberlin College and his Ph.D. in Psychology from Indiana University.

G. Shane Pitts is an assistant professor of psychology at Birmingham-Southern College. Dr. Pitts is a recent graduate of the University of Alabama where he received his Ph.D. in cognitive psychology. As a graduate student, he received several awards for teaching excellence and research fellowships. His research focuses on unconscious cognitive processes and stereotyping. His teaching interests include Introduction to Psychology, Cognitive Psychology, Social Psychology, Critical Thinking, and Research Methods. Dr. Pitts may be contacted by e-mail at spitts@bsc.edu.

Nnamdi Pole earned his masters and doctoral degrees in Clinical Psychology from the University of California, Berkeley and is currently a postdoctoral fellow at the University of California, San Francisco. Dr. Pole's research interests include psychotherapy process, posttraumatic stress disorder, minority mental health, and psychophysiology of emotion. While at Berkeley, he was a TA for numerous courses and designed two popular undergraduate seminars: The Scientific Basis of Psychotherapy, and Culture, Ethnicity, and Mental Health. For these efforts, he has been awarded both the Outstanding Graduate Student Instructor Award and the Teaching Effectiveness Award.

Steven Prentice-Dunn is Professor of Psychology at the University of Alabama. Among the courses he teaches is a required doctoral practicum in Teaching of Psychology. He has received the College's and University's highest awards for teaching excellence. Dr. Prentice-Dunn has published over 70 articles on violence and on health psychology. He currently investigates interventions to promote preventive health behaviors. He has been named to a list of researchers most frequently cited in social psychology textbooks and is a Fellow of the Society for Personality and Social Psychology. Dr. Prentice-Dunn may be contacted by e-mail at *sprentic@bama.va.edu*. or through regular mail at the Department of Psychology, University of Alabama, Box 870348, Tuscaloosa, AL 35487-0348.

Lauren Silver earned her doctorate in developmental psychology from the University of California, Berkeley and is currently the Associate Curator of Education, at the Iris and B. Gerald Cantor Center for the Visual Arts, Stanford University. Her research interests center around cognitive and linguistic development in preschool children, with a particular focus on the development of symbolic representation in children's art and language. While a graduate student, she taught extensively in the psychology department and led a number of campus-wide teacher training activities for graduate students and faculty; she was awarded the Outstanding Graduate Student Instructor Award in 1995-1996.

Patricia Keith-Spiegel is the Reed D. Voran Honors Distinguished Professor of Social and Behavioral Sciences and Director for the Center for the Teaching of Integrity at Ball State University. In 1994 she received the Distinguished Teaching Award from the American Psychological Association. The second edition of *Ethics in Psychology* (with Gerald Koocher), was published by Oxford University Press in 1998.

Pamela Trotman Reid is a developmental psychologist and professor of psychology and education, and research scientist at the Institute for Research on Women and Gender at the University of Michigan, Ann Arbor. A Fellow of the American Psychological Association with more than twenty five years of academic experiences, her scholarship focuses on issues of ethnicity, gender and social class. Her interest in preparing future faculty led her to develop a series of workshops and seminars for doctoral students interested in teaching.

Bernard E. Whitley, Jr. is Professor of Psychological Science at Ball State University. He received his doctoral degree in social-personality psychology from the University of Pittsburgh in 1983. His research interests include attitudes toward homosexuality and academic dishonesty. He is the author of *Principles of Research in Behavioral Science* (1996).

Arno F. Wittig is Professor of Psychology and Dean of the Honors College (Emeritus) at Ball State University. A Fellow of Divisions 1 (General Psychology), 2 (Society for the Teaching of Psychology), and 47 (Exercise and Sport Psychology) of the American Psychological Association, he has authored or co-authored five books and over eighty articles and convention presentations. He has served on the Executive Committees of APA Division 1 and the National Collegiate Honors Council and was President of the Mideast Honors Association in 1988-1989. He has 36 years of college teaching experience.